Help Desk Practitioner's Handbook

Barbara Czegel

Help Desk Practitioner's Handbook

WILEY COMPUTER PUBLISHING

John Wiley & Sons, Inc.

New York • Chichester • Weinheim • Brisbane • Singapore • Toronto

Publisher: Robert Ipsen
Editor: Theresa Hudson
Assistant Editor: Kathryn A. Malm
Managing Editor: Brian Snapp
Text Design & Composition: NK Graphics

Designations used by companies to distinguish their products are often claimed as trademarks. In all instances where John Wiley & Sons, Inc., is aware of a claim, the product names appear in initial capital or ALL CAPITAL LETTERS. Readers, however, should contact the appropriate companies for more complete information regarding trademarks and registration.

This book is printed on acid-free paper. ∞

Published by John Wiley & Sons, Inc.

Published simultaneously in Canada.

This publication is designed to provide accurate and authoritative information in regard to the subject matter covered. It is sold with the understanding that the publisher is not engaged in professional services. If professional advice or other expert assistance is required, the services of a competent professional person should be sought.

Library of Congress Cataloging-in-Publication Data
Czegel, Barbara, 1953-
    Help desk practitioners handbook / Barbara Czegel.
      p. cm.
    Includes bibliographical references and index.
    ISBN 0-471-31992-9 (alk. paper)
    1. Computer industry—Customer services—Management.
    2. Electronic office machine industry—Customer services—Management.   I. Title.
    HD9696.2.A2C96   1999   98-31159
                                                               CIP

10 9 8 7 6 5 4 3 2 1

To my dear friend Di Regendanz, who took over my barn chores so I could finish this book.

Contents

SECTION ONE Expectations of the Business 1

CHAPTER ONE Roles 3

CHAPTER TWO   Focusing on the Business   34

SECTION TWO   Supporting the Help Desk Structure   61

CHAPTER THREE   Structure   63

SECTION THREE   Managing Problems   93

CHAPTER FOUR   When Problems Become Dangerous   95

CHAPTER FIVE   Listening to Resolve and Prevent Problems   129

CHAPTER SIX   Getting and Giving Information   162

CHAPTER SEVEN   Proactive Problem Control   191

CHAPTER EIGHT   Using Tools   222

SECTION FOUR   Understanding the Business of Help Desks   253

CHAPTER NINE   Everything You Need to Know about Performance   255

CHAPTER TEN   Cost Justification Made Easy   293

CHAPTER ELEVEN   Can I Interest You in Marketing?   328

SECTION FIVE | **Thriving in a Help Desk Environment   365**

CHAPTER TWELVE   It's All in Your Attitude   367

Preface

This is a practical book for Help Desk practitioners. There is no magic in it, only information that will make you a more effective Help Desk practitioner. The book has five sections: Section 1, Expectations of the Business; Section 2, Supporting the Help Desk Structure; Section 3, Managing Problems; Section 4, Understanding the Business of Help Desks; and Section 5, Thriving in a Help Desk Environment.

The first section, Expectations of the Business, contains two chapters. The first, "Roles," discusses the impact of the Help Desk practitioner on the profitability of the business. It considers the roles practitioners must play on the Help Desk and the skills each role requires. The second, "Focusing on the Business," discusses the Help Desk practitioner's involvement in getting and keeping the Help Desk focused on the business.

The second section, Supporting the Help Desk Structure, contains only one chapter, Chapter 3, "Structure," which discusses how the various levels in a support structure relate to each other and how to improve working relationships between levels so as to minimize resolution times and lessen the chance that calls will fall through the cracks.

The third section, Managing Problems, deals with problem control and elimination. The first chapter in this section, Chapter 4, "When Problems Become Dangerous," discusses avoiding common support mistakes and getting into a cycle of ongoing evaluation and improvement. Chapter 5, "Listening to Resolve and Prevent Problems," focuses on improving listening in the problem-solving process. It discusses how factors such as negative filters can make us miss what our customers are saying and can cause us to work on the wrong problems. The chapter also presents eleven effective listening habits to improve our problem solving. Chapter 6, "Getting and Giving Information," talks about the overall cycle of information exchange on the Help Desk. It discusses how to optimize this cycle of listening, questioning, and delivering information so as to increase the speed and accuracy of problem resolution, reduce calls to the Help Desk, and have a positive impact on the profitability of the business. Chapter 7, "Proactive Problem Control," discusses how to be proactive by understanding customer needs, using early warning systems, and applying layered strategies for problem and dandelion control. Tools play a large part in problem solving, and Chapter 8, "Using Tools," gives an overview of tools that can be used to reduce calls and eliminate problems. This chapter also describes how to get the most out of tools such as the Internet, Help Desk management systems, and knowledge bases.

The fourth section is Understanding the Business of Help Desks. It contains three chapters. The first, Chapter 9, "Everything You Need to Know about Performance," explains what performance is and gives the Help Desk practitioner an understanding of the data required to identify and carry out improvements and plan for the future. Chapter 10, "Cost Justification Made Easy," teaches the Help Desk practitioner a simple process for doing cost justifications and works through three examples. Chapter 11, "Can I Interest You in Marketing?" shows the Help Desk practitioner the value of marketing in reducing and eliminating calls and how to use every Help Desk interaction as a marketing opportunity. This chapter also discusses the role of a Help Desk Web site in marketing and gives suggestions and examples for setting up such a Web site.

The final section, Thriving in a Help Desk Environment, contains only one chapter, Chapter 12, "It's All in Your Attitude," which discusses how a Help Desk practitioner can thrive, instead of just surviving, on the Help Desk. It talks about getting a Help Desk attitude, improving tolerance of stress, and taking responsibility for making things happen.

Throughout the book I make extensive use of scenarios and examples to illustrate the ideas presented. My goal was to create a book that was somewhat entertaining, easy to read, and full of useful information for becoming a more effective Help Desk practitioner and for getting more enjoyment out of the Help Desk practitioner's role. I hope I've succeeded. Enjoy the book.

Acknowledgments

Thank you to my many students. You taught me more about Help Desks than I could have learned in a lifetime of practical experience. Your feedback and ideas shaped this book.

Thank you to my late father, for teaching me how to pull dandelions out by the root.

Thank you to my mom, for teaching me that appearances don't count for very much.

Thank you to my children. To Chris for being understanding always, even through times of pretty incredible change. To Care for her encouragement, her music, and her company.

Thank you to my new family. To Ray, for being so very supportive and for not letting me take myself too seriously. To Kristina for keeping me company while I worked on this book and she worked through hours of Final Fantasy. To David for being gracious about not being able to use my PC on the weekends (because I was using it), even after I upgraded to 128 MB of memory. To Julia for making sure Risky got enough exercise. To Buffy and Prince for the dead mouse. (Next time just draw me a picture.)

Thank you to my good friends Megan, Shelley, and Risky, for being perpetually cheerful and encouraging (and for not eating the cats).

Thank you to John Neill and Bari, Jonno, Phoenix, and Toy, for teaching me so much about patience, understanding, and relaxation.

Thank you to my friends Di and Judy for holding the fort when I got swamped.

Thank you to Terri Hudson for this third opportunity.

About the Author

Barbara Czegel is president of SIRIUS3, a Toronto-based company that provides training for Help Desk professionals and facilitates improvement initiatives for technology support areas. She has over 22 years of experience in both the technical and human facets of the computer industry. Ms. Czegel has been involved in the planning, development, analysis, and support of retail business systems, planning systems, and manufacturing systems. She has justified, established, and managed Help Desk operations in corporate environments and is an experienced communicator and facilitator.

Ms. Czegel received her bachelor of science in computer science and mathematics from the University of Toronto in 1975. She is a member of the Help Desk Institute and the Toronto local chapter of the Help Desk Institute.

Barbara Czegel can be reached at bczegel@sirius3.com. The SIRIUS3 Web site is at www.sirius3.com.

Note from the Author about the "Help Desk Practitioner"

Over the course of several years spent working with and training Help Desk professionals I have come across a wide variety of titles given to people who work on a Help Desk. These include Help Desk analyst, Help Desk operator, Help Desk officer, service representative, support representative, and so on. Few of the titles are indicative in any way of the roles played by the people holding them. For the purposes of this book I wanted to use a term that would cover all of these titles without implying that any one was in any way better than the others. I did not want the term to imply any specific role because there are so many roles that must be fulfilled on a Help Desk. I selected the term Help Desk practitioner and use it to refer to anyone who works on a Help Desk on a day-to-day basis.

SECTION ONE

Expectations of the Business

Roles

Being a Help Desk practitioner involves much more than just answering the phone. A Help Desk practitioner has a direct impact on the profitability of the business he or she supports. You seem surprised. Perhaps you haven't considered the impact you have on the business you support. How many businesses can you think of today that do not rely on some form of technology to keep them running? Not many, if any at all. And who keeps that technology up and running? Who keeps the users of that technology working? That's right, you, the Help Desk practitioner, do.

In This Chapter

In this chapter I will attempt to show you how important your role on the Help Desk is and how complex it can be. I will discuss the following topics:

- Profitability scale of a company
- Roles you play on the Help Desk
- Skills you need on the Help Desk

Profitability Scale of a Company

All companies operate on a profitability scale somewhere between prosperity and bankruptcy. Hopefully, the business you support is closer to prosperity than bankruptcy. When company employees are contributing at their full potential, the profitability of the business is at a certain point, as shown in Figure 1.1. When employees are not contributing at their full potential, the profitability of the business moves down, as shown in Figure 1.2. The company is not as profitable as it could be if the employees were fully productive. This also means that when a Help Desk customer is unable to work, whether because the technology is not functioning properly or the customer does not know how to do something, the profitability of the company decreases. That company is getting zero return

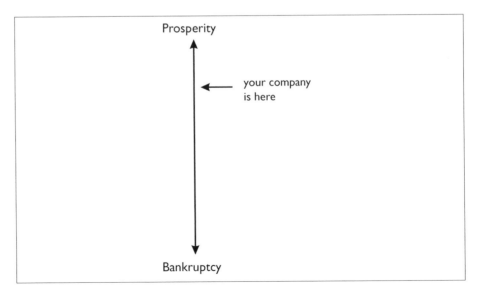

Figure 1.1   Profitability scale.

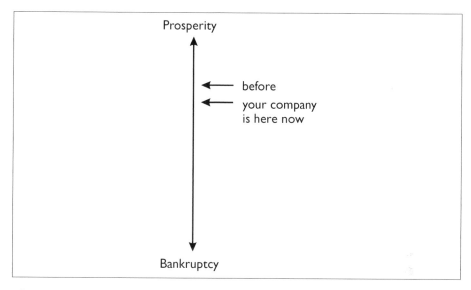

Figure 1.2   Impact on profitability when employees are unable to work.

for the salary the employee is being paid. You might think that this is not a significant amount, since the employee is rarely down for long, but that is not the case. One employee unable to work for ten minutes has a fairly minor impact on profitability, it's true. However, one thousand employees each unable to work from ten minutes to one hour over the course of a month becomes a very significant cost, certainly more than enough to impact the profitability of the business.

What does all of this have to do with you? You often have direct control over how long a customer is unable to work. If you are not as effective as you could be in getting that customer up and running as soon as possible, you are negatively impacting profitability. If, on the other hand, you have consciously made the effort to become as effective a Help Desk practitioner as possible you will have that customer up and running as quickly as possible, minimizing any negative impact on profitability. Just in case you still don't believe me, let's look at some scenarios that illustrate this point.

SCENARIO 1

Dianne is a Help Desk analyst for an insurance company. She is technically oriented and very eager. Midge calls Dianne with a problem. "Dianne," she says, "I can't print this spreadsheet out. I've got to go to a meeting in 15 minutes and I need to distribute copies of it, so I'm kind of desperate here." "No problem," Dianne replies. "I'll just pop over and see if I can find the problem." Dianne pops over to Midge's workstation and after about five minutes or so proclaims herself stumped. "This is really weird. I just don't understand what the heck is going on. This sure is an interesting problem."

Midge is starting to get upset because the meeting time is creeping closer, but Dianne persists in checking and rechecking because this is really the most interesting problem she has encountered since leaving school. There appears to be some kind of conflict between the network software and the spreadsheet software.

After 15 minutes have passed Midge is almost frantic. "I need this spreadsheet for the meeting! Please, just print it out!" Dianne is apologetic: "I'm sorry, I can't find the problem. Just give me a few more minutes." A "few more minutes" turns into 15 more minutes and still no spreadsheet. Midge goes to the meeting very stressed, with a few scribbled notes. She manages to get through the material but must set up another meeting the next morning to review the correct figures.

Discussion

What was the cost of Scenario 1? The meeting lasted one hour, with six people. Six hours of employee time were wasted. No one got anything accomplished. Midge found that she really could not make any decisions without the real numbers. Dianne wasted at least two hours outside of the meeting. The project has now taken eight person-hours longer than it should have, eight hours that people could have spent working on another company initiative. The business paid for those eight hours of employee time with zero results. The profitability of this company has definitely moved down. But consider Scenario 2.

SCENARIO 2

Once again, Midge calls Dianne with a spreadsheet problem. "I need it for a meeting in 15 minutes!" she says worriedly. "No problem," says Dianne, but this time she means it. "Let me just use my remote control software to do a quick check. . . . Well, the problem is certainly not obvious, so I'll just copy your spreadsheet to another network drive and then print it off on one of the printers in this area." Dianne matches action to word and soon the spreadsheet is printing out. "You can pick the spreadsheet up here on your way to the meeting," Dianne tells Midge, "and I'll have to look into why you can't print it from your workstation. I'll let you know what the problem is as soon as I find out." The whole interaction has taken approximately seven minutes.

"That's not that important," Midge tells her, "I've got the spreadsheet. That's what's important." Midge goes off to the meeting, which proceeds as if she had not had a problem.

Discussion

Dianne's actions prevented any significant negative impact to the company's position on the profitability scale.

The way you handle each Help Desk call makes a difference in how profitable the business you support is. Very simply, the more effective you are, the more effective your customers are and the more profitable the business you support will be.

Roles You Play on the Help Desk

To be effective on the Help Desk you need to understand all the roles you must play and be effective at performing each of them. The major roles that Help Desk practitioners must play are as follows:

- Partner
- Problem eliminator
- Communicator
- Marketer
- Data gatherer
- Expert
- Customer service representative

Let's examine each of these in more detail.

Partner

Playing the role of partner means believing in and working to fulfill the mission, services, and objectives of your Help Desk. It means taking the time to understand how the Help Desk fits into the business, supporting all Help Desk initiatives, and working for the benefit of the whole Help Desk, not just yourself. It means scrutinizing each action you take to determine whether or not it is in the best interests of the Help Desk. For example, say you are on your way to a customer's workstation to help with a problem. Another customer stops you and says, "Could you please come by my desk and help me? It will only take a few minutes!" You think about it. If you go with the second customer you will be working against the Help Desk in several ways. First, you will be making the first customer wait unnecessarily. Second, you will be working on an unlogged call, which means valuable call statistics will be lost. This will impact performance measurement and any cost justifications that the Help Desk needs to do, such as justifying more staff. Third, you will be setting a precedent. The second customer will expect this kind of service next time, and, worse, that customer may tell several other customers who will all start expecting that kind of service. As a partner, your decision is easy. "I'm sorry," you tell the second customer, "I cannot work on any problems that have not been logged and scheduled by the Help Desk."

A Help Desk practitioner that does not really believe in or support what the Help Desk is doing can sabotage the success of the Help Desk without even realizing it. Scenario 3 illustrates how this can happen.

SCENARIO 3

Gene is a Help Desk practitioner on a very busy Help Desk. The Help Desk has just installed an automated voice response system. The automation was installed to eliminate several mundane, repetitive tasks, the most repetitive of which were password resets. One of the challenges Gene's Help Desk faces is getting the customers to use the automated system. Customers have not had to deal with any automation from the Help Desk to date.

Frank from Accounting calls the Help Desk and gets the automated voice response system. He listens to the options, decides he doesn't want to talk to a machine and doesn't trust the machine to reset his password, and bypasses the automated options to get a Help Desk person. He gets Gene and proceeds to tell Gene his problem. "Hi, this is Frank, and I've forgotten my password. I've been on holidays for a few weeks, and I just can't remember what I changed my password to before I left. Can you please reset it for me?"

"We have an automated system that will . . . ," Gene starts.

"Please," Frank replies, "I don't want to use that automated machine thing. I don't like talking to a machine. Please just reset it for me. It won't take you long."

Gene hesitates for a moment, then capitulates. He has never really supported the automated voice response system. It makes him feel somewhat replaceable, and, like Frank, Gene much prefers interacting with humans to interacting with machines. He understands how uncomfortable Frank feels about using the automation. "Hey, I know what you mean," Gene says. "I prefer talking to people too. I'll just reset it for you now." Gene resets the password and Frank hangs up, satisfied.

Discussion

Was the interaction in Scenario 3 successful? From Frank's point of view, yes. He got his password reset, and he didn't have to deal with the machine. From Gene's point of view, yes as well. He helped Frank, and he felt good about that. From the point of view of the Help Desk, absolutely not. Without realizing it, Gene has undermined the success of the automation project. Frank will be more reluctant than ever to use the new technology because now he has someone on the Help Desk who supports his point of view, who will accommodate his desire for personal service. He sees absolutely no reason to use the automation now. To make matters worse, Frank is going to tell his colleagues, "Hey, you don't really need to use that machine thing. Those Help Desk people will still reset your password for you, no problem!" Gene's coworkers on the Help Desk will not be impressed. They don't want to spend their days resetting passwords for customers; they want to do more interesting work. If they had heard Gene's interaction with Frank they might have had something to say to him about it.

How should Gene have handled the interaction? Gene should have encouraged Frank to use the technology.

Let's look at Scenario 4.

SCENARIO 4

Once again, Frank calls the Help Desk to get his password reset. Once again, he bypasses the automation to get to a Help Desk person. "Hi, this is Frank, and I've forgotten my password. I've been on holidays for a few weeks, and I just can't remember what I changed my password to before I left. Can you please reset it for me?"

"We have an automated system that will . . . ," Gene starts.

"Please," Frank replies, "I don't want to use that automated machine thing. I don't like talking to a machine. Please just reset it for me. It won't take you long."

This time Gene does not capitulate. He understands how important this project is to the Help Desk. He empathizes with Frank but remains firm. Gene understands that his own time could be much better spent doing things that can't be easily handled by a machine.

"I know you aren't comfortable with the new system yet," he tells Frank, "but I really encourage you to try it out to get used to it. We'll be adding more and more functions to the automation, and we won't be able to do this for you because of our workload. Let me walk you through the procedure. This time we'll do it together, but next time I'd like you to try it on your own. If you have any problems using it you can call us."

Discussion

In Scenario 4 Gene played the role of partner by supporting the automation initiative and encouraging Frank to use the new system even though it would have been easier to give in to Frank. Gene was helping ensure the success of the automation initiative, which will free up time for the Help Desk staff to focus on the work most important to the business. Gene also played a customer service role by helping Frank through the automation process and reassuring him that help would be available should he need it.

Problem Eliminator

I have yet to encounter a Help Desk that has time to waste, yet I often encounter Help Desks that spend time solving the same problems over and over. Time spent solving the same problems repeatedly is time wasted. It is not enough for Help Desk practitioners to be problem solvers; they must be problem eliminators. Help Desk practitioners must learn to ask themselves, "What can I do to make sure this problem does not recur?"

Unfortunately, when you know how to fix something it is easier to keep fixing it than to do something to prevent it from breaking. Each time you fix it you think, "this will only take a few minutes." All those minutes can add up to a significant amount of time, however, time that you could be spending on things that are more important to the business and affect its profitability. Also, as technology changes, new problems will keep emerging. If you don't get rid of the old ones you are not going to be able to handle the problem load.

SCENARIO 5

Natalie is a Help Desk practitioner. She receives a call from Bill, a customer on the second floor. "My PC is frozen," Bill tells her. "I can't do anything." Natalie knows how to fix the problem. "Just reboot," she says. Bill reboots and everything is fine. During the course of the day Natalie gets six more calls from the second floor, all with the same problem.

Discussion

You may be wondering, "What's wrong with this scenario? It looks fine to me. Natalie got the customer back up." Yes, Natalie did get the customer back up, and she did not take too much time doing it. But consider the amount of disruption for Natalie, her coworkers, and the customers over the course of a month if the problem keeps recurring. It becomes significant. It becomes even more significant as new problems occur, and the Help Desk has less time to spend with each caller. But consider Scenario 6.

SCENARIO 6

In this scenario, Natalie plays the role of problem eliminator. Instead of just telling Bill to reboot and leaving things at that, Natalie decides to do something about the recurring problem. She creates a problem log outlining the problem and puts it into the project queue, giving it the priority that is reserved for recurring problems. The project staff reviews the problem, determines the cause (the version of software being used needed a vendor patch), and installs the required fix. The Help Desk stops getting those calls.

Discussion

The problem eliminator role described in this scenario is vital to those Help Desk practitioners who want to improve and succeed. There is no room for wasting time in an environment where both time and people are in short supply.

Communicator

Your role as communicator is not as simple as it might seem. Not only do you need to communicate with at least the five groups shown in Figure 1.3,

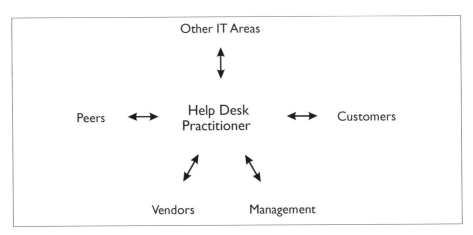

Figure 1.3   Five groups you need to communicate with.

but that communication needs to be two-way. When communication fails there is a corresponding negative impact on the profitability of the business.

The five groups you need to communicate with are as follows:

1.   Your peers
2.   Your customers
3.   Other information technology (IT) groups
4.   Management
5.   Vendors

Your Peers

On a Help Desk, it is vital that you exchange information with your peers. A problem that occurs in one area could affect several other areas. If you take the call for the initial problem and don't pass the information on to your peers in some way, they will be missing a valuable piece of information. They might waste time trying to solve the problem, not knowing where the problem originated. Similarly, if you come across something different, a little strange, or not quite right—for example, a batch job running much longer or shorter than usual or sudden decreases in response time—it is important that you pass that information on to your peers. It may help someone prevent a problem or help resolve one later on.

I still encounter situations in which people on the Help Desk are sitting next to each other working on the same problem without even knowing it. Having the most up-to-date, feature-filled Help Desk management software is no guarantee that the required communication will take place. Sometimes, there is no substitute for simply telling someone something they may need to know.

To play the role of communicator effectively with your peers you need to do the following:

- Include all the information you know about a problem when you log it. The time you take to key in a few vital facts could save someone else much more time when they need to solve that problem or a related problem.

- When you resolve a problem, log the complete solution. Include all of the important components of the solution and do not simply key in "Done" or "Completed."

- When you notice something strange, something odd, or something of note that might affect the Help Desk—for example, a virus—tell your peers. Choose a communication medium that is appropriate for your Help Desk, one that your peers will read or listen to. It really doesn't matter whether you stand up and shout it, put it on a message board, or put it on a Web site, as long as you get the information across.

- Listen to and act on information that your peers pass on to you.

Your Customers

Communicating with your customers typically involves listening to them describe their problems, asking them questions to clarify information, and then explaining solutions to them or updating them on the status of problems. Doing a poor job in any of these three areas means that you may not hear the problem correctly, you may not get all of the information necessary to solve the problem, or your customer may not understand your instructions or explanation. The problem will not be resolved, and the Help Desk will get at least one more phone call about it.

As Scenario 7 shows, doing a poor job in any aspect of communication with the customer can increase call volume unnecessarily and have a negative impact on the profitability of the company.

SCENARIO 7

At 8 A.M., Carolyn, a practitioner on the Help Desk, gets a call from the accounting department. "My spreadsheet isn't working, and I really have to get these numbers to Finance by 2:00!" shouts Marlene, in panic. "OK. Leave it with me, and I'll look after it for you," Carolyn tells her. Carolyn looks at the problem, decides it's going to take a while to resolve, and decides to put it aside for 20 minutes or so while she finishes a smaller problem she had been working on. When the smaller problem is done, Carolyn decides to go and explain it to the customer.

While she is gone, Marlene calls back. "I called ages ago!" she says, still panicked. "The problem should be fixed by now but it isn't!"

Madhu, who takes the call, checks the log and sees that nothing has been done on the problem.

"I'm sorry, it's not done yet," he tells Marlene. "What's going on!" she cries, even more panicked. "I need that spreadsheet! Carolyn said she'd do it!" "Let me look into it for you. I'll call you back in a few minutes," Madhu promises, somewhat overwhelmed by Marlene's panicked tone. Madhu gets off the phone and starts looking into Marlene's problem.

After about 15 minutes, Marlene calls back again. "Well? Have you finished the problem?" she asks impatiently. Madhu assures her he is working on it. "It's just going to take a while, but I am working on it right now. I know what the problem is. I'm just fixing it." Marlene hangs up, somewhat appeased. Carolyn returns and is greeted by a disgruntled Madhu. While he is explaining the situation to her, Marlene calls back again. Madhu updates her on his progress and promises to call her back when he's done. "It won't take long now," he assures Marlene, while glaring at Carolyn, who has taken the problem over and is working furiously to make the necessary changes.

Marlene calls two more times, at 10-minute intervals, before the problem is finally resolved and tested, well in time for her Finance meeting.

Discussion

After reading Scenario 7 you may be thinking how annoying it must have been for Carolyn and Madhu to have to deal with such an unreasonable customer—that Marlene was a pain in the neck. You may be thinking that you have too many customers like Marlene. I need to interrupt your line of reasoning. Marlene is not the one at fault here. Carolyn must take credit for the first mistake. She told Marlene that she would look after her problem but did not tell her that she wouldn't be working on it right away.

When I am a customer and someone tells me they are looking after my problem, I assume they will be looking after it right away. That may be unreasonable on my part, especially since I am a Help Desk person and should know better, but unless someone tells me something different, that is what I assume. Madhu compounds the first problem when he tells Marlene that he will call her "in a few minutes." What does "a few minutes" mean to a customer? When I am trying to get help from a service provider, whether an insurance company or an appliance repair company, "a few minutes" means 10 minutes tops. After 10 minutes, if I don't hear back, I call. That's what Marlene did. In fact, as a customer with things to do, I would probably behave exactly as Marlene did.

What could Carolyn and Madhu have done differently? They could have communicated more effectively to Marlene. Carolyn could have told Marlene that she had something else to do before working on her problem. She could have given Marlene an estimate as to when her problem would be resolved. Similarly, Madhu could have been more specific about how long he would take to get back to Marlene. Scenario 8 shows how Carolyn and Madhu could have handled the whole situation more effectively.

SCENARIO **8**

Once again, Marlene calls the Help Desk in a panic. "My spreadsheet isn't working, and I really have to get these numbers to Finance by 2:00!" "OK. Leave it with me, and I'll look after it for you," Carolyn tells her and starts looking at the problem. After a few minutes, Carolyn realizes it's going to take a while to resolve and decides to put it aside for 20 minutes or so while she finishes a smaller problem she had been working on. She knows Marlene is very concerned about getting the problem resolved, and she knows that Marlene expects it to be resolved in a few minutes, so Carolyn gives her a call.

"Marlene, this problem is going to take longer than I thought, and I do have another important issue to work on. I should be finished working on your problem in about an hour and a half. That should give you plenty of time to get ready for your meeting. I'll give you a call to confirm that everything is done and to have you check it out on your end." "An hour and a half? You can't do it any faster?" "No, Marlene, I'm afraid that's the best I can do for you. I'll call you when I get it done."

Exactly one hour and twenty minutes later, Carolyn finishes Marlene's problem and calls her back. "Marlene, I've fixed your problem. You should be able to get into your spreadsheet just fine. Can you try it now?" Marlene tries her spreadsheet software and agrees that the problem is fixed. "Yes, thanks, it seems to be working just fine." "Great. If you have any more problems, just give us a call."

Discussion

In Scenario 8, Carolyn communicated effectively to Marlene, and Marlene did not have to call back even once. When Marlene complained that an hour and a half was too long, Carolyn was not tempted to capitulate and give a shorter time. She knew that an hour and a half—including 15 or 20 minutes as a buffer for unforeseen issues—was the time she needed. If Carolyn had not understood the problem she would have told Marlene that she would investigate the problem first, then call her back with an estimate on how long it would take to fix. That conversation might have gone something like this: "Marlene, I've looked at your problem, and I don't understand yet what's causing it. I need to do some more investigation before I can tell you how long it will take to fix. I'll call you back in an hour and give you an update."

In Scenario 7 Marlene called the Help Desk six times in the course of getting her problem resolved—five times more than in Scenario 8, five times more than was necessary. The profitability of the company was negatively impacted. Customer time and Help Desk time were unnecessarily wasted.

Other Information Technology Groups

Other IT groups that you need to communicate with might include technical support areas, development areas, other Help Desks, or operational areas. You are passing problems and information on to these groups and getting information from them. Any time there is a break in communication, problems may take longer to solve, unnecessary calls may come into the Help Desk, and time will be wasted. Chapter 3 addresses the communications challenges involved in interacting with other levels of support and with other Help Desks.

Management

Depending upon your particular position, communicating with management might include letting your own manager know about the status of Help Desk activity or about escalating problems. It might include passing on situations that might need to be addressed in the future or making suggestions for improvement. Your role as a communicator also means listening to management, learning where the business is going, and absorbing suggestions and requirements.

Vendors

The vendors you need to communicate with include the vendors of any Help Desk software, hardware, and services you are using or thinking about using as well as the vendors of the software and hardware you are supporting. You need to keep these vendors informed of any problems you are having and of any special requirements you have. You also need to keep up to date on any new releases, fixes, published problems and solutions, recalls, available training, new service offerings, and so on. The more information you have about the products and services you use and support the quicker you can resolve problems for your customers. Similarly, the more information you pass on to your vendors about requirements and problems the greater the chance that those requirements will be met and those problems will be resolved.

Addendum to the Communicator's Role

When managers are hiring people for the Help Desk they sometimes minimize the role of communicator by describing it as "someone who can deal with people." I hope I've been able to show you that the role of communicator encompasses at least five groups of people as well as the myriad communications activities that are involved in interacting with each of those groups—being a communicator means much, much more than just "dealing with people."

Marketer

On a Help Desk, every customer interaction is a marketing opportunity. The marketer's role involves taking advantage of these opportunities to promote a professional Help Desk image, to sell the Help Desk's performance and successes, to communicate information about the technological environment, and to teach customers how to use technology more effectively. If you don't give this marketing role enough importance or don't even realize that it is a role you must play, you could be jeopardizing the effectiveness of your Help Desk, as illustrated by Scenario 9.

SCENARIO 9

Shaunna's day starts badly. She gets a speeding ticket on the way to work and she's 15 minutes late. As she rushes to her desk, her manager gives her an admonishing look. The light on her phone is flashing so Shaunna picks up her first call.

"Good morning, Help Desk, Shaunna speaking." A hesitant male voice comes across the line. "Hi, this is Chris from Human Resources. I'm having trouble using this PC. It doesn't seem to work." Shaunna sighs to herself. She is still wound up, hasn't had time for her first coffee, and her first call is a particularly trying one—probably a customer unfamiliar with his PC. "Can you be more specific," she asks, "what makes you think it doesn't work?" "The light isn't on." "Which light?" "The light on the screen thingee." *I need a coffee,* Shaunna thinks to herself, *why is this guy being such an idiot?* "Can you just check the on/off switch for your screen?" Shaunna suggests to Chris. "I want to make sure that it's working properly." The problem does indeed turn out to be a monitor that has not been turned on.

Shaunna spends several minutes more with Chris explaining what he needs to do to log onto the network. Chris does not seem to know anything, and Shaunna gets increasingly frustrated. "Oh. I think I'm on now, things are happening," Chris finally says. "Great! Any more problems, give us a call!" and without giving Chris a chance to say another word, Shaunna hangs up and races over to the coffee machine with her mug. She is back at her desk before the next call comes in. "Chris sure needs to take one of our introductory PC courses" is her final thought before picking up the next call.

Unfortunately, Chris has not managed to get on to the network and spends most of the morning wandering around his department trying to find someone who can help him. He finally does manage to get onto the network but starts running into problems using the word processing software and again turns to his colleagues. By the end of the day he has accomplished very little and has wasted several hours of his colleagues' time.

Discussion

Fulfilling the role of marketer means educating the customer. This does not mean that it's up to you to teach the customer what to do, but it is up to you to help him or her use technology more effectively. Shaunna had a great marketing opportunity to suggest some courses to Chris, but she didn't take advantage of it. As a result, Chris wasted several hours of his own and his colleagues' time. The profitability of the business was negatively impacted.

Despite the fact that she hadn't had her first coffee of the morning, what Shaunna should have done was to let Chris know that training was available and who he should contact to sign up for it. Chris may still have wasted some time until he actually took the training, but the sooner he was signed up, the less time he would waste. Scenario 10 shows how Shaunna could have done some marketing to minimize the negative impact on the profitability of the business.

SCENARIO **10**

Shaunna arrives at the Help Desk late, breathless and craving coffee. "Good morning, Help Desk, Shaunna speaking." A hesitant male voice comes across the line."Hi, this is Chris from Human Resources. I'm having trouble using this PC. It doesn't seem to work." Uh-oh. A customer unfamiliar with his PC. "Can you be more specific," she asks, "what makes you think it doesn't work?" "The light isn't on." "Which light?" "The light on the screen thingee."

"This guy is in desperate need of training," decides Shaunna. She resolves the monitor problem and walks Chris through the process of getting on to the network. She makes sure he is actually on the network then broaches the subject of training. "Chris," she asks, "how long have you had your PC?"

"Just got it this morning," he admits. "We like to tell all of our new PC users about all of the great PC training the company offers. Just so you'll know what's available. Have you taken any PC training yet?" Shaunna asks, knowing what the answer will be. "What PC training?"

Chris wants to know. Shaunna goes on to explain what training is available and, when Chris expresses interest, transfers him directly to the training department. Then she goes for coffee.

Discussion

Scenario 10 did not take much, if any, more time than Scenario 9, yet the impact on the business is very different. Scenario 9 left Chris a completely nonfunctioning employee, while Scenario 10 got Chris onto the network and signed up for some training. Chris soon becomes more functional.

Each day that an employee is nonfunctional means working hours lost, which means the business is being negatively impacted. The sooner you can get an employee productive, the less loss there will be. Chapter 11 looks at the Help Desk practitioner's role as marketer in more detail.

Data Gatherer

On a Help Desk you are exposed to a barrage of data. This data contains valuable opportunities for improvement, for preventing and resolving problems, and for cost justifications. The data typically comes from your customers or from your Help Desk system. Your customers might be telling you what services or improvements would make it easier for them to do their jobs, or they may be giving you feedback about your performance as a Help Desk. As a data gatherer you would not ignore this data but would collect it and either do something with it, such as make improvements, or pass it on to someone who would act on it.

In Scenario 10 in the previous section of this chapter, Shaunna, the Help Desk practitioner, could have been even more effective by playing her data-gatherer role and making sure that the interaction with Chris was properly logged as a training-type call. When Chris called in the future, Shaunna and her colleagues would see the logged information and could help Chris more effectively. If Chris did not take the recommended training, the Help Desk manager could use the logged calls as proof that Chris needed training and could approach Chris's manager with the data.

If Shaunna and her colleagues logged all training-type calls, statistics generated by the Help Desk management system would show the total percentage of calls that were from customers requiring training, and this statistic could be used to justify customer training initiatives.

Expert

Your customers expect you to know the products you support. You are expected to have a certain level of technical expertise. To fulfill your role as expert you need to keep up with all of the new products and services you support and get the training you need.

Getting the training you need does not mean waiting for your manager to suggest it to you. It means identifying the training you require, doing some research to find out when and where the training is offered, and approaching your manager with some suggestions. In your data-gatherer role, you could also collect the statistics necessary to prove that training would be beneficial. Chapter 10 provides an example of using data gathered on the Help Desk to justify required training.

Customer Service Representative

The situations you deal with on a Help Desk are often tense and fraught with emotion. Customers call you when they cannot get their work done. They may be facing impending deadlines, angry managers, or other stresses that you know nothing about. You need to be able to get problems solved while dealing with their reaction to these stresses. This may mean dealing with anger, frustration, unhappiness, or panic.

Playing the role of customer service representative also means looking for ways to make things better for the customers and improve customer satisfaction. This means constantly evaluating your environment and looking for ways to eliminate service problems that crop up and prevent future service problems.

SCENARIO 11

Phil hangs up the phone, somewhat concerned. David, a Help Desk customer, has just called complaining that his PC has not been delivered yet. He had been promised a delivery time of two weeks exactly two weeks ago. Phil had checked the log while David was talking, and, sure enough, David had done all of the right things. He should have received the PC today at the latest, but according to the log the PC had not even arrived yet.

Phil calls the technology receiving department. "Yes, it's sitting right here," is the answer he gets when he inquires about the missing PC, "I think it just came in this morning." "Great!" he says, relieved. "I'll send someone down to pick it up right away." As soon as Phil is off the phone he asks one of the PC technicians to pick up the equipment from receiving and configure it. "It arrived really late, and David is pretty upset. If we can get it to him by the end of today that would be great. Today was the install date." The technician nods and hurries off.

Within two hours she has the PC unpacked and configured and is on her way to David's desk. Phil calls David and lets him know the PC is on its way. David is pleased. "Whew!" thinks Phil. "That was close! I sure handled that well!"

Discussion

You might be asking "So what's the problem? Phil got the PC installed on the due date." True. Phil got this particular PC installed on the due date. However, Phil ignored a very important point—why was the PC delivered late? Something had happened to make that PC late. If that something was an event that had crept into the PC ordering and delivery process then chances are the event will recur, possibly with each PC order. What had been an isolated incident could turn into a full-scale service problem.

Phil could have averted a major problem by taking the time to find out why the PC order was late and then taking action to resolve the problem. If he could not prevent all orders from being late, he could at least alert customers to the fact that they would have to wait longer than expected for their PCs. Scenario 12 illustrates what Phil could have done.

SCENARIO 12

As in Scenario 11, Phil gets a call from David who complains that his PC, which should have been delivered today, was not yet at his desk. Phil calls the technology receiving department. "Yes, it's sitting right here," he's told when he inquires about the missing PC, "I think it just came in this morning." "Just came in this morning? Are you sure?" Phil is concerned. The Help Desk has several PC orders still outstanding, and if this one was late others could be also. "Hang on. Let me check the packing slip . . . delivery date . . . yup, it came in today. Want us to send up the paperwork?" "No, no, I'll send someone down to pick everything up right away."

Within a few minutes Phil is reading through the paperwork while a technician works to set the PC up for David. The paperwork is in order, and Phil starts to trace the PC order to see where it got held up. Four phone calls later Phil has his answer. The manufacturer was having problems getting certain parts and as a result is behind in manufacturing and delivery. The PC order had not been shipped until this morning. The part availability problem will be continuing for some time.

Phil finds all the affected orders and lets his manager and the other Help Desk staff know about the problem. They arrange for an alternate source for the most important orders (the logistics project) and for the regular orders alert the customers that their PCs might be late. Phil's manager researches another PC supplier in case the problem becomes permanent.

Discussion

In his customer service role, Phil was concerned about the impact of any service problem on all of his customers, not just David. He kept his eye out for potential problems and did what he could to head them off. In Scenario 12, Phil prevented a negative impact on a mission-critical project and minimized the inconvenience to customers. He communicated to his team and management so that everyone could work together to minimize the negative impact on the profitability of the business.

Playing All the Roles

The roles you play on the Help Desk are most effective when they are integrated. The more of these roles you fulfill at the same time, the more effective you can be. In Scenario 12 in the previous section of this chapter, Phil played several roles to get the service problem resolved. Besides the role of a customer service representative, he played communicator and partner roles by letting coworkers and management know about the problem and working with them to resolve it. He played a problem eliminator role by investigating the service problem and taking action to address the cause, not just the symptom.

Skills You Need on the Help Desk

Each of the seven roles discussed in the previous section of this chapter requires certain skills. These are the skills you need to focus on acquiring or improving to be an effective Help Desk practitioner:

- Proaction
- Focus
- Problem solving
- Communication
- Technical expertise
- Customer service

To play all Help Desk roles most effectively a Help Desk practitioner requires all of the skills in this list, but as a practitioner you may not yet have all these skills to the degree that makes you most effective. Figure 1.4 shows the three most important skills in each of the roles a practitioner takes on. You may notice that the role of customer service representative has four "top three skills." Each of the four is simply too critical to leave out.

Proaction

The skill of proaction can be defined by the following characteristics:

- Taking initiative
- Taking responsibility
- Making things happen
- Fixing things before they break

Roles \ Skills	Proaction	Focus	Problem Solving	Communication	Technical Expertise	Customer Service
Partner	✓	✓		✓		
Problem Eliminator	✓		✓	✓		
Communicator	✓			✓		✓
Marketer		✓		✓		✓
Data Gatherer		✓		✓	✓	
Expert	✓		✓		✓	
Customer Service Representative	✓	✓		✓		✓

Figure 1.4   Top three (plus) skills required for each role.

- Always asking "Why are we doing this?" and "Could we be doing this better?"
- Not being a sheep

The skill of proaction is the most important skill a Help Desk practitioner can have. Without proaction you will never be anything more than mediocre, run-of-the-mill, reactive. Without proaction you will be just a sheep, following unquestioningly. With proaction you make things happen. You make your Help Desk more effective. You positively impact the profitability of your business.

I will use the example of a tie company to illustrate the application of the skill of proaction. (Don't ask me why a tie company. It just works.) Scenario 13 describes a company that is sadly reactive.

SCENARIO 13

Ray is the owner of a fairly successful tie company called Ray's Ties. His sales were fairly steady until two months ago, when they started to fall (see Figure 1.5). Ray is puzzled by the sudden decline. He decides to send one of his top tie salespeople, Kristina, out into the marketplace to see what the problem is. It doesn't take Kristina long to get back to Ray. "Ray," she says, taking the bull by the horns, "your ties are too fat." "What!" cries Ray, "I thought fat ties were all the rage!"

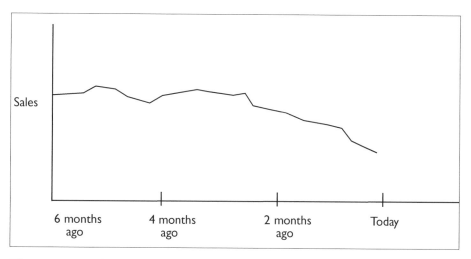

Figure 1.5   Sales at Ray's Ties decrease.

"Everyone is wearing thin ties now. They are buying thin." Kristina explains. "We need to start manufacturing thin ties."

Ray listens to Kristina, has his tie patterns changed, and starts production of the new thinner tie. From the time Ray talks to Kristina it takes two months for the first thin ties to come off of the production line. Ray's sales gradually recover, and he manages to recover the costs of the change (see Figure 1.6). Just as Ray is starting to relax, however, his sales start to drop again. He calls Kristina in immediately. "What's going on?" he cries, "I thought people loved my thin ties! Find out why people aren't buying my ties!" Once again Kristina goes out to the tie stores to see what is happening. She returns to Ray with bad news. "Bow ties," she says. "Everyone wants bow ties."

Ray shakes his head, speechless. Customers are so unpredictable. "OK," he finally says, "let's change." Tie production undergoes the necessary changes, and two months later Ray is producing bow ties. But because switching over to bow ties is expensive, it takes longer for his sales to recover.

Discussion

If I continued the sad story of Ray's Ties, we would see periods of declining sales with longer and longer recovery times and Ray finally fad-

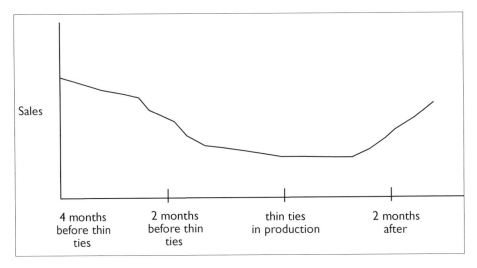

Figure 1.6 The first recovery.

ing into oblivion. Ray's Ties is heading very purposefully toward the bankruptcy mark on the scale of profitability. What is Ray doing wrong? I'll give you a hint: "Baa." Ray is being completely reactive, waiting until the market changes before he changes his business. What difference can proaction make to Ray? Check out Scenario 14.

SCENARIO **14**

We're back in the office of Ray's Ties, and Ray has just finished hearing Kristina describe the problem with the fat ties. Ray has also just read a book (I won't mention which one) about being proactive. "Kristina," he says, "I have a new job for you." Kristina perks up. It hasn't been much fun working for such a reactive company. In fact, she's been secretly job hunting for something more exciting. "I want you to be our tie market analyst. I want you to stay out in the marketplace, check what ties are selling, go to fashion shows, and find out what's coming in tie trends. I want us to be ahead of everyone else. I want Ray's Ties to know what consumers will be buying six months from now. In fact, I want Ray's Ties to be setting trends!"

Kristina is elated but a little concerned. After all, she has been reactive for a long time. "Isn't that risky?" she asks tentatively. "Hell, yes!" cries Ray. "But it sure beats slowly sinking into oblivion! I'm sure we'll make some mistakes, but if we learn from them we'll just get further and further ahead." Kristina accepts the job, Ray lends her his book on proaction, and Ray's Ties launches itself into a period of growth and prosperity. As tie market analyst, Kristina attends the latest fashion shows and brings back information about upcoming trends. She starts making suggestions for tie designs based on what she has learned about the market and seen on the runways and on potential customers. A few of Ray's Ties designs fail (no one really wanted to wear a tie shaped like a watermelon), but most are wildly successful (Kristina learned to stay away from fruit shapes).

Discussion

A proactive Ray's Ties is going to be in business for a long, long time. Even if ties completely go out of style Ray will know about it well ahead of time and will be able to launch his business in a new direction, toward a new trend.

The lessons of Ray's Ties can be applied to any business, to any Help Desk. Help Desks that are proactive, that are constantly looking ahead at what business requirements and technology are emerging, are going to be prized by the businesses they support and are going to be around for a while. Help Desks that are reactive, wait for the business to change before they change, and are constantly struggling to keep up with change and immediate problems, will eventually fade into oblivion—replaced, outsourced, or forced out of business along with the business they supported.

Throughout this book I refer constantly to proaction, giving you suggestions on where and how to apply it on the Help Desk. Becoming proactive is not easy. It requires a conscious change of mindset, a different way of thinking in every aspect of your life. Chapter 12 discusses the change in attitude that is required. Reactive practitioners make reactive Help Desks. Proactive practitioners make proactive Help Desks. It's up to you.

Focus

The skill of focus can be defined as follows:

- Understanding what the business requires
- Making decisions and doing work based on what is most important to the business
- Promoting and supporting Help Desk initiatives at every opportunity
- Fostering a professional Help Desk image

The skill of focus requires an understanding of the Help Desk's whole reason for being. It requires an understanding of and belief in the Help Desk's mission, objectives, and services. It requires an understanding of the Help Desk's customers, senior management, and other IT groups. All of these areas are covered in detail in Chapter 2.

Problem Solving

Four of the main activities involved in the skill of problem solving are as follows:

- Being able to interact with the customer to get the required information and to relate status and instructions—in other words, good communication skills.
- Research and analysis. The ability to use problem resolution tools and other resources such as the Internet.
- Solution selection and testing.
- Addressing root causes, not just symptoms.

Chapter 7 tells you how to enhance your problem-solving skills with a new strategy that addresses root causes through the use of a layered approach.

Communication

The skill of communication has several component skills. The three main ones are the following:

- Listening effectively
- Getting your message across effectively
- Getting beyond challenging behavior to find out what the customer really wants or needs

Chapters 5 and 6 address communication in problem solving. Chapter 11 discusses marketing, an application of communication on the Help Desk.

Technical Expertise

The skill of technical expertise can be defined as having the technical knowledge you need to support the systems you are responsible for in a specific amount of time. This definition means that you may need enough technical expertise to resolve most customer problems at the point of call. It also means that you need to get the training required to keep your skills up as the technology you support changes.

Technical skill should never be undervalued. I have heard people say, "Anyone can learn the technical stuff," but that just isn't true. Some people cannot or do not want to learn the technical stuff. Putting such a person on a Help Desk would be a painful experience for both the person and the Help Desk.

Customer Service

Having the skill of customer service means being able to do the following:

- See things from the customer's point of view
- Understand that the customer is not an interruption, that the customer is your job
- Focus on giving customers what they need to get their jobs done
- Practice respect and professionalism

The key to having good customer service skills is being able to put yourself in your customers' shoes and understand why they are feeling the way they are, what they need, and why they need it. This should be easy. We are all someone's customers, and we have all experienced good and bad service. Unfortunately, we seem to have very short memories. Take teenagers, for example. When your teenager exhibits a specific behavior, for example, simulating nuclear war in his or her bedroom, what is your reaction? Do you say, "Ah yes, I can put myself in my teenager's shoes. I remember what it was like to be 16. I was going through a lot of weird emotions. My room was always a disaster"? Probably not. Your reaction is more likely to be "Clean up your room! We didn't raise you to be a pig! Why are you such a slob?"

We carry these short memories into our work at the Help Desk. When someone calls, upset or anxious, wanting something in a hurry, do we say, "This customer has stresses, deadlines, an irate manager, pressures that we know nothing about. That's why this customer is behaving this way or making this particular request"? Typically not. We say, "What a jerk! Why is this guy upset? Why should we give him this just because he's the assistant to the president? Who does he think he is?" Meanwhile, the assistant may be totally stressed out by the unreasonable requests being placed on him by the president of the company, who needs everything in a huge hurry. When we understand what pressures our customers might be under we can put things into perspective, react more calmly, and be of more help to our customer. Learn to walk in your customers' shoes. Practice by walking in your teenagers' shoes. If you can walk in their shoes you can walk in anyone's.

Chapter 4 discusses using customer service techniques to avoid the most common support mistakes. Chapter 7 discusses getting beyond challenging behavior during problem solving to find out what the customer really needs. Chapter 7 also discusses resolving service problems by using a layered approach to problem solving.

Checklist

In this chapter we talked about your importance as a Help Desk practitioner to your business, the roles you need to play on the Help Desk, and the skills you need to have. As you start to apply this material to your work, keep asking yourself the following questions:

✓ Do I understand how important I am to the business and the impact I have on the profitability of the business? Is this knowledge reflected in my behavior, my attitude?

✓ Do I understand the following seven roles I must play on the Help Desk?

- Partner
- Problem solver
- Communicator
- Marketer
- Data gatherer
- Expert
- Customer service representative

✓ Am I fulfilling all of these roles? How could I be doing this better?

✓ Do I understand the following skills I need to play the seven roles of the Help Desk practitioner?

- Proaction
- Focus
- Problem solving
- Communication
- Technical expertise
- Customer service

✓ Do I have or am I getting the skills I need? How will I keep them up to date?

✓ Am I putting myself in my customers' shoes? Am I learning to see things from their point of view? Am I able to understand what they need?

✓ Am I being a sheep? What do I have to do to stop being one?

Focusing on the Business

A Help Desk that is focused on the business is a Help Desk that is set up for success. It is providing the services that are most important to the business within a budget that the business can afford. Why do you, the Help Desk practitioner, have to worry about focus? You need to understand the focus of your Help Desk because all of your responsibilities and activities should be determined by that focus. If you work outside of your Help Desk's focus you are working against the Help Desk.

A focused Help Desk is a strong Help Desk. It is concentrating its strengths on those things that are most important to the business. An unfocused Help Desk is weak. Its resources might be spread too thinly and working on too many things, many of which just aren't that important to the business. Or it may not be keeping up with the demands of the business.

A Help Desk practitioner who understands focus and works within it is setting the Help Desk up for success.

In This Chapter

In this chapter I will talk about the components of focus, its importance, and how you can ensure that your Help Desk keeps it. The topics I will cover are as follows:

- What is focus?
- Focus and customers
- Focus and senior management
- Focus and other information technology (IT) groups
- Mission, services, and objectives
- Focus, success, and you

What Is Focus?

The following two scenarios illustrate the difference focus can make to a Help Desk.

SCENARIO 1

Alexis works on a newly formed Help Desk. It has only been in existence for a couple of months, and its staff members are often unsure of exactly what they're supposed to do. This morning the phones are ringing constantly as usual, and an already flustered Alexis takes a call from a customer in Finance who wants to borrow a laptop computer. Alexis is in a quandary. No one has made that request before. Is the Help Desk supposed to loan out laptops?

"Well, when can I pick it up?" Loren, the customer, snaps, "I need it for this evening." Alexis makes a decision. She is already feeling pretty frazzled, she does not want to disappoint Loren and face his anger, and she wants to make a good impression. She decides to give

Loren one of the shared laptops that the Help Desk team isn't using at the moment. "I have one sitting right here," Alexis starts. "I'll be right down!" Loren says and hangs the phone up before Alexis can say another word. Loren arrives, checks out the laptop, and is very annoyed to find that it isn't loaded with the software he needs. Alexis apologizes and spends the next hour loading the correct software. Unfortunately, while Alexis is working on the laptop calls accumulate, and other, more important problems sit waiting. The laptop is finally ready, and Alexis delivers it to Loren, who promises to have it back the next morning. Alexis then scrambles to get to the other calls. Several of the customers are annoyed at having had to wait.

The next morning the laptop isn't returned. Alexis calls Loren.

"Oh, I thought I'd keep it for a couple of days—it's really coming in handy," he explains. Alexis hangs up the phone, worried. A few minutes later her worries are justified. Judy, Alexis's manager, appears and asks, "Where's our laptop? I need it for a presentation to the logistics department." Oops. Alexis's heart sinks. She explains that she loaned the laptop. Judy is not very happy and tells her so. The people in the logistics department who were promised a presentation but didn't get one are also unhappy. When her lunch break arrives, Alexis spends some time checking out the career classifieds.

Later on in the day another customer calls and says to Alexis, "I hear you loan out laptops—I need one for tonight." Alexis is not about to make the same mistake twice. "We don't lend laptops out," she says. The customer argues. "You don't lend out laptops? Sure you do! Loren got a laptop just yesterday!"

Alexis does not back down. She persists with "We do not loan laptops out," and the customer finally hangs up, irate and dissatisfied.

Discussion

To satisfy one customer Alexis made a significant number of customers as well as her manager unhappy. By trying to do something that was beyond what the Help Desk could handle, Alexis not only alienated several customers but created unrealistic expectations and wasted a lot of time. There wasn't much business value in what Alexis did.

Alexis did not do all of this intentionally. She thought she was doing a good job, helping the customer. In reality, she was jeopardizing the success of the Help Desk. She was not focused on the business. The manager had not done a good job of focusing the Help Desk when it was being set up.

Now let's turn Scenario 1 around. Let's assume that Judy, Alexis's manager, had taken the time to define to her staff what the Help Desk should be doing, including the services it should be providing. Consider Scenario 2.

SCENARIO 2

Loren calls asking to borrow a laptop. Alexis takes the call. She knows what the Help Desk services are, and loaning out computer equipment is not one of them. "No," she says, "we don't have any equipment for loan, but I can look up the name of a company that does rent out hardware." Alexis looks up the information and calls Loren back. "If you decide to use this company let us know how satisfied you are with them." Loren isn't completely happy with this, but Alexis has given him an alternative and has taken the course of action that is best for the business. Alexis then goes one step further and records the name of the loaner company in the online Help Desk library so the next time a call comes in the information will be there for quick reference by any Help Desk employee. She also sends out a note to her colleagues to let them know about the information she has added.

Discussion

In Scenario 2 Alexis very quickly handles a request that took hours in Scenario 1. She helps the customer without detracting from the focus, the strength, of the Help Desk.

Components of Focus

On a Help Desk, the three components that define focus are mission, services, and objectives:

- A Help Desk mission defines how you will handle each customer interaction and how you will approach each problem.

- Services describe the realm of the Help Desk's responsibility, the functions that you must perform for the business. In Scenario 2 we saw the positive effect of defining services and staying within that definition.

- Objectives are sales quotas that define the goals you should be working toward. These goals should be moving the Help Desk forward in the same direction as the business.

The Needs of the Business

A Help Desk that has a mission, objectives, and services may be focused, but being focused isn't enough. The focus of the Help Desk must reflect the needs of the business. A Help Desk cannot have its own agenda. Your agenda needs to be the agenda of the business. There are three groups that need to be involved in setting the Help Desk's focus. They are customers, senior management, and other information technology (IT) groups.

Customers and senior management represent the business. They can tell your Help Desk what the business expects from you and what direction the business is taking.

Other IT groups need to be involved in setting the focus of your Help Desk because you share the same customers and your responsibilities may overlap. You need to clarify who does what so no customer problems or requests are left without ownership.

Figure 2.1 shows the relationship between the groups that need to be involved in setting the Help Desk's focus and the components of that focus.

What Focus Looks Like

If your Help Desk is focused on the business then your environment can probably be described as follows:

- You, your colleagues, and your manager share a common understanding of how each call is to be handled as well as of the Help Desk's mission.

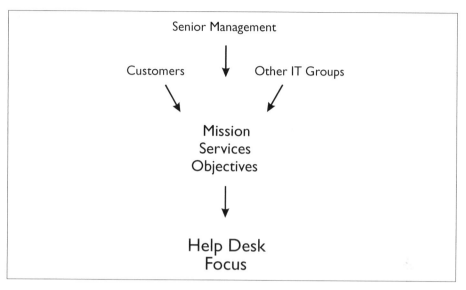

Figure 2.1   Relationship between the needs of the business and the components of focus.

- You have a clear picture of your objectives (which is a good start toward attaining them!).

- You and your customers understand what your responsibilities are, which makes it easier for you to keep customers satisfied.

- Your Help Desk has the support of senior management and customers because you are adding value to the business.

- You have the support of other IT groups and have defined lines of responsibility. Getting a response from secondary levels of support is much easier, which makes your job easier.

As a Help Desk practitioner you would probably very much appreciate the opportunity to work in an environment like the one described in this list. The benefits of focus are worth the effort you must put out to get and/or keep the Help Desk focused. In Chapter 1 we looked at the roles you have to play on the Help Desk. In the following sections of this chapter we will look at how you will use some of these roles to interact with customers, senior management, and other IT groups to keep your Help Desk focused on the business.

Focus and Customers

Your customers are your reason for existing. You need to have a very good idea of what your customer profile looks like so you know what your customers need and expect. As a problem eliminator you want to be prepared to solve the problems they call you with. As a data gatherer you want to be gathering information about their changing requirements. As a communicator you want to be passing this information on to management and other appropriate groups.

A profile of your customers (see Figure 2.2) includes the following types of information:

Who your customers are, how many of them there are, and where they are. You don't want to be in the situation where all of a sudden you are getting calls from customers you didn't even realize existed. You need to know where your customers are and how to support them, particularly if they are at remote locations. Take the time to find out just exactly who your customers are and what, if any, special support procedures are in place for any specific groups of customers.

What technology they use, what they use it for, and when they use it. If you know what technology customers use you can take steps to make sure you are trained in it so you can be more effective when they call. Knowing how customers apply their technology will give

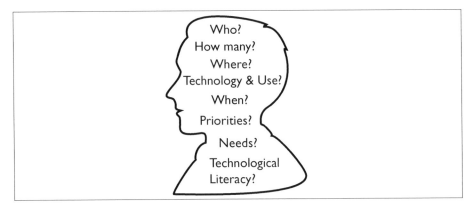

Figure 2.2 Profile of customers.

you an idea of how knowledgeable you need to be in any specific piece of software. Answering a question about changing fonts in a word processor requires a much different skill level than answering questions about setting up data templates, linking and embedding, doing mail merges, and so on. If you know customers have a light requirement in one area you can forgo more detailed training in that area to concentrate on other software that they do require more help in. Knowing when your customers use technology can help not only in terms of scheduling but also in terms of meeting business requirements. Remember, your customers are your reason for existing. If your customers are calling you requesting extra hours of support or a different time for support then you want to collect that information and pass it on to your manager so your Help Desk can continue to meet the needs of the business.

How technology literate and technology friendly they are. If you make yourself aware of how technology literate your customers are you can start to gather data about their training requirements. You can then pass this on to management or whoever is responsible for training, so the right training courses can be set up or sourced. Not only will this help your customers do their jobs more effectively, it will lighten the load on your Help Desk. The more familiar your customers are with technology the less they will have to call the Help Desk.

Their priorities. You need to know which problems or requests coming into the Help Desk are the most important to the business. This dictates what you will work on first, especially when you have several requests coming in at once. A word of caution here. You need to differentiate between the priorities of a specific customer and the priorities of the business, that is, of all customers. In Scenario 1 Loren was focused very much on his own priority. His priority did not necessarily reflect the needs of the business, only himself. In giving in to Loren's priority, Alexis actually went against the needs of the business. Make sure you understand what the business priorities are. If you don't know, ask.

Their needs. As a Help Desk practitioner you are very close to your customers. You hear their complaints, their questions, and their requests. You need to gather this data and pass it on to management so they can make sure the Help Desk is meeting the needs of the customers. Those needs will change as the business changes.

Focus and Senior Management

Senior management knows where the business is going and what its critical needs are. The information provided by senior management will help you choose the things you should be doing for the business from all those you could be doing. In your role as partner you need to make an effort to find out what direction senior management is taking the business in, and what impact that new direction will have on the Help Desk.

If senior management dictates that costs and head count must be reduced, you might want your Help Desk to be highly automated with several self-service options for customers. As a Help Desk practitioner and a partner, this would mean that you would encourage self-sufficiency among your customers, as in Scenario 4 in Chapter 1. Alternately, if you are supporting external customers and senior management is concerned about providing personal service to customers, then your Help Desk may have more human intervention and less automation. You would offer the customers a greater degree of hand-holding.

Sometimes the direction the business is taking is not one you particularly want to travel. Consider the following scenario: Your Help Desk is focused on providing support for packaged desktop applications. Senior management knows that changes in the business will necessitate the purchase of several specialized applications. These applications are critical to the business and require 24-hour support.

"This shouldn't be our job," you say, fearful of the new responsibilities and increased support hours. Senior management responds by saying, "This is our critical support requirement. Standard desktop software is not. This is what the business needs. If you can't provide it perhaps somebody else can."

Senior management plays a very powerful role in determining Help Desk focus, and you need to be aware of this in your role as partner. Knowing what senior management wants and where the business is headed will help you make better decisions about what is best for the business.

Focus and Other IT Groups

Your Help Desk will typically have some responsibilities that overlap with those of other groups within IT, such as supporting applications developed internally. Whenever there is an area of unclear responsibility, there is a chance that a customer request or problem may "fall through the cracks" and end up in oblivion, as shown in Figure 2.3. Customers might be left waiting for a solution that no one is working on and that no one has taken responsibility for, or they could find themselves being bounced between IT areas.

Consider Scenarios 3 and 4.

SCENARIO 3

Justin calls the Help Desk. He is having trouble with his Alpha communications software. "Hi," he says to Sheena, who happens to answer

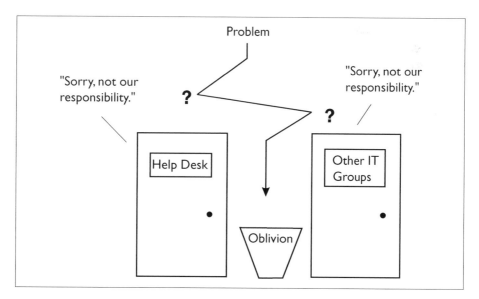

Figure 2.3   Customer requests going into oblivion.

his call. "I can't get my Alpha software working. Can you help me?" Sheena is working a double shift on the Help Desk because one of her colleagues has contracted measles. She is tired and a little resentful at having been asked to put in the extra working time. She really does not want to handle any more calls than she has to. She listens to Justin's request with some relief. Alpha was communications software, and communications problems were the responsibility of the Communications Help Desk.

"No," Sheena says, "I'm sorry, I can't help you. You need to call the Communications Help Desk." "Oh. Can you transfer me?" Sheena obliges and Justin is soon talking to Paul on the Communications Help Desk. "I can't get my Alpha software working," Justin repeats. "Alpha software?" Paul says, "That's PC software. You have to call the PC Help Desk." "But I just called the PC Help Desk, and they asked me to call you," Justin points out reasonably. "Sorry, but they shouldn't have transferred you here. We don't deal with PC software issues. I'll transfer you to the PC Help Desk." Justin hangs up in disgust before Paul can complete the transfer.

Discussion

I have experienced scenarios similar to this one, and to say the experience was frustrating is to severely understate the reality. Justin's downtime was much longer than it should have been (we have to assume that he did finally find someone to help him), and at least one of the Help Desks got one or more calls it didn't need, all of which negatively impacted the profitability of the business. The situation also damaged the image of each of the Help Desks. Let's see in Scenario 4 how Sheena could have avoided the situation, even if she was not sure whose responsibility the problem was.

SCENARIO 4

"Hi," Justin says to Sheena. "I can't get my Alpha software working. Can you help me?" "Alpha software," Sheena says thoughtfully as she tries to figure out how to handle the request. Her Help Desk supports PC software, but it does not deal with communications issues. She decides to take ownership of the problem. She will deal with the Communications Help Desk if she has to.

"Why don't you explain the problem to me, and I will try to help you," Sheena answers, and Justin complies. Sheena suspects that the problem is a communications issue, but she does not put Justin off. "I'm not sure what the problem is right now, but let me look into it and I'll get back to you within an hour."

When Sheena gets off the phone she calls the Communications Help Desk and talks to Paul about Justin's problem. Sure enough, it does turn out to be a communications issue. Paul takes ownership of the problem from Sheena, resolves it, and calls Justin back to explain what the problem was and that it had been resolved.

Discussion

In Scenario 4, Sheena took responsibility for an unclear area because it was in the best interests of the business.

Lines of responsibility between the Help Desk and other IT areas are often unclear. A good manager will work with other IT areas to clarify responsibilities as much as possible, but there will always be gray areas. As a Help Desk practitioner, it is your responsibility to take ownership of a gray area whenever this makes sense for the business and then communicate the gray area to management and/or the other IT areas involved so it can be clarified if possible. In this way, there will be less of a chance that customers will wait futilely for someone to take responsibility for their problem or request and thus less chance of a significant negative impact on the profitability of the business.

Mission, Services, and Objectives

You should now understand well how customers, senior management, and other IT groups are your partners in achieving focus and that you can only achieve it with their input. In this section, we are going to look at the three components of focus on a Help Desk—mission, services, and objectives—and your role in creating and fulfilling them.

Mission

People tend to run away screaming when I say "mission statement." It seems as if you've had your fill of mission statements. But when I say "mission statement" I mean something quite different from what you've probably been exposed to. Before you run away screaming, let me clarify.

What a Mission Is Not

Several years ago mission setting was a very popular corporate activity, and motivational speakers and facilitators were finding the whole process quite lucrative. Whole departments would go off site, play corporate games, and brainstorm a mission statement. Not only would they brainstorm content but wording as well. Wording was important. Hours and hours were spent discussing which words were most appropriate, for example, *effective* versus *efficient*. After several days, people would emerge exhausted, and a new mission would be born. The mission statement was framed, hung on corporate walls, and never thought of again. It was, as I heard someone once say, "missing in action."

The scenario I've just described has nothing to do with what a real mission statement is.

What a Mission Is

A mission is your strategy for handling customers, for doing business. It is not your manager's strategy or senior management's strategy but your strategy. It governs each interaction you have with your customers. It determines how you will deal with a call, problem, or request. It is your "modus operandi." As an analogy, I have a mission statement that I use to live my life from day to day. I don't think of it as something special, something to hang on my wall, I just do it. My mission is "I am responsible for my own life." This means that if I want things to happen I need to make them happen. I cannot blame anyone else for things that happen to me. That's a bit rough sometimes because on occasion it sure would be easier to blame someone else, but in the long run it does me a lot of good. I take the learning I gain from mistakes I make and then move forward, leaving the mistakes behind. Even the simplest decisions I make are based on my mission of taking responsibility.

A Help Desk mission should not be much different. It should guide your simplest decisions, and it should be a natural part of your job. You should just "do it." A mission is most effective when it is created by the people who will be fulfilling it. That means you and your colleagues. If you have not created the mission for your Help Desk but have inherited it then you must be prepared to accept it as your own, to just "do it." A mission does not need to be written down. As Figure 2.4 illustrates, a mission needs to be in your head, governing your actions.

Creating a Mission

If you are fortunate enough to be participating in establishing a mission for your Help Desk there are a few things you should know about mission statements. First, there is no rule for what a mission statement looks like. A mission is typically one to five paragraphs long. Sometimes it will be a statement only, and sometimes it will be a statement followed by values, that is, how you plan to achieve your mission. You decide what your mission statement looks like and what works best for you.

Second, there is no need to pack a mission statement full of sophisticated words. The words should be your own and should be meaningful to you. There is a Web site somewhere on the Internet that contains a mission statement generator. You just click on the Generate key and a new mission statement appears full of mission statement-type words. I must say the site generates some pretty sophisticated looking mission statements. If you concentrate too much on wording and try to make your mission sophisticated you might as well just visit that site and gen-

Figure 2.4   A mission needs to be in your head.

erate a statement there. It will probably be as meaningful as the one you come up with and will take a lot less of your time. And, no, I will not give you the name of the site. I'm afraid you might be tempted to use it, especially if you have an anxious manager breathing down your neck to "hurry up with that mission statement."

Third, a mission is never finished; it is constantly being fulfilled. It is a declaration of purpose, values, and direction. It sets out what your Help Desk should be trying to achieve with each call that is answered.

Fourth, your mission must be believable. A mission such as "Exceed customer expectations" is not very believable if you are currently not even meeting customer expectations. If you do not believe in your mission you will most likely not play the role of partner very effectively. You won't be working to fulfill your mission with each call, which means you will be working against the Help Desk.

Fifth, your mission must be achievable. Remember, you actually have to do what the mission says you will. I have seen mission statements such as "Strive to thrill the customer at every opportunity." Realistically, I don't think you are going to be able to thrill your customers unless you are offering a lot more than technology support.

Finally, your mission must be recognizable. If you can't recognize when you are fulfilling the mission then it's not much use having one. It is very easy for me to look at any part of my life, business or personal, and answer the question "did I take responsibility?"

The following are a couple of ideas for the actual process of mission creation:

- Write your suggestions down individually, then get together as a team to discuss a strategy for running the Help Desk, that is, how you feel you should be handling each call. A mission will come out of this.

- Get together as a team and think of comments you would like to hear customers making about your Help Desk. Work these into a mission.

Of course, you must remember that it is necessary to take customers, senior management, and other IT groups into account. Let's look at

Scenario 5 for an example of the process of establishing a mission statement.

SCENARIO 5

As part of the process of getting focused on the business, the staff of the Help Desk for Grace Hospital decided that they needed to solve more problems at point of call, in other words, without having to pass them on to someone else. Problem resolution times were very high. About 40 percent of problems were not being resolved at point of call but were being passed on to the technical support department. That department was very busy and contributed significantly to the high resolution times for problems received from the Help Desk.

The Help Desk manager went through the process of getting focused, which involved gathering input from customers, senior management, and other IT groups. She then sat down with her team and gave them a summary of her findings.

"Customers really need shorter resolution times from us. Their work is being impacted by significant downtimes whenever they have a problem. Senior management wants to lessen the impact of technology and usage problems on the financial success of the hospital. It also wants the technical support department to focus on technology architecture. Technical support wants us to send them only the problems that we don't have the authority to fix, and they've even given me a list."

The five Help Desk practitioners listened in silence and then started to ask questions. Fortunately, they had all been trained in being proactive, and once their questions were answered they began to discuss the ways in which they could perhaps satisfy the needs of the business. The meeting closed with the manager giving her team an assignment. "I'd like you to set a mission statement for the Help Desk," she said. "Remember, it's something you're all going to have to live by so work as a group and don't rush it. I'd like to see your mission in two weeks. Give it a top priority and let me know if you need help."

The group sat on after their manager left and decided how to approach the mission setting. They would each take a few days to think about a mission and then have a meeting to present their ideas. A few days later they had their meeting, and after a few hours they came up with a mission. Their mission was to be "Best value, first time." They felt that the most important thing they could do for the customer was to solve the problem at point of call. They did not want the customer to have to wait for a solution, and they did not want the customer to have to have multiple interactions with various support levels.

The Help Desk team also discussed what they could do to make sure that the customers got "Best value, first time." It set up some learning exchange sessions with the technical support group so the Help Desk could learn to do some of the things the technical support group wanted to hand off. It also identified training seminars Help Desk members needed to take to become stronger in specific technical areas. By the end of the whole mission-setting process, the Help Desk team was very clear on what its mission was, and all the team members were willing to play the role of partner in fulfilling it.

Discussion

Scenario 5 illustrates a good way of setting a mission. The points I would like to emphasize are as follows:

- Get input from customers, senior management, and other IT groups. You cannot set a mission without input from these groups because they determine what you should be doing for the business.
- "DYI." Do it yourselves. A mission should be set by the people who will be living it. If your manager tends to be of the interfering kind or wants to impose a mission on you, give her or him the day off while you do the job. The mission must be yours; you must believe in it.
- Is the mission "Best value, first time" believable? I'd have to say yes. The Help Desk team is easily able to believe in "Best value, first time" largely because they understand the business needs behind the mission.
- Is the mission achievable? Absolutely. The team knows what it has to do to fulfill that mission. Team members are taking training and exchanging information with the technical support

group. As they use the mission they might find that they need to have procedures around it to make it more easily achievable. For example, the team might have to set a time limit on calls so other calls don't pile up while one call is being handled. "Best value, first time" does not mean spending an infinite time on one call to the detriment of numerous other calls.

• Is the mission recognizable? Let's look at Scenario 6 to see.

SCENARIO **6**

Jody on the Grace Hospital Help Desk gets a call from Edwina in Patient Services. "Jody, my PC is hung up again. It's unusually busy here, and I've got a long line of people waiting. This is the fourth time in the last 15 minutes or so. Can you please do something to resolve this problem?" Jody thinks about what the best value to Edwina would be—a PC, loaded with patient registration software, that works. But which would be quicker, getting Edwina another PC or doing some analysis to determine the underlying problem of her current PC? Jody does a quick check on the asset management system to see if there are any other PCs configured like Edwina's. Yes, one in the adjacent office in fact. It was marked "Public," which meant it was shared.

"Edwina, if we could borrow the PC from the office next to you and set it up on your desk, would that be a good solution?" "How long would that take?"

"About five minutes. Tim could do it for you right now." Jody had checked Tim's availability on the work scheduling system. "Great. Hang on while I check with Mary to see if it's OK. She sometimes uses that PC." Edwina determines that the suggestion is in fact OK with Mary, and Tim is dispatched. Within ten minutes, Edwina is using the new PC and has no lockup problems for the rest of the afternoon. Tim takes Edwina's old PC away for closer scrutiny.

After getting a call from Tim informing her that everything was working, Jody hangs up the phone and considers whether she gave Edwina "Best value, first time." She comes to the conclusion that yes, she did: She got Edwina up and running in the quickest possible way. Borrowing the PC wasn't much of a risk because the configurations were identical. Sending someone out to investigate the PC would have been much more of a risk—there was just no telling how long it would have taken to find the problem.

Discussion

Jody was easily able to see that she gave Edwina "Best value, first time." She had two options, and she chose the one that was most likely to satisfy Edwina. She focused on giving Edwina value rather than on the actual technical problem. Let's look at another example.

SCENARIO 7

Raoul is one of the Grace Hospital Help Desk's team members. He gets a call from Darwin, an executive in Administration. "My outpatient trend report on my executive information system (EIS) isn't printing. It accepts my print request and then just goes away. It does not print." Raoul considers the problem. The EIS system had been generating a lot of calls lately. Here was a chance to have a closer look to see what the root problem was. He could use the remote control software, and maybe he could finally put an end to the recurring problems.

"I'm going to shadow your PC," he tells Darwin. "I'd like to find out what's causing the problem." "I'll leave you to it," Darwin says and goes off to a meeting. Half an hour later Raoul is no closer to a solution. He has managed to spend almost all of that time on Darwin's problem because the afternoon has been particularly quiet. He is doing some further checks when Darwin calls.

"Raoul, where the hell is my report? I thought you'd be done by now! I need that report right now. I've got the outpatient team in my office for a meeting, and we can't do a damn thing without that report!"

Raoul is embarrassed. He promises to hand-deliver the report in five minutes and then proceeds to export the report from the EIS system into the word processor. From there he has no problem printing it. After delivering the report Raoul walks back to his desk and scores himself on his response to Darwin. He did not give Darwin "Best value, first time." He should have asked Darwin how urgent his reporting requirement was, and he should have printed it off first, then worked on the deeper problem. Raoul decides he will never make that mistake again.

Discussion

Raoul was able to recognize, very easily, that he did not fulfill his mission. Fortunately, the experience was not a total loss. Raoul learned something from the incident—he would never repeat his mistake of focusing on the problem before the business, and he would think more carefully about "Best value, first time" with each customer call that came his way.

When you set a mission statement, recognize that there will be times when you make a mistake, when you do not fulfill it for whatever reason. When that happens, do as Raoul did: Learn from the experience and apply it to all your future calls. Put the negative portion of the experience behind you. You will be a more effective Help Desk practitioner for it.

Examples

People are always asking me for examples of mission statements. You should never have to look at someone else's mission statement to set your own. The mission should be yours and yours alone. Since we established earlier that the format and sophistication of the mission's wording do not matter you should not have to look at other mission statements. I know, however, that there will be those of you who will absolutely insist on having samples to work from. I therefore offer you the following two mission statements. I hope you don't take the attitude of "Hey, this looks good enough for me" and copy them. Use them to generate your own ideas.

Example A

Mission:
- To help the customer make the best use of technology in support of the business.

Values:
- We resolve problems, not symptoms.
- We are proactive, actively seeking to prevent problems and eliminate reasons for calls.

- We treat customers courteously and professionally.
- Our top priority is to minimize the downtime of our customers.

Example B

Mission:
- Focus on the business needs first.

A Mission Is Not Forever

As the business changes, so will your focus and your mission. The mission you have while your Help Desk is in startup mode will most likely be very different from the mission you have two years later when your environment is more mature and your support structure is in place and working well. Revisit your mission every year or in whatever time frame makes sense for you. Don't bother getting your mission statement framed. It will change.

Services

The second component of Help Desk focus is services. The services your Help Desk provides should be determined by your customer profile, senior management, and other IT groups. The more services your Help Desk offers and the more things you support, the more thinly spread your staff and resources will be. You need to focus on providing those services that give the best value to the business.

Unfortunately, the very characteristics that make you a good Help Desk practitioner will be your downfall when it comes to providing services. You like to help people. You find it hard to say no to someone who has a need. As a result, you may say yes to too many requests, which is the same as expanding your services. What happens then? When you try to provide too many services and support too broad a range of products, you spread yourself too thinly and you are setting yourself up for failure. You could end up in the situation where customers with important needs are forced to wait while you provide a service that is not as important. Consider Scenario 8.

SCENARIO 8

Diana works on a Help Desk in the corporate headquarters of a large retailer. She is rushing down the hall on her way to help Michelle with a PC problem when she meets Grant, a regular Help Desk customer. "Diana! Just the person I wanted to see. Have you got a minute? I'm having a problem with my PC."

Diana hesitates. "I'm just on may way to another customer." "Oh, they can wait for a few minutes. This won't take long, I promise, and you're right here. It's kind of silly not to come and help me. Please?" The "please" does Diana in. She really hates to say no. "OK. But only for a few minutes."

Unfortunately, "a few minutes" turns into half an hour. "Thanks, Diana," Grant says, pleased to have his PC problem taken care of. "I told you it wouldn't take long. Diana runs off, anxious about Michelle's PC. When she gets to Michelle's office she is met with anger. "Where have you been? The Help Desk person said you were on your way!" Diana apologizes. "I'm sorry, I stopped to help someone else with a problem." "You were helping someone else? But you were supposed to be working on my problem! I was told I was next in the queue. I've wasted half an hour sitting here waiting for you!"

Diana mumbles another apology and then finds and fixes the problem. When she gets back to the Help Desk, Glen, a colleague, motions her over.

"Diana, Grant called to say that you didn't take care of his PC problem. It's back. I can't find the problem log though so I can't reopen it." Diana explains what happened and Glen logs a new problem.

Discussion

In this scenario, the service that Diana provided was what I call "drive-by Help Desk." Diana succumbed to something we've all been subjected to: Help Desk customers snatching you out of the hallway, accosting you in elevators, even cornering you in washrooms to demand instant, in-person Help Desk service. Diana found it hard to say no. But she might not find it so hard next time if she considers the following:

- The cost in terms of time wasted of customers who have to wait, which has an impact on the profitability of the company.
- The cost to the Help Desk of losing valuable Help Desk statistics. If Diana and her colleagues made a regular practice of "drive-by Help Desk," the Help Desk's call volume would appear to be lower than it really was. This would make it harder for Diana's manager to justify extra staff or improvements or to prove value.

What should Diana have done? Let's look at Scenario 9.

SCENARIO 9

Once again, Diana is on her way to service a customer's PC. Again, Grant stops her and says "Diana! Just the person I wanted to see. Have you got a minute? I'm having a problem with my PC." This time Diana doesn't hesitate. She smiles, steps around Grant, and says over her shoulder, "Sorry, Grant, I'm tied up now. I'm on my way to see a customer who's waiting in her office for me. And anyway, I can't work on your problem until you've logged it with the Help Desk. We need to keep track of all of our calls."

Diana's confident tone and body language do not invite any further entreaties on Grant's part. He goes back to his desk and calls the Help Desk, realizing that's the only option if he wants his PC fixed.

Discussion

Diana stayed within the Help Desk's agreed-upon services. She played the role of partner, working within the focus of the Help Desk. She made it clear to Grant that the only way to get Help Desk service was to go through the Help Desk. Grant will no longer be negatively impacting service provided to other Help Desk customers. Diana also helped make life easier for her colleagues. Grant will most likely not try to get drive-by Help Desk service from any of them.

Creating a List of Services

If you are involved in putting your Help Desk's list of services together, there are a few things to remember:

Services must be manageable. Make sure your Help Desk doesn't take on more than it can handle.

Services must support the business. Your Help Desk has limited resources. Make the best use of them by focusing on the services that deliver the best value to the business. You need to look at input from customers, senior management, and other IT areas.

Even if you aren't involved in putting together services, as a partner it is your responsibility to ensure the following:

Services must be well defined and well understood. If they aren't, customers may have expectations far beyond what you can possibly provide. The closer your customers' expectations are to reality the more satisfied they will be. Services also need to be well defined to ensure that you are clear about what you should be focusing on and are not distracted from the important calls by requests or problems of lesser importance. If you are not clear about what services you should be providing, go to your manager to get them defined or to at least start the process. You cannot function effectively if you don't know what you are supposed to be doing. If your customers do not understand your services then communicate this to your manager and suggest ways you might market this information to your customers.

When Things Change

As the business you support changes and as your customers' requirements change, the services your Help Desk provides must change also. As a data gatherer and communicator you need to collect any changing customer requirements you become aware of and pass them on to management. As a Help Desk practitioner you are very close to your customers. You will often see changing requirements before anyone else does.

Objectives

Objectives are the third component of focus on a Help Desk. Objectives are the targets you are aiming for. If you don't know what target you are aiming for, chances are you aren't going to hit it. Objectives give you direction. Objectives are enablers of improvement. Some of the first indications of a Help Desk in trouble, that is, in an out-of-control problem cycle (see Chapter 4), include the absence of objectives or objectives that are not being achieved. If you aren't improving, if you don't have targets for improvement, you are in trouble.

As a Help Desk practitioner, you may or may not be involved in setting objectives. If you are, there are some points to remember:

Objectives should be clear. There should be no ambiguity in your objectives. People should understand what you're trying to achieve. For example, "Bring in training for customers" is not very clear. What training? Which customers? Does training need to be enforced? The objective is not at all clear. Alternatively, consider "Arrange for basic spreadsheet training for the 40 customers in Finance, starting in September. Ensure that each person in the department is trained within four months." This is clearer because the responsibility is clear. If you have an objective that is not clear, clarify it.

Objectives must be measurable. Objectives are not much use if you can't measure whether you've attained them. If you don't know how you will measure an objective, don't set it. "Increase percentage of calls resolved at point of call" is not measurable. Have you succeeded even if you increase this percentage by .04 percent? "Increase percentage of calls resolved at point of call from 60 percent to 80 percent" is better but not good enough. It does not give you a time frame. "Increase percentage of calls resolved at point of call from 60 percent to 80 percent by January 4" is best of all. This objective will be very easy to measure.

Even if you aren't actually setting objectives, there are things you need to do to fulfill your partner role and be an effective Help Desk practitioner:

Make sure you understand what your Help Desk's objectives are. Ask your manager to clarify any fuzzy objectives. Be sure you understand your role in each objective.

Give objectives the priority they deserve. Be clear about how important each is and how each fits in with the other things you may be doing. Play your partner role by doing your part to achieve Help Desk objectives.

Learn from objectives that you do not meet. When you fail to meet an objective, make it your business to understand what happened and why the objective was not met. Decide what you need to do to meet the objective next time. This might involve training, avoiding previous mistakes, or even making the objective more reasonable (if that was really the reason you did not meet it). As an example, your manager might ask you how long it will take to upgrade memory in all of the PCs in a specific department. You say "Two weeks." At the end of two weeks you have only managed to upgrade half of the PCs. You did not realize that scheduling time to work on customers' PCs would be a problem. The next time you have to upgrade PCs you will be able to give a better estimate and set a more realistic objective. You will take into account the fact that you have to schedule upgrade time with your customers.

Focus, Success, and You

Focus is critical to the success of your Help Desk. One Help Desk practitioner can do a lot of damage to a Help Desk and push it a great distance toward failure. But this is not a book about failure. One Help Desk practitioner can also do a lot of good for a Help Desk and push it a great distance toward success. This chapter has given you a plan. Play the role of partner fully. Push your Help Desk toward success.

Checklist

Focus is the formula for success for your Help Desk. If you don't follow the formula you can jeopardize the success of your Help Desk. To ensure that you are supporting the focus of your Help Desk you have to keep asking yourself the following questions and make sure you can answer them positively:

✓ Do I have a good understanding of the profile of my customers?
✓ Do I collect changing customer requirements and pass them on to my manager?

✓ Do I understand what senior management expects of the Help Desk? Do I understand why? Do I understand the direction the business is taking?

✓ Am I doing my best to ensure that any gray areas of responsibility between my Help Desk and other IT groups are covered and clarified? Do I take responsibility when a call in the gray area comes my way?

✓ Have I made the Help Desk mission my modus operandi? Is it governing how I handle each Help Desk call?

✓ Is my mission believable, achievable, and recognizable? If it isn't, have I made an effort to get it changed?

✓ Do I have a good understanding of the services my Help Desk provides? If not, have I made the effort to get them defined?

✓ Am I making sure that I stay within the services that my Help Desk has defined?

✓ Do my customers understand our services? If not, have I made an effort to get them clarified?

✓ Do I know what the objectives of my Help Desk are? Do I understand my role and my responsibilities in achieving these objectives?

✓ Am I working to achieve my objectives?

✓ If my Help Desk has no objectives, have I done anything to encourage the creation of objectives?

✓ Are my objectives clear and measurable? If not, have I done anything to get them clarified?

✓ When I do not achieve an objective, do I make an effort to understand why and then use this information to improve my performance next time?

Supporting the Help Desk Structure

CHAPTER THREE

Structure

The structure of a Help Desk is a reflection of its focus. In Chapter 2, "Focusing on the Business," we discussed how mission, services, and objectives determine the focus of a Help Desk and how we should not try to copy these from other Help Desks. The same goes for structure. The structure of your Help Desk should be determined by your focus, by your environment, and by your business, not by someone else's Help Desk.

Setting up the structure of your Help Desk was most likely not your responsibility. Making the structure work, however, is. Even if someone created the perfect Help Desk structure for your organization it would only succeed if the Help Desk practitioners in it understood the structure, worked within it, and used it as it was designed.

In This Chapter

In this chapter I will discuss how you can work within the particular Help Desk structure you have to make your Help Desk as effective as possible. The topics I will cover are as follows:

- Levels in a Help Desk structure
- Relationships between support levels
- Making distributed Help Desks work
- Consolidating Help Desks
- Your career

Levels in a Help Desk Structure

Figure 3.1 shows the structure of a typical Help Desk and the levels within it. Calls come into the front line, the first level of support. If the practitioners on the front line can't resolve a call it is passed on to the second level of support or to a third level, which might be a specialized area such as hardware maintenance. If the second level can't resolve the call or if the call requires specialized skills, the call is passed to the third level, which is typically another IT area or an area external to the organization, such as a vendor's support department.

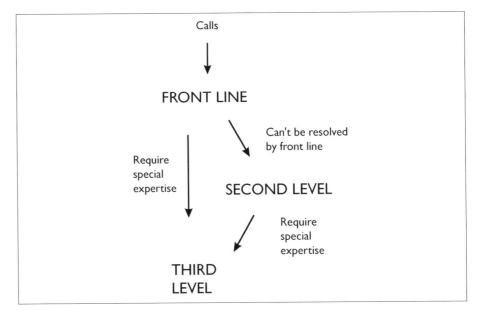

Figure 3.1   Typical structure of a Help Desk.

The Front Line

The structure of the front line is critical to the overall success of the Help Desk. It is the point of first contact with the customer, the first opportunity to help the customer. Front lines are usually structured as either Dispatch, in which the call is answered and then dispatched to a second level, or Resolve, in which the Help Desk practitioner tries to resolve the call, only passing it on if it cannot be resolved within a certain amount of time. A Resolve front line may dispatch calls that require specialized support, such as hardware maintenance.

Let's look more closely at each of the Resolve and Dispatch front lines; at their characteristics, advantages, and potential weaknesses; and at what you can do to make each more effective.

Resolve Front Line

If you work in a Resolve front line you try to resolve each call that comes in. You know the products you are supporting, and you have good problem-solving skills. You have tools such as remote control software or knowledge bases to help you resolve problems quickly.

Characteristics and Advantages

The biggest advantage of a Resolve frontline structure is the resolution time. A call that you resolve at point of call, in other words, while the customer is still on the phone, will have a much shorter resolution time than a call that is passed on to someone else who may or may not look at it right away. Customers get their answers before they get off the phone. Not all calls can be resolved at point of call, but on a Resolve front line, most are.

Another advantage of the Resolve front line is higher customer satisfaction. Customers talk to the actual problem solvers and do not have to repeat their problems again to someone else unless the frontline practitioner cannot resolve the call. Even if the call has to be passed on, responsibility for it typically sits with the person who initially took the call, so there is less chance of the problem being passed on to someone who sits on it forever. There are at least two people looking out for the welfare of that call.

A Resolve front line is typically an interesting working environment. As a Help Desk practitioner on a Resolve front line you have the opportunity to get an overview of all the systems in the corporation, talk to customers in all areas of the business, and learn what is most important to the business. You are constantly learning and keeping current with the technology your customers use and with any tools, such as knowledge bases, that your Help Desk uses.

A Resolve front line offers excellent career prospects. Working on a front line you develop or enhance a very marketable set of skills. You are constantly enhancing your technical and problem-solving skills, and you are gaining business knowledge. You have an ongoing opportunity to practice and enhance your communication skills and customer service skills. You can practice proaction. All of these skills are in great demand. If you are a successful Help Desk practitioner working on a front line you will not have any problem moving to another job, be it technically or business oriented.

Potential Weaknesses

One thing that Resolve front lines need to look out for is escalating call duration. When you are trying to resolve a call at point of call, you sometimes don't know when to let go. Spending half an hour resolving a customer's problem over the phone may be good for that customer but not for the other customers who are waiting to get through to the Help Desk. A company's profitability could be negatively impacted if you are spending too much time with each customer.

Critical Success Factors

The three things that are absolutely critical to the success of a Resolve frontline structure are skills, training, and tools. If you want to be able to answer calls at the point of call you need to have the skills to resolve the problems that come your way. Putting someone on the front line who does not have the skills to resolve the problems or answer the questions is courting failure. That person will not be able to answer most calls at the point of call and will function as a dispatcher until those skills are gained. For example, someone with poor problem-solving skills or poor technical knowledge simply will not be able to resolve any but the simplest problems.

The technology you support is changing rapidly. You need ongoing training to keep current in the products you are supporting. If you aren't getting the training you need you won't be able to resolve the problems that come into the Help Desk. For example, if a new release of software is rolled out to your customers before you are trained in it you will not be able to resolve calls for those problems (unfortunately, this happens far too often). You will have to revert to Dispatch mode.

To make your Resolve front line successful you need tools that allow you to solve problems quickly and without leaving your desk, even problems you may not be familiar with. For example, remote control software allows you to take over a customer's PC and troubleshoot problems that would otherwise require a site visit. Knowledge bases give you solutions to problems that you might otherwise not know how to solve.

Making It Work

As a Help Desk practitioner, the success of your Resolve front line is largely up to you. There are several things you can do to make sure your Resolve front line works. First, get the training you need. Don't expect it to be offered to you. Decide which areas you need training in, do some research on courses offered (someone may do this for you depending on your organization), and then present a proposal to your manager.

Second, know your tools. Make an effort to understand them. Make sure you are using them properly and know what they are capable of. This might mean more training for you. Third, know when to escalate a call. You do want to resolve calls at point of call, but you do not want to resolve one call at point of call to the detriment of scores of others that need to wait. If your Help Desk does not have a time limit for calls suggest one. For example, if you have not resolved a call in 10 minutes pass it on.

Fourth, always be on the lookout for ways to get more calls resolved at point of call. You need to get yourself into an improvement cycle in which you find an area for improvement, make the improvement, find the next area for improvement, and so on.

Dispatch Front Line

If you work in a Dispatch front line you are not necessarily familiar with the products that customers are calling about. You don't typically have the knowledge to resolve the problems or questions you get. You take the call, log the information, and then pass the log on to the next support level or the appropriate area for resolution.

Characteristics and Advantages

A Dispatch front line offers the customer fast initial response. Time per call is low because all you are doing is taking down the information. You are not trying to resolve the problem.

Potential Weaknesses

The downfall of many dispatch front lines is high call resolution times. On a Dispatch front line you may be giving the customer fast initial response, but you typically have no control over the actual resolution time. You just pass the call on, and, unless you have dedicated second and third support levels, you simply hope for the best. Dispatching calls is a low-interest job. It requires few skills, and it's probably not something you'd like to do for a significant amount of time. From a career point of view, a Dispatch frontline position does not open many doors for you.

Customer dissatisfaction is something else you are more likely to be faced with on a Dispatch front line. Unless the problem is very simple, customers will have to repeat their problem at least twice: once to you, the dispatcher, and once to the person who will actually be resolving the call. Customers may therefore try to contact the resolver directly instead of going through the front line.

Critical Success Factors

The three most important factors in making a Dispatch front line work are a good understanding of where to send each call, service level agreements (SLAs) with resolvers, and realistic customer expectations. A good understanding of where each call should be sent will help to ensure that you keep resolution times as low as possible. Sending a call to the wrong place will significantly increase resolution times. Someone will have to take the time to find out where the call should have gone and then reroute it.

Setting up SLAs with each area that calls are passed to will ensure that calls are resolved within a specific time frame. Figure 3.2 illustrates what can happen when Help Desk calls are not given a high enough priority. Calls sit and wait while the assigned resolvers work on other things. SLAs would clarify agreed-upon resolution times for such calls. Resolvers would understand the urgency of Help Desk calls in relation to their other work, and their performance could be measured against SLAs.

Realistic customer expectations go a long way toward ensuring customer satisfaction. Customers need to be aware of the fact that their problems will not be resolved at point of call. They need to understand the call resolution process so they do not develop false expectations. Customers with unrealistic expectations are customers who are dissatisfied, complain to higher places, try to contact resolvers directly, and keep calling the Help Desk back to ask what is happening to their problem.

Figure 3.2   Calls sit and wait while resolvers work on other things.

Making It Work

If you are a Help Desk practitioner on a Dispatch front line, there are several things you can do to make that front line more effective. First, make sure you understand exactly where to send each type of call. If you have any questions about where a call should go, ask someone for clarification. Don't just guess and send the call off to potential oblivion.

Second, if your Help Desk does not have an SLA with each area you send calls to, suggest to your manager that these be set up. See Chapter 9 for more information on SLAs.

Third, if you find that your customers have unrealistic ideas about how long it takes to resolve a call or about the call resolution process, suggest a marketing initiative to your manager. Chapter 11 talks extensively about marketing. If your Help Desk is not focused on the business, your manager will have to go through the process of getting focused (as described in Chapter 2), which will involve getting input from customers.

Finally, do a good job of logging the call. Enter in as much information as possible so the resolver can do some or all of the problem resolution before getting back to the customer. This will also lessen the customer's frustration since he or she will be less likely to have to repeat the problem or start from scratch when he or she is contacted by the resolver. Scenarios 1 and 2 illustrate this point.

SCENARIO **1**

Julia works on a two-person Dispatch front line. It's a fairly busy morning, and the phone rings constantly. She is determined to meet her quota of calls and tries to get through each call as quickly as possible. Gina from Human Resources (HR) calls the Help Desk, and Julia takes the call. "This is Gina from HR. I've got a really strange problem with my PC. Something very weird is happening." Gina then starts to explain the problem.

Julia enters the call as Gina speaks and misses most of Gina's explanation. "OK, Gina, I've assigned you a ticket number of A2341. Someone will be getting back to you about your problem." Julia finishes the conversation, assigns the problem to the appropriate queue, and takes the next call. Later on in the day the call is picked up by Yuri, who works in one of the secondary levels of support. Yuri looks at the call description that Julia entered. It reads, "Customer experiencing intermittent problem with her PC." "Great," Yuri thinks, "that sure doesn't give me much to go on." He gives Gina a call. "Gina, this is Yuri from support. I understand you're having an intermittent problem with your PC." "Yes," Gina acknowledges, "I explained it all to the Help Desk. Have you got a solution for me?"

Yuri sighs to himself. He knows what's coming next. "Could you please explain it to me again? I want to make sure I understand exactly what's happening." Gina is annoyed. She thought the problem should have been resolved by now. She very much resents having to repeat her long explanation. "I already told the Help Desk! I talked to Julia. I know she keyed it in because I heard her entering it as I was talking to her. Can't you just read her explanation?" Yuri persists, and Gina finally explains the problem again. When she's finished, Yuri realizes that someone will have to visit Gina's PC. He breaks the news to her. She is not happy. "What? You mean I have to wait longer? Why couldn't Julia have sent someone out?"

Discussion

In Scenario 1, Julia not only increases the customer's dissatisfaction, she makes Yuri's job unpleasant. The customer's PC is also down longer than necessary, which negatively impacts the profitability of the business. Let's look at Scenario 2 to see how Julia could improve the situation.

SCENARIO 2

Julia gets the call from Gina in Human Resources. "This is Gina from HR. I've got a really strange problem with my PC. Something very weird is happening." Julia replies, "Gina, I want to make sure that I get all of the facts straight. If you describe the problem, I'll key it in so the support rep has as much information as possible." Gina proceeds to describe the problem. Julia asks her a few questions to clarify the symptoms and soon has the whole description keyed in. She finishes the conversation with Gina and puts the call into the appropriate queue.

Later on in the day the call is picked up by Yuri, who works in one of the secondary levels of support. Yuri looks at the call description that Julia entered and realizes immediately that the call will require a short site visit. He calls Gina to make sure she is there and then goes to her office. He has most of the information he needs to fix the problem and makes the required changes quickly.

Discussion

By getting all of the relevant information from the customer and logging it along with the problem, Julia lessens the customer's downtime and minimizes any negative impact on the profitability of the company. The customer's level of satisfaction is higher, and the support person's job is easier and more pleasant.

Second Level of Support

The second level of support in a Help Desk usually consists of Help Desk practitioners who are doing other things besides resolving problems passed on by the front line. Practitioners in the second level of support may actually take turns rotating through the front line, so they get a chance to experience both the problem resolution and the project side of the Help Desk.

If you are a practitioner at the second level of support you are probably doing such work as testing and installing software, conducting customer surveys, or performing tasks related to call elimination and marketing initiatives. You might also be involved in maintaining Help Desk Web site information such as hints and tips, frequently asked questions (FAQs), standards and policy information, and system information.

Help Desk improvement or call elimination initiatives are usually carried out by the second level of support. These improvement initiatives have the highest business value of just about any of the tasks you perform on the Help Desk. If you aren't working to eliminate calls, your calls will simply keep increasing. Your Help Desk will lose effectiveness and eventually fail.

If you are working on the second level of support, make sure you give call elimination work the priority it deserves. If you find that other work is eating away at your time, let your manager know. I talk more about improvement initiatives and their importance in Chapter 4.

Third Level of Support

Third levels of support typically involve areas outside of the Help Desk such as technical support, database administration, program development, and network administration. Depending on the Help Desk's services, some of these areas may actually reside within the Help Desk. Third levels of support might also include third parties who are providing services such as hardware maintenance to Help Desks as well as vendors of Help Desk tools and products that Help Desk customers use.

The terms of support outside of the Help Desk need to be formalized so there is a clear understanding on both sides regarding the responsibilities that are involved in passing on and receiving Help Desk problems. A problem that may seem important to a Help Desk analyst who has actually spoken to the desperate customer may not seem as important to the network administrator on whose desk it may eventually fall (see Figure 3.2). A weakly defined third level of support can completely undermine strong first and second levels. I discuss the relationships between support levels in the next section.

Relationships between Support Levels

In the previous section we saw that there were three levels in a typical Help Desk structure (see Figure 3.1). The quality of the relationships between the different levels goes a long way toward determining how effective the Help Desk will be. The quality of the relationships is based on the following factors:

- Understanding responsibilities
- Willingness to fill service gaps
- Commitment to ongoing improvement

Let's look at each of these factors more closely.

Understanding Responsibilities

When you pass calls on to another level of support you have certain expectations regarding how those calls will be handled. You expect certain tasks to be carried out and certain results to be achieved, and you probably expect all of this to be done within a certain amount of time. Now consider the person who picks up the call you passed on. Will that person do what you expect? Will that person carry out the tasks and achieve the results, all within the time you expect? The answer is no, that person will probably not do what you expect unless you and that person (or your respective mangers) have decided what your responsibilities are in terms of tasks, deliverables, and time frames. Let's look at Scenarios 3 and 4 for an illustration of this concept.

SCENARIO 3

Marianne works on the front line of a Resolve Help Desk. She has just spent about 15 minutes on the phone with a customer, Derek from Real Estate, trying to solve a network access problem. "Derek, I'm afraid I'm going to have to contact the Network people for help on this one. I'm going to pass this call on to them, and either a Network person or I will give you a call back." "Oh. OK. Any idea when?," Derek worries. "I've really got to get working on this stuff. We've got to make a decision about that deal, and I can't do that without all of my information, and I can't get to that until you fix my network problem." "I realize how critical network access is to you," Marianne assures Derek. "I've given this problem a very high priority. You should be hearing from someone within a couple of hours."

"A couple of hours . . . that's not too bad," Derek says. "I'll get some of my phone work done, and I've got a few visits to make. It can't be too much longer than that though . . ." "It won't be," Marianne assures him. "Let me get this over to Network, and I'll probably be talking to you later." "Fine. Thanks."

Marianne adds some notes to the logged call then puts it in Network's queue, assigning the highest nonemergency priority. She then calls the Network group and leaves a message on their voice mail, urging them to get to the problem as quickly as possible.

The Network group, unfortunately, is out. One of the four staff members is ill at home, and the remaining three are working on a network upgrade. John, the most senior, is doing some cross training, teaching Michelle and Salido, the two juniors, some of the basic upgrade tasks so they can take them over for the remaining networks. Marianne forgets all about the call because of the high call volume. She barely has time to put the phone down from one call, when it rings again. After about three hours, a disgruntled Derek calls the Help Desk. Marianne takes his call again. "I've been waiting and no one has gotten back to me," he says. "The problem still hasn't been fixed. You told me a couple of hours! If this is what you consider a high priority then a normal priority must take days!"

Marianne promises to look into the status of his call and get back to him immediately. She calls the Network group. She gets a voice mail message. Maybe someone is there but on the phone. Marianne decides to pay the Network group a visit. When she arrives, Salido is at his desk, listening to phone messages and making notes. John and Michelle are still off somewhere. Marianne waits for Salido to finish, which he does in a few minutes, and then attacks. "Where have you guys been? Derek from Real Estate hasn't been able to log on all day! I passed the problem on to you ages ago, but it hasn't been done yet." Salido logs on to the call management system and, sure enough, there's the call, at the top of the queue. "I'll get to it right away," he tells Marianne. "We were doing a network upgrade, and we just got back. I'm just checking our voice mail now. Maybe you should have paged us." "No," replied a very exasperated Marianne, "I could not have paged you because pages are only for priority 1 emergencies. You guys give us hell if we page you for something that's not an emergency." Salido promises to work on the problem right away, and Marianne leaves to go back to the Help Desk to call Derek.

Discussion

In Scenario 3 Marianne expected the Network group to pick the problem up almost immediately and to resolve it within two hours. She based this expectation on the fact that she gave the call a high priority and that she left a voice mail message reiterating the importance of the call she had passed on. Unfortunately, these two things did not have the same meaning for the Network group as they did for Marianne. They would certainly have taken problem priority into consideration, but there was no structure in place for determining response times or for checking voice mail on a regular basis. Marianne and the Network group were each working from a completely different understanding of what the Network group's responsibilities were. The result was a disgruntled and inconvenienced customer and a negative impact on the profitability of the business.

In Scenario 4, let's look at how Scenario 3 might have played out had John, Marianne, and Marianne's manager first taken the time to clarify their understanding of responsibilities.

SCENARIO 4

Marianne has tried to solve Derek's problem but has finally given up. She tells him she has to pass the call on. "Derek, I'm afraid I'm going to have to contact the Network people for help on this one. I'm going to pass this call on to them, and either a Network person or I will give you a call back." "Oh. OK. Any idea when?," Derek worries. "I've really got to get working on this stuff. We've got to make a decision about that deal, and I can't do that without all of my information, and I can't get to that until you fix my network problem." Marianne assures Derek: "I realize how critical network access is to you. I've given this problem a very high priority. You should be hearing from someone within a couple of hours."

Marianne has a high level of confidence in the truth of what she has just told Derek because she and her manager spent time with John of the Network group clarifying the call-handling process between the Help Desk and the Network group. She puts the call into the Network queue after adding a few notes. Since it is a particularly important call she calls the Network group and leaves a voice mail. Sure enough, although one Network staff member is ill at home and the other three are working on a network install, Marianne's confidence is justified. Salido and Michelle take turns every 30 minutes picking up their voice mail to check for calls that cannot wait for them to finish their work. Salido hears Marianne's message, returns to the Network area, and picks the call off the queue. He resolves Derek's problem, then gives Derek a call to get him to try the connection. Everything works, so Salido closes the call log, which generates a closure message to Marianne. Salido then goes back to join his colleagues.

Discussion

In Scenario 4 both the Help Desk and the Network group had the same understanding of how the Network group would handle calls. As a result, things played out as Marianne, Derek, and the Network group expected. There was minimal negative impact on the profitability of the business, and the customer was satisfied with the Help Desk's service.

What Can You Do?

The more clearly responsibilities are defined between support levels, the less likely it is that calls will fall between the cracks and the higher the levels of service will be. A Help Desk with a base of support it can rely on is a strong Help Desk, one that can do more for each customer and for the business.

If your Help Desk has not taken the time to define responsibilities with other levels of support, it may be time for you to do something about it. Talk to your colleagues and your manager. It might be difficult or inappropriate for you to talk directly to the other levels of support, although this can work in smaller organizations. As long as there is a gap in understanding, there will be room for dropped calls, for failures in service, and for a negative impact on business.

Willingness to Fill Service Gaps

Even when people have the best of intentions and responsibilities have been clarified, things can still go wrong. When they do, it is your responsibility as a Help Desk practitioner and in your role as partner to temporarily fill the gap in service and then follow up to make sure it is addressed. It is very easy to say, "Well, I've held up my side, now it's up to them. If they don't carry out their responsibilities, then they'll just have to take the blame." It may be easy, but, unfortunately, it's not very good for the business. It's also a cop-out and not at all a reflection of the partner role you should be playing. If you find yourself saying those words then either start learning how to play the partner role or start looking for another career. If you can't play the partner role you'll never be an effective Help Desk practitioner.

It's much harder to say, "Well, I've held up my side, but it doesn't look like they're carrying out their responsibilities. Maybe I'll look after things this time and then let them know that something went wrong." Taking this attitude is good for the business because there are fewer cracks for problems to fall into. It is also good for you. Your Help Desk will be stronger and more effective, and, as a result, your working environment will be much more pleasant.

Let's look at Scenario 5 and Marianne's Help Desk for an example.

SCENARIO 5

Marianne is having a frustrating morning. One of her colleagues is taking a course and another is home ill. And, of course, almost all of the calls coming in require site visits.

"It looks like no breaks and no lunch today," she thinks dejectedly as she answers the phone one more time. Her mind is not quite on the call, and as the customer, Ursula, is speaking, Marianne notices that the call-waiting light is flashing. Ursula's problem sounds like a network problem, Marianne tells herself. "I'll transfer it to the Network Group right away," and without hesitating she finishes logging the call and puts it into the Network queue. She says goodbye to Ursula and picks up the next call.

In the Network group, Michelle picks up the call, reads it, and frowns. "Hmm. This sure doesn't sound like a network problem." Michelle calls Ursula up and agrees to visit her office. Michelle finds the problem and discovers that she was right: The Help Desk had not installed the correct software. The problem was not network related. From Ursula's desk Michelle calls the Help Desk, gets Jim, Marianne's colleague, and the new software is downloaded. Michelle then configures it properly and gives Ursula some instructions for using it. Ursula thanks her, and Michelle returns to her office. She adds some notes to the call log and closes it. She sends an e-mail to Marianne letting her know what happened. The e-mail reads, "Marianne: Just to let you know, when I went out to visit Ursula I found that the ABC software hadn't been loaded. With Jim's help I got it onto Ursula's PC, configured it, and showed her how to use it. All seems fine now."

Discussion

Michelle did a great job filling a service gap. When she suspected the problem was not network related she might have simply sent it back to the Help Desk. Instead, she did what was best for the business. She solved Ursula's problem and minimized a potential negative impact on the profitability of the business. She also addressed the potential for future recurrences by sending Marianne a note. If the problem had been more severe or kept recurring, then Michelle would have had to go to her manager who would then have gone to Marianne's manager to resolve the issue. Michelle's actions also strengthened relations between the groups. Marianne will now certainly be willing to bridge service gaps for the Network group in the future.

What Can You Do?

When you encounter a service gap that you have the power to do something about, like the one described in Scenario 5, there are several steps you can take:

Bridge the gap. It may not be your responsibility, but think in terms of the impact on the profitability of the business. If your involvement will minimize a negative impact, then get involved.

Address the gap. You want to prevent a recurrence. If the event was an unusual occurrence, as in Scenario 5, let the person directly involved know what happened. If you feel that responsibility is unclear, clarify it. Don't feel you have to go through your manager. If, however, the matter is more serious or recurs, you'll need to go through your manager.

Be tactful. Don't crucify people for making mistakes. Assume that the person did not mean to make a mistake. Too often, especially when we're busy and stressed, we tend to immediately think, "What an idiot! Why did she send it over here? She did this on purpose! Why should we do this? It's not our job!" Give the person involved the benefit of the doubt. In Scenario 5, Michelle's note was very tactful. It was simple and did not try to lay blame but rather informed and reassured.

Commitment to Ongoing Improvement

A third factor in making the relationships between the different support levels work is making a commitment to ongoing improvement. The stability of the Help Desk is very much affected by the support base on which it sits. If you can't get the support you need, your customers won't get the support they need, and the whole Help Desk structure becomes weak. The stronger the relationships between the support levels are, the stronger the support base and the more effective the Help Desk will be. If you continually look for ways to improve relationships, you will be continually strengthening that base.

Ongoing improvement is a cycle. You find something that could use improving, improve it, then find the next thing that needs improving, and so on. What kinds of things should you be looking for? Relationships might be improved by sharing information, clarifying responsibilities, or taking advantage of opportunities to improve a process.

Sharing Information

Could you improve your Help Desk's performance by giving more information to the other levels of support? This might mean telling them about unusual occurrences or problems that might affect their areas or simply taking the time to be more thorough when logging calls so they have more information when they pick up a call.

It might also mean requesting that they share information with you. You might approach this from the following point of view: "We may be able to save you some work if you keep us informed on these specific issues." Anyone who works in support appreciates anything that will save work.

You might attend some of their meetings or invite them to attend some of yours.

Clarifying Responsibilities

Any time you notice a responsibility that is not clear or a customer being bounced from one support area to another, instead of taking offense take the opportunity to make an improvement. Resolve the issue with the person involved or through your manager. Communicate the resolution to all Help Desk practitioners and other support staff so everyone is clear on the responsibility. If it seems to be a onetime thing, don't belabor it. It might be enough just to speak to someone.

If your Help Desk is large, if you interact with several support areas, or if you are having trouble getting cooperation when you try to clarify responsibilities then your Help Desk might do well to create SLAs with the support areas it interacts with. An SLA is an agreement between the Help Desk and another area—another support area in this case—that spells out the responsibilities of each. The agreement also provides a way of measuring compliance with the agreed-upon responsibilities. For example, the agreement might specify that when you pass a call to the network support group they must pick it up and respond to the customer within 30 minutes. The agreement might also specify that you have to include a detailed description of the problem when you log the call. Specific details that you need to include in the description might be also specified in the agreement.

SLAs are valuable, but they are time-consuming to set up and difficult to enforce unless everyone in the company believes in them. Initiatives to create SLAs often fail because people simply do not realize how much work is involved in the process. You first have to figure out exactly what you do and then reach agreement with all of the other support areas on what they should be doing. To say that is not an easy thing to do is to grossly understate the situation. Setting up separate SLAs with each support area you interact with might be an onerous chore, but if it will give your Help Desk a stronger base and make you more effective, it is certainly worth the effort. SLAs are discussed further in Chapter 9.

Process Improvement

If it makes sense for you to be doing something that another support area is doing or vice versa, try to do the thing that makes the most sense. (If you understand that then you have obviously been on a Help Desk too long!) If you have a suggestion for improving a process, your reasons are valid, and you can present them unemotionally, chances are you can get the process improved by bringing your reasons to your manager or to the other support area involved. For example, if you are constantly getting calls for security changes after the security group has gone for the day, you might want to suggest that the Help Desk take on at least some security functions. The Help Desk could handle the later calls and minimize the negative impact of downtime caused by security issues on the profitability of the business. If customers can't get the security system to do what they need it to do, then the business is certainly being negatively impacted.

Making Distributed Help Desks Work

Working effectively with other support groups is a challenge that is sometimes intensified by having another Help Desk in your organization. Working in an environment in which you are one of two or more Help Desks is more challenging than working in an environment in which you are the only Help Desk. There are a number of reasons for this, some of which are described in the following section.

Challenges Faced in an Environment of Multiple Help Desks

In an environment of multiple Help Desks you typically do not have all the information about the technological environment at your disposal. For example, if you are working on a PC Help Desk and your company also has a mainframe Help Desk, you might not know when there is a problem on the mainframe. Customers might call you with a problem, and you might waste a lot of time before you realize the mainframe is down.

If you have multiple Help Desks in your organization then chances are you are using different Help Desk tools and find it difficult to transfer calls and information back and forth. This is an interesting phenomenon. In my work with various Help Desks, I have found that it is almost a certainty that if one Help Desk gets a tool first and finds that it works, the second Help Desk will repeat the discovery process and stubbornly purchase a different tool that will be difficult to interface with the first tool.

In an environment of multiple Help Desks each Help Desk will typically have processes that differ from the others. One Help Desk might misunderstand how another works, and false expectations might arise as a result.

Similarly, each Help Desk might give its customers a different level of service. In a multiple environment, you run the danger of not meeting customer expectations and of having your image affected by the performance of the other Help Desk.

What Can You Do?

If you are in an environment with more than one Help Desk there are things you can do to help ensure that communication between the Help Desks does take place and that neither the customer nor the business suffers.

First, have regular meetings between the Help Desks. Talk about problem trends, new technology or techniques being employed, and anything unusual that has occurred. Review the effectiveness of the communication between the Help Desks. You may think that suggesting meetings is your manager's job, but in your role as partner (remember Chapter 1?) you are taking responsibility and doing what is best for the business you support. If you can't get meetings going on your own, you might have to enlist the help of your manager.

Second, if all the Help Desks can't use the same software and tools, try finding a way to pass problems back and forth. This may involve developing some kind of conversion or import/export functions. If possible, get access to the other Help Desks' databases and give the other Help Desks access to yours. The work I've just described could be incorporated into your Help Desk improvement initiatives.

Third, ensure that each Help Desk understands what its own responsibilities are as well as those of the other Help Desks. Knowing who does what will help ensure that customers aren't bounced between Help Desks and that there are no cracks for problems to fall through. The ideas contained in "Clarifying Responsibilities" earlier in this chapter apply here also. Set up procedures for keeping each other informed of problems and new developments. If your manager launches an initiative to create such procedures, participate enthusiastically. Make sure you understand procedures and their importance. Get clarification if you don't. If you are a PC Help Desk and there is a problem on the mainframe, it is important that you know about the problem because you will likely be getting calls about it.

Consolidating Help Desks

If you work in an environment that has multiple Help Desks you may, at some point in time, be faced with an initiative to consolidate all the Help Desks into one. Such an initiative will only succeed if it has your full support and understanding. In this section I will attempt to give you an understanding of the advantages of consolidation, the process of consolidation itself, and your responsibilities in that process.

Advantages of Consolidation

The words *we're going to be consolidating all of the Help Desks* tend to make Help Desk practitioners nervous. Although it may seem to you that the decision to consolidate was not based on any logical thought, there are in fact several good business reasons for consolidating multiple Help Desks:

One source for information. In a multiple Help Desk environment, there is always the danger that one Help Desk does not know when another has detected a problem in its particular piece of the environment. This could result in the wasted effort of trying to resolve a problem that has already been recognized and addressed. Without knowing it you could be giving out false information to customers.

Better use of staff. In a Help Desk consolidation, the resulting Help Desk typically requires fewer staff members than the sum of the component Help Desks. I won't try to hide the fact that some people may lose their jobs or be moved to other areas because of a consolidation initiative. This is a fact of life. Not many businesses have money to throw away in today's economic climate. Businesses must keep their operating costs to an absolute minimum, and the Help Desk is usually part of those operating costs. If you want to ensure that you will keep your Help Desk job in a consolidation initiative become as effective a Help Desk practitioner as you can. If you are an effective Help Desk practitioner then even if you do lose your job you will not have much trouble finding another. Take the energies that you would otherwise have invested in worrying about losing your job and put them into making yourself as effective as possible.

Even if the consolidation does result in staff layoffs, the resulting Help Desk should end up with a more effective staff complement. The combined call load will be easier to balance among the staff and will be less susceptible to dramatic fluctuations.

A more interesting environment for staff. If you end up being part of the consolidated Help Desk you will have the opportunity to develop a broader base of skills. You will have a more complete picture of what is happening, which will make it easier for you to resolve problems. You will gain experience in a broader base of technologies and will most likely find that the consolidated Help Desk is a more interesting place to work.

Better use of technology. On a consolidated Help Desk, the duplication of Help Desk tools will be eliminated, and tools can be more easily integrated so their functionality and accuracy increases. Tools for one Help Desk generally cost less than the sum of tools for several individual Help Desks.

More consistent service. A consolidated Help Desk makes it easier to provide consistent service to customers. Putting procedures in place to ensure consistent service is easier to do in a single Help Desk than across multiple Help Desks. Similarly, monitoring and managing these procedures is easier in a single Help Desk environment.

Increased Help Desk value. One consolidated Help Desk is typically less expensive to run than several smaller Help Desks. Savings can be realized on tools, on staff, and on office space.

I am not saying here that it is always wrong to have more than one Help Desk. If you have separate customer bases with separate requirements and support needs, more than one Help Desk might well be the way to go. In the following three examples multiple Help Desks were necessary to satisfy the business's needs:

- A bank that had 90 Help Desks before consolidation ended up with 3 after consolidation. Each of the 3 supports a different client base in a different part of the country.

- A pharmaceutical company with 5500 PC customers spread among several buildings decided to create several satellite Help

Desks to bring support closer to the customers. The Help Desks are administered centrally and draw on the same resources.

- A retailing organization found it advantageous to have one Help Desk for its home office and a separate Help Desk to service the support requirements of its numerous stores. The stores have their own computer systems and are hooked into the corporate network. The stores' Help Desk provides help 17 hours a day, across the country, in two languages. The support staff must have detailed knowledge of the stores' systems—including the cash register systems—and are, in fact, required to have actual store experience.

The Process of Consolidation

Consolidating existing Help Desks is not an easy task. There are several processes that you need to work through, and you will survive them better if you understand them. They include the following:

- Analysis of the consolidation, ensuring that it is in the best interests of the business
- Gathering information from all the Help Desks being consolidated
- Gathering information from the business
- Designing the new Help Desk

These processes are explained in the following sections.

Analysis of the Consolidation

Before the business makes any moves toward consolidation, management needs to determine if consolidation is something the business should be doing. This involves answering such questions as "What is the business looking to accomplish through consolidation?" and "What are the current biggest support issues or concerns? How will consolidation help resolve them?"

Gathering Information from All Help Desks

The people involved in the consolidation project need to look at what each of the Help Desks does and what resources each uses. This involves gathering information such as functions performed, technology supported, Help Desk technology used, and the skills and strengths of the people on the Help Desks.

The project staff will also talk to the current Help Desk staff to try to uncover any potential problems or oversights.

Gathering Information from the Business

The consolidation project staff will talk to the customers of the future Help Desks to get a good understanding of the customer profile so they can ensure that the new Help Desk is focused on the business and to address any concerns customers have about the consolidation.

Designing the New Help Desk

The consolidation team uses all the information it has gathered to start designing the new Help Desk. It will be considering such factors as the following:

First-level call resolution. In a consolidated support area people might be required to support a wider range of products. This could decrease first-level resolution rates (the percentage of calls resolved at point of call) significantly.

Call handling. In a consolidated environment call handling might be more complex, for example, passing calls on to other levels of support. Clear procedures and SLAs may need to be set up with all secondary levels of support.

Impact on customers. Customers hate surprises. Anything that will change their current levels of service or what the Help Desk does for them now needs to be marketed so they are aware of it ahead of time.

Tools. A Help Desk that is supporting a wider base of technology may need new tools.

Focus. The consolidation project staff needs to make sure that the new Help Desk is focused on the business. The project staff needs to consider the new customer profile, what management expects from the consolidated Help Desk, and what the responsibility splits are with other IT areas.

Your Responsibility in the Consolidation

Taking part in a Help Desk consolidation is not an easy task, especially when your job is changing and the future of your Help Desk, and possibly your job, is uncertain. If you want to be an effective Help Desk practitioner you must be effective even during a consolidation. You must continue to play all of your Help Desk roles. In a Help Desk consolidation, you have four major responsibilities.

Be cooperative. Give information willingly, and give more than you're asked for. Don't take the attitude that "I'll answer only what I'm asked." If you think the consolidation project will benefit from certain information, then offer it. Play your partner role to its fullest. Always put the needs of the business before any fears you have over changes or of losing your job.

Make constructive suggestions. If you think there is a better way of doing something that perhaps hasn't been thought of, suggest it. If there is something that someone has forgotten, bring it to the consolidation team's notice. If you know of anything that would make the consolidation more successful, make sure the consolidation team knows about it.

Voice concerns positively. It may be difficult at times, but try not to whine. Whining tends to deafen people to the message you are trying to get across. If you have a concern, make sure you have valid reasons for it and that you state them along with the concern. Don't fall into the trap of voicing concerns only to your colleagues. What you are doing then is fear mongering. If your concern is valid then the consolidation team needs to hear about it. If your concern is not valid you should keep it to yourself so you don't alarm your colleagues unnecessarily.

Keep your skills sharp. In times of change people tend to become almost paralyzed and stop participating in any kind of self-improvement. This is the worst thing you can do. You need to keep moving and make sure that you don't fall behind. If there are skills that you think will benefit you on the consolidated Help Desk or in another Help Desk position, work on acquiring them. This doesn't only mean that you should go to your manager and ask to be sent on training. You might not get it until things have settled. What you should do is start seeking out training on your own. You might try self-training through books, audio, video or online sources, or after-hours training. You might even be able to get a few hours a week off to take classroom training at a community college. Don't let yourself stagnate. It will do nothing for your morale or for your career.

Your Career

In working to make the structure of your Help Desk as effective as possible, you are enhancing your career options. I realize I've probably already said this many times, but I have the feeling that you don't believe me yet so I'll say it again. If you have the skills (we discussed them in Chapter 1) that are required to fulfill all Help Desk roles enthusiastically and effectively then you will have little problem getting a job just about anywhere, doing just about anything. Look at the jobs advertised in the classified section of your favorite daily paper. What do employers ask for? "Good problem-solving and communication skills, good technical skills, proactive, customer service oriented, good with customers in person and on the phone, willing to learn about the business." Sound familiar? It should sound like you if you've taken to heart what we've discussed so far in this book.

What can you do to improve your career opportunities? First, keep your skills sharp. Make sure you address all of your training needs, not just technical training. You need to include personal training, such as communication, and procedural training, such as project management or problem solving. Second, widen your experience wherever possible. Take advantage of opportunities to work in other areas, learn new things, work with new people, and try things you haven't tried before. Finally, learn as much as you can about the business you support. Even if you do not pursue a career within the business, learning more about it will help you tremendously in analyzing and solving problems.

Where might you look for career opportunities? Your choices here are unlimited. Some career paths you might consider are as follows:

- Technical roles in areas such as network design, program development, or other specialized support roles

- Management roles such as project management or Help Desk management

- Roles in areas that involve working closely with people, such as training, human resources, customer service, or marketing

By now I hope you finally believe me and are grateful for the day you decided, for whatever reason, to work on a Help Desk. You may even decide to make it a lifetime career.

Checklist

In this chapter we discussed how you could work within your Help Desk's structure to make your Help Desk as effective as possible. Use the following checklist to make sure you are applying the principles you learned here and that you are doing as much as you can:

✓ If I work on a Resolve front line am I getting the training I need? Do I have the tools I need?

✓ Do I know when to escalate a problem? Do I make sure I do not work on problems for too long, forcing other customers to wait?

✓ Am I constantly looking for ways to resolve more calls at point of call?

✓ If I work on a Dispatch front line do I know exactly where to send each type of call? Do I have SLAs with each of the areas I send calls to? If not, have I suggested this to my manager?

✓ If my Dispatch customers have unrealistic expectations, have I considered suggesting a marketing initiative to my manager?

✓ Am I doing a thorough job logging each call so the person it is passed on to gets as much information as possible?

✓ Do I understand the responsibilities of other support areas? Do they have the same understanding that I do?

✓ Do I willingly fill in service gaps? Do I address the reasons for the gaps? Am I always tactful?

✓ Am I constantly looking for ways to improve relationships with other support areas? Have I considered better ways of sharing information and clarifying responsibilities? Are there processes that can be improved?

✓ If I work in a distributed Help Desk environment, do I regularly meet with the other Help Desk(s)? Have we made the effort to share tools, information, or databases? Are our responsibilities clear? Do we have processes in place for keeping each other informed about what is going on in our respective environments?

✓ If I am going through a Help Desk consolidation, do I understand all of its potential advantages?

✓ If I am going through a Help Desk consolidation, am I being cooperative and playing the role of partner to its fullest? Am I making constructive suggestions? Am I voicing concerns positively? Am I keeping my skills sharp?

✓ Am I doing all I can to further my career? Am I constantly upgrading my skills? Am I doing what I can to widen my experience? Am I taking every opportunity to learn about the business my Help Desk serves?

Managing Problems

When Problems Become Dangerous

As Help Desk practitioners, problems are our business. We are dealing with problems from the moment we step into the office to the moment we leave. We are so used to problems we often don't recognize until it's too late when they start becoming dangerous and start taking control.

In This Chapter

In this chapter I want to help you understand how vigilant you must be about staying on top of your problems and the things you must do to keep them from spinning out of control. The topics I will cover are as follows:

- The out-of-control problem cycle
- Keeping or regaining control
- Avoiding common support mistakes
- Focus, structure, and tools

- Priorities and procedures
- A cycle of evaluation and improvement

The Out-of-Control Problem Cycle

I suspect that at least some of you have experienced the anguish of an out-of-control problem cycle. If you haven't, good for you, you'll proba-bly live a lot longer than the rest of us. If you have, you are very familiar with the symptoms, which include the following:

- You can never seem to finish one thing before something else be-comes more important.
- Customers are rarely satisfied and are always demanding faster service.
- You can never catch up with your backlog.
- Priorities seem to change on a day-to-day basis and are largely de-termined by who screams louder.
- The number of calls keeps increasing.
- You are completely stressed. Your stomach starts to hurt every time you hear a phone ring. You wake up at night thinking the phone is ringing.
- You dread answering the phone, even at home.

These symptoms describe a very unpleasant environment, to say the least. They also describe a Help Desk that is offering less than optimal business value to the organization it supports. Unfortunately, getting into an out-of-control problem cycle is very easy.

Each call coming into the Help Desk means that a customer is work-ing at less than optimal productivity. Your job as a Help Desk practi-tioner is to get that customer up to full productivity as soon as possible. When the calls start coming fast and furiously, this becomes more diffi-cult. Consider Figure 4.1. You start working on one problem, and then you get a customer who is absolutely frantic and demands your imme-diate help. How do you decide who gets served first? "First come, first served" doesn't allow for the fact that some problems are more important than others. You decide, for example, that the second call must be more important because the customer sounds so frantic, and you put the first request aside to work on the second. Before you get started, however, another call comes in that sounds even more frantic than the previous one, and the cycle starts over. You find yourself with several things on hold while you work frantically on several more. Calls start coming in from customers asking why their work hasn't been completed. You haven't logged anything because you haven't had time.

Your Help Desk is now totally out of control. The problems have taken control and are doing a good job managing you. You don't have a chance to resolve one problem before you have to drop it and start on another one—a cycle that's difficult to get out of. The number of calls will keep increasing because you won't be able to finish everything properly, and you aren't doing anything to make things better. You might not be logging many calls, so you don't have statistics that can help you get a handle on what you're dealing with.

As if this situation weren't bad enough, the calls that you have put aside onto the Help Desk's pile of unresolved problems start taking on a life of their own, as Figure 4.1 shows. Some become urgent and come back into the Help Desk. Others cause more problems that come back into the Help Desk as new problems. Theoretically, if you waited long enough you wouldn't need any new external problems coming in; your cycle would be generating enough problems to keep you busy full time.

Keeping or Regaining Control

What can you do as a Help Desk practitioner to avoid an out-of-control problem cycle? What can you do to get out of such a cycle once you're in it? Probably the most common reason for getting into an out-of-control problem cycle is sheer volume of problems: You simply are getting more problems than you can handle. One of the most effective ways to avoid an out-of-control problem cycle is to minimize the number of problems coming into the Help Desk. Your role as problem eliminator comes into play here. The more time you spend on call elimination initiatives, the

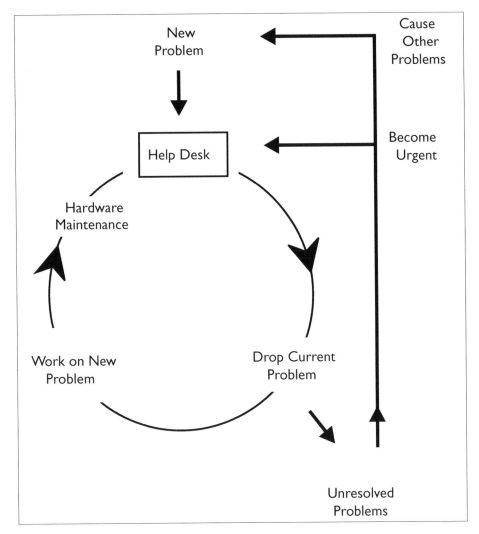

Figure 4.1   An out-of-control problem cycle.

less chance there is that your Help Desk will lose control. How do you eliminate problems and at the same time get out of an out-of-control problem cycle—and stay out? You do the following:

- Make an effort to understand what the most common support mistakes are, how they can become dangerous, and what you can do to avoid them.

- Stay focused on the business, make your Help Desk structure work as effectively as possible, and use problem-solving tools effectively.
- Follow well-defined priorities and procedures.
- Start a cycle of ongoing evaluation and improvement.

Each of these approaches is covered in more detail in the following sections.

Avoiding Common Support Mistakes

There are five mistakes that as Help Desk practitioners we tend to make over and over. Our customers see them as service mistakes, but their roots run to the very core of our Help Desk: its focus; its structure; its tools, priorities, and procedures; and its cycle of evaluation and improvement, or lack thereof. In this section, I will discuss five of the most common support mistakes, why they happen, how they can become dangerous, and how to avoid them.

Five of the most common support mistakes are the following:

Not delivering *when* you promised. You tell the customer you'll have a problem fixed by a specific time or a service, such as a new PC, delivered by a certain time, and then you don't meet that deadline. You're late.

Not delivering *what* you promised. You tell the customer the problem is fixed, and it isn't. You promise one kind of PC system and deliver another.

Appearing rude or unfriendly. You might make the customer feel stupid, you might be too abrupt, or you might pass his or her call on to someone who isn't there.

Not listening. You jump to conclusions or ignore the customer's explanation.

Refusing to help the customer. Customers might feel you are doing this when they get bounced back and forth between support areas or when you simply say no without offering an explanation or any alternatives.

Why These Mistakes Happen and How to Prevent Them

Now we'll look at each of these five problems, why they happen, and what you, the Help Desk practitioner, can do to prevent them.

Not Delivering When You Promised

At one time or another we've all been guilty of promising the customer a delivery time that we did not meet. Oddly enough, one of the reasons we tend to do this is because we want to tell customers what they want to hear. We don't want to have to give them the truth if the truth will annoy them. What are the consequences of undelivered promises? Look at Scenario 1.

SCENARIO 1

Mario works on the Help Desk. He has just received a call from Rita, who has a problem with her PC. "What seems to be the problem, Rita?" Mario asks cheerfully. He's still fairly new. "My word processor can't find the spell checker! I can't spell check anything. I'm just trying to do the final edits for the catalog, and I can't finish until I've spell checked all of the sections." Mario asks Rita a few questions about the problem's symptoms and quickly determines that this is not something he can resolve over the phone. "Rita, I'm going to have to send someone out to have a look at your PC." Mario pauses, checking the schedule.

Rita interrupts him. "It had better be soon, I need this right away!" Mario, who was just about to say, "How about 3:00 this afternoon?" stops himself. Rita is not going to be happy with that. He looks at the schedule again. "If Leonard takes a late lunch, maybe he can squeeze Rita in this morning," he muses. Leonard is the PC technician on call this week. "Well? When can I expect someone?" Rita asks impatiently. "I have to get that catalog finished!" Mario makes his decision. No way is he going to give Rita bad news. "I'll have someone there later on this morning," he promises. "Is that the best you can do?" Rita asks.

"That's the best I can do," Mario assures her. Rita accepts the time, and the conversation ends.

Mario's "the best I can do" turns out to be "much better than I can actually do." Leonard has already booked something for his lunch hour so he cannot take a later lunch, and he is too busy to squeeze in a visit to Rita.

Mario hopes for a miracle. Unfortunately, as is often the case with miracles, one doesn't happen. At 11:59 Rita calls the Help Desk. "You said someone would come later in the morning. How much later can it get than 11:59? What happened? I still don't have my spell checker!" Mario explains what happened. Rita is furious. She calls back two more times in the afternoon, until finally Leonard arrives at 3 P.M. Unfortunately for Leonard, Rita is at her desk when he arrives. Leonard weathers her wrath and fixes the problem. Leonard is not very happy with Mario.

Discussion

Mario made Rita fairly happy with his promise of a morning visit, but that happiness was very short lived. When Rita discovers that Mario's promise is not going to be met, she is livid. Mario could have saved himself, his customer, and the rest of the Help Desk a lot of grief if he had just bitten the bullet and told Rita the truth. She may have kicked up a fuss, but unless she was willing to escalate the problem into an emergency to get a higher priority, she would have had to accept the 3 P.M. time slot.

Scenario 1 is typical of what happens when we make a promise we can't meet. The customers are happy with the promises we give them, but it is only a temporary reprieve for us. When customers realize we are going to be late, they are less than happy, and they keep calling and calling. They may have arranged their work schedules around the time we gave them, or they may have promised a deadline based on that time. Our original aim of not wanting to annoy our customers starts to look pretty silly. What we've managed to do, besides inconvenience our customers and possibly embarrass our coworkers, is negatively impact the profitability of the business.

Let's look at some of the reasons why we do not deliver when we promise:

We are poor estimators. When we give an estimate of how long it will take to fix a problem, we tend to estimate the shortest possible time, that is, with nothing going wrong, no problems occurring during the testing that we need to do, no possibility of being pulled off to work on an emergency, and so on. Given the environment we work in we certainly are an optimistic bunch when it comes to estimating. We're almost embarrassed to give customers a real estimate.

We simply don't know, so we guess. Perhaps our manager has not given us the data we need to do our day-to-day jobs. I wish I could say that this is a rare occurrence, but unfortunately it is not. All too often, managers have not taken the time to get the Help Desk focused on the business and to get services defined, which involves setting delivery times and passing all this information on to Help Desk practitioners.

We hate to give customers bad news. If you tell the customer, "Your PC should be here in three weeks" and the customer gives you grief, you are tempted to say, "We'll try for two." If you actually do say that, what the customer hears is "We'll have it for you in two weeks for sure." We are afraid of our customers.

We don't speak the same language. When a Help Desk practitioner says, "I'll have this ready in a few minutes," what does he or she mean? They mean somewhere in the neighborhood of 30 minutes or so. What does the customer hear? If I were the customer I would think, "A few minutes . . . that's about five minutes, ten minutes tops." After ten minutes, I'd be calling back demanding to know "Why isn't it fixed yet? It's been ten minutes!" (If you're thinking that I am a very demanding customer, you are correct.) We use words such as *few, a while, not too long,* or *in a jiffy* and expect the customer to know what we mean.

There is a gap between customer expectations and what we can deliver. Perhaps we don't give the customer a time, but he or she simply assumes one. This can happen even when there are service level agreements (SLAs) in place. If a customer does not know such an agreement exists—something that happens too frequently—or does not understand the terms, he or she may have his or her own expectations about how long the task should take. The customer usually has a much more optimistic view of how long something should take, and inevitably the reality is a disappointment.

We depend on other people whose time and scheduling are out of our control. This takes us back to Chapter 3, where we discussed the relationships between support levels. If we depend on other areas for support we must understand the kind of response times we can expect from them. Ideally, we have some kind of agreement in place that spells this out. We cannot give out a delivery date with any kind of assurance until we know the delivery times of the support groups we rely on.

How can you avoid promising times you cannot meet?

First, learn to estimate your time realistically. Let's say you are fixing a problem for someone. You figure that if you sat down and started fixing it right away, without interruption and with everything going the way it should, it should take you 30 minutes. Now, consider all the things that might happen to increase this time. A colleague might interrupt you with a question. You might get pulled on to an emergency. The test data you need may not be there. A utility you need to use may not work properly. You could probably add many more items to this list. All of a sudden that 30 minutes is looking more like 60 or even 90. If you tell the customer "30 minutes" and it takes you 60, you're in trouble. You've generated extra calls because that customer will be calling back, and you're now dealing with an irate customer. If you tell the customer "90 minutes" and it takes you 60 or even 30, you have not generated any more calls, and the customer will be very pleased to get the result earlier than expected. I am often asked, "Isn't this just padding the estimate?," as if that were something negative. My answer is "No, you are not indiscriminately padding the estimate, you are making it more realistic. You are giving the customer a more honest answer."

Second, if you don't know or are unclear about expected delivery times, ask your manager. Make sure you know about all SLAs your Help Desk may have with customers or with other support areas. Don't be forced into guessing because you will be wrong at least 50 percent of the time, and you will be generating negative calls that you do not need.

Third, learn to play the role of communicator effectively. Convince yourself that it is much better to tell the truth and get a little grief from the customer than to tell a lie and get much more grief from the customer later on. If you're going to give a time, make sure there is no ambiguity and that the customer hears what you say. Chapters 5 and 6 deal with communicating effectively. You should find lots of ideas in these two chapters to help you out.

Fourth, if there is a gap in what customers expect and what you can deliver, start bridging it. This might mean letting your manager know about the problem and putting some kind of marketing initiative in place. This will be much easier if you have some kind of SLA with the customers. If you don't, you'll have to market the times that you can meet. Chapter 11 will give you ideas on how to market effectively.

Finally, you need to establish some kind of service agreements with the support areas that you depend on. You'll need your manager's help here, but you can certainly be the instigator. In Chapter 3, we talked about several ways of improving the relationships between support levels. If you need to depend on external vendors such as PC suppliers then you should have written SLAs with these organizations. If you are giving out times based on their delivery you have to be very sure what their delivery time is.

These are only some of the things you can do to avoid promising times that you can't meet. Chapter 7 provides a whole strategy for addressing problems such as this one as well as an example of not meeting agreed-upon delivery times.

Not Delivering What You Promised

Let's look more closely at what "not delivering what you promised" means. You do something to fix a customer's problem and tell the customer, "It's fixed now." Ten minutes later you get a call back: "The problem is still happening! You didn't fix it!" Not only have you wasted the customer's time and increased the number of calls coming into the Help Desk, you've also caused the customer to lose confidence in you and in the Help Desk, and you now have to spend more of your own time fixing the problem again. You have negatively impacted the profitability of the business.

Why don't we deliver what we promise? The reasons might include the following:

We don't listen. Sometimes we're too busy to listen attentively, and we don't hear everything the customer is saying. We may stop listening after the first few words, thinking that we've heard this particular problem so many times before that it must be the same one. We may end up working on the wrong problem. (I also discuss failing to listen in a later section of this chapter.)

We jump to conclusions. When we start to investigate the problem we think it looks so much like another familiar problem that it must be the same thing, so we put in the usual fix without taking the time to analyze further.

We don't test. When things get busy on the Help Desk and we see the same problems again and again, we sometimes get careless. We assume we understand a problem because it looks similar to one we've fixed many times before. We don't bother testing the solution because testing takes time.

What can we do to avoid delivering something other than what we promised? First, we need to slow down and listen. The extra few seconds we spend listening can save us much time and grief later on. If you aren't sure about something the customer has said, ask for clarification or paraphrase it back to the customer to make sure you understand what the problem is. Chapters 5 and 6 deal extensively with communication in problem solving.

Second, we need to slow down and analyze. Again, take a few minutes to make sure this problem is exactly like the one you are familiar with before you slap the familiar solution onto it. Third, don't even think of letting a solution go until it's tested. If you feel you cannot test it effectively anywhere but on the customer's PC, call the customer up and have him or her try it out while you are on the phone. Explain what you are doing so the customer does not expect an immediate solution. Customers will be very cooperative if they realize you're trying to help them.

Appearing Rude or Unfriendly

None of us come in to the Help Desk in the morning and say, "Today, I'm going to be as rude as I can to my customers." Most of the time when we come across as rude or unfriendly, we simply don't realize the impression we're creating. What do we do that makes our customers think we are rude or unfriendly?

We make them feel stupid. If you inadvertently talk down to someone, you make that person feel stupid. If you indicate by your words or even by the slightest change in your tone that the customer should have known better, then you make that customer feel stupid. The result? Customers will feel offended, will feel you have no respect for them. If they feel you have no respect for them, they will certainly have little for you. There goes your image, and there goes the customer's cooperation when you need it. If customers are afraid of appearing stupid they will often say "I understand" when they do not. This will translate into more calls to the Help Desk. The customers will have to call back to get clarification and a clearer explanation.

We are abrupt or distracted. Think of how you feel when you go into a doctor's office and she makes you feel like she hardly has time for you. You are explaining a very personal problem in detail, for example, when the phone rings. "Excuse me," she says and takes the call. After a few minutes she puts the phone down, apologizes and asks you to continue. You gather your thoughts and start again. Your doctor nods as you speak but looks at her watch every few seconds. Before you're quite finished she says, "Yes, yes, I understand. Now, let's just check you over before we go any further," and without giving you a chance to respond she throws you a dressing gown, says, "Just change into that and I'll be back in a jiffy," and then is gone for 15 minutes or so while you wait shivering in the flimsy paper gown. You feel like you are very near the bottom of that doctor's priority scale. She obviously has many more important things to do than listen to your problems.

You decide to look for another doctor, a doctor who listens to you no matter how many other patients are waiting. A doctor who tells you with her or his actions that you are important. On a Help Desk we are always in a hurry. We might speak quickly or try to get people off the phone as soon as possible. We might be working on more than one problem at the same time. As a result, we might be making our customers feel unimportant, as if they are very low on our scale of priorities.

We transfer them into oblivion. Someone calls the Help Desk. You answer the call. The person needs a security change. You tell them you'll transfer them to that department. Again, you're in a hurry. You transfer them and hang up, without waiting to see if there is anyone there to answer. The customer feels very unimportant, very expendable. You are probably going to get another call from that same customer, now more than slightly irate.

What can we do to avoid coming across as rude or unfriendly? First, if you do not understand why people are commenting on your rudeness or unfriendliness, have an honest colleague listen to a few of your interactions and then give you some constructive feedback. Be willing to hear the truth or people will be afraid to give it to you.

Second, before you start each working day, look into the mirror and say (don't worry, this is not turning into a fairy tale), "My customers are not interruptions. My customers are the most important part of my job." You have to carry that attitude into work each day and into each customer interaction. If customers are the most important part of your job, you need to respect them. If you respect them, you cannot make them feel stupid. You take care not to make them feel stupid. Respect is an interesting thing. It works in a cycle, as Figure 4.2 illustrates. If you respect your customers through their impatience, irritation, and worry, they will eventually start to respect you. Having your customers' respect means that customers will believe what you tell them. They will not try to shout their way into a higher priority; they will be cooperative when you tell them you cannot get to their problem just yet. They will help you stay out of an out-of-control problem cycle.

Third, when you answer a customer's call, remember your distracted doctor: Make your customer feel as if he or she has your complete attention. Listen actively; ask questions. Don't be working on

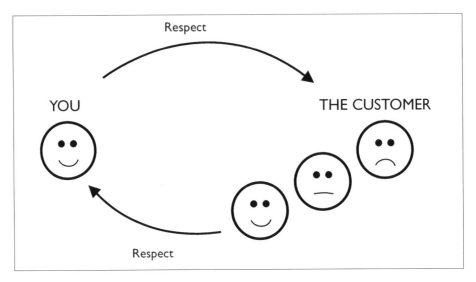

Figure 4.2 The respect cycle.

several things at once. You won't save time; you'll make mistakes. Chapter 5 has several suggestions for improving your listening skills.

Fourth, don't ever leave customers hanging or facing a wall. If you try to transfer them somewhere and no one picks up the phone, don't leave them. You can either give them the number to try later or you can offer to call for them, depending on what your particular Help Desk does and the service they are requesting.

Not Listening

Have you ever tried explaining something to someone who just wasn't listening? It's a very infuriating experience. I once was trying to explain a problem I was having with a virtual e-mail ID to an Internet service provider (ISP) I used for a while. The support person could only hear the words *e-mail ID*. He would not listen when I tried to explain that, yes, I knew my regular ID was working; it was my virtual ID that was the problem. He kept interrupting with suggestions; he simply would not listen. I did finally get the virtual ID problem resolved, but by that time I'd had enough and I changed Internet providers (which turned out to be a good thing because the provider I had been using went out of business).

Why didn't this person listen to me? Why are there times when we choose not to listen to our customers? A common reason is the following:

We think they don't know what they are doing. That might be a tough one for some of you to swallow, but there it is. All of us, at one time or another, feel that we know a lot more than our customers. After all, we work in technology day after day; they just work in the business. How could they possibly know something that could help us out? If you feel like that it's very easy to tune someone out, to interrupt them, to tell them what the problem is. Unfortunately, that isn't much of a solution for them, and they will call back and probably ask to speak to someone other than you.

I would like to be able to list several less-damning reasons for not listening, but I really can't think of any. I'm not talking about being too busy or too distracted to listen; I'm talking about consciously choosing not to listen. When you are simply not listening to a customer's explanation, when you are choosing to ignore it, then you are obviously thinking that you know better than the customer, that the customer does not know what he or she is talking about.

What can you do about this? This isn't just a matter of listening effectively; it is a matter of learning to respect the customer and realizing how important the customer is. The customer may not understand technology the way you do, but the customer does not need that level of understanding. It is not the technology that brings the business financial gain, it is the customer's use of technology, what the customer does with that technology. The customer needs to understand the business and how the technology can support the business. It is up to you to provide the deeper level of understanding that can fix that technology when it stops working and can help that customer use the technology more effectively.

Refusing to Help the Customer

I'd like to spend a few paragraphs clarifying this particular problem. If a customer calls the Help Desk and says, "I want to order some blinds for my office. Can you help me?," the Help Desk practitioner who takes the call should certainly answer, "No, I'm sorry, we do not handle blinds" (unless, of course, that Help Desk has defined window coverings as one of the services it provides!). Unless that Help Desk practitioner happens to know which department handles window coverings, he or she should not spend the time researching the information because it is something quite out of the realm of that Help Desk's expertise.

There are times when, to focus on the business, you are going to have to say no to the customer. Sometimes you will be able to at least point the customer in a good direction, as Alexis did in Scenario 2 in Chapter 2, when she looked up the name of a company that loaned out PC equipment. Loaning PC equipment is a request that the Help Desk might get again in the future. Other times—as with requests for help with blinds—you will have no idea where to find what the customer is asking for, the request is totally unrelated to what you do, and the business value of taking the time to provide that information to the customer is minimal at best. Spending time on that would mean taking time away from other customers and making them wait, which would negatively impact the profitability of the business.

This, however, is not what I mean by refusing to help. "Refusing to help" refers to a situation in which customers call the Help Desk with a technology-related or Help Desk-related request and are left with the feeling that the Help Desk does not want to help them. This might happen for the following reasons:

The customer is bounced between support areas. For example, in an environment with multiple Help Desks, the PC Help Desk might tell the customer, "This is a mainframe problem; call the mainframe Help Desk," and the mainframe Help Desk might tell the customer, "This is definitely a PC problem; call the PC Help Desk." The customer has uncovered a service gap, a gray area of responsibility. The customer has also uncovered Help Desk practitioners who are unwilling to fill service gaps, as we discussed in Chapter 3, and who are not playing the role of partner very effectively.

The customer has false expectations of service. In Scenario 1 in Chapter 2, Alexis set a false expectation for her customers by loaning out a laptop to Loren. By the time Alexis realized her mistake, another customer had already picked the expectation up from Loren and expected to get Alexis to loan him or her a laptop. When Alexis told the customer that was not a service the Help Desk offered, that customer probably felt, with justification, that Loren was refusing to help.

The problem of "refusing to help" will go away when the Help Desk is focused on the business, its services are clearly defined, and all Help Desk practitioners are working as partners and are willing to fill service gaps while building or strengthening relationships with other support areas.

How These Mistakes Can Become Dangerous

Each time you give a customer a service delivery time that you cannot meet you are generating extra calls to the Help Desk. That customer will call you when the time you gave (or the time the customer heard) passes and you have not delivered. The customer may call back more than once, depending on how persistent he or she is, how badly he or she needs the service, and how long you actually take to deliver it. These calls are also not regular calls. The customer is unhappy and wants some kind of satisfaction that you cannot deliver. If the customer complains loudly enough, you may be intimidated into bumping someone else out of the queue and trying to satisfy the disgruntled customer. Does this sound familiar? Look at the out-of-control situation pictured in Figure 4.1; the situation I have just described fits that model exactly.

The same holds true when you deliver something other than what you promised. Customers will keep calling back until they get what they want, and they will be more unhappy each time they call. These kinds of calls readily feed an out-of-control problem cycle.

When we appear rude or unfriendly to customers, they may call back and be more annoyed than before, if, for example, we had transferred them into oblivion, or they may go and complain to someone else at a higher level. In the latter case, the perception of the customer and the customer's senior manager will be that the Help Desk does not offer good value. This will get back to the Help Desk, and there will be more pressure than ever to help anyone who yells loudly so as to avoid any more complaints. This provides even more nourishment for the out-of-control problem cycle. If a Help Desk manager cannot get problems under control and senior management has the perception that the Help Desk does not offer good value the days of the Help Desk are numbered. Outsourcing is always an option.

When we don't listen to customers, when we refuse to help them, we are just begging for more calls, and we are asking customers and management to have a poor perception of the Help Desk's value. When you are in a busy environment, barely holding your own, and you start generating more calls—calls you do not need and cannot handle, negative calls that are not easily resolved and demand immediate service—you are in danger of losing control. Add on top of this senior management's low estimation of the Help Desk's value, and you have the formula for disaster and failure. You need to stop this situation before it gets to the point of crisis and avoid these kinds of mistakes.

Preventing These Mistakes

The way to prevent these mistakes from becoming dangerous and taking you into an out-of-control problem cycle is to stop them from happening altogether. Awareness is the first step. You now will know what these problems are and the danger they pose. The next step is evaluation and improvement—constantly evaluating your environment to see if these problems exist and looking for ways to eliminate them. The evaluation and improvement process is discussed in more detail later on in this chapter.

Focus, Structure, and Tools

Focus, structure, and tools can play a major role in getting you out of an out-of-control problem cycle—and keeping you out. In your role as partner, you need to do what you can to ensure that the Help Desk stays focused on the business and to ensure that the resources of the Help Desk are focused on what is most important to the business. Any effort you expend that is not geared toward that focus makes your Help Desk weaker, leaving greater room for loss of control. You need to fulfill the Help Desk's mission, work toward the Help Desk's objectives, and provide and stay within defined Help Desk services. Chapter 2 discusses your responsibility to maintain focus.

You also need to do what you can to make the Help Desk's structure work effectively. As we discussed in Chapter 3, there is much you can do to improve the relationships between support levels and strengthen your support base. If you are filling service gaps, clarifying relationships, and working to improve relationships, you are creating less opportunity for customer calls to fall through the cracks. You are eliminating the need for customers to call back, which means fewer calls into the Help Desk, which in turn helps to prevent an out-of-control problem cycle. You can also make sure that your front line works as effectively as possible. If you are on a Resolve front line, get the training you need, learn when to escalate calls so you are not spending too much time on any one call to the detriment of others, and work to resolve as many calls as possible at point of call. If you are on a Dispatch front line, you can make sure you know where each call should be transferred, do a thorough job logging each call, address any unrealistic customer expectations, and sell your manager on SLAs for customer areas.

Problem resolution tools such as knowledge bases and remote control software can help you resolve more calls at point of call and can shorten the time you spend on a call. They can help you get out and stay out of an out-of-control problem cycle. If you have problem resolution tools, make sure you know how to use them properly. You want to get the maximum possible value out of each tool in terms of the number of problems it can help you with and the time it can save you. If you don't have the right problem resolution tools, or if you don't have any, it's up to you to convince your manager of their worth. Chapter 8 discusses problem-solving tools in detail.

Priorities and Procedures

Priorities will help you identify what problems, requests, questions, and work are most important to the business. Setting priorities will help prevent the scenario in which a call becomes an emergency if the caller sounds upset enough but is then dropped midstream when a caller who sounds even more upset comes along. When that happens, we're back to the out-of-control problem cycle shown in Figure 4.1. How angry a customer is should not play a part in the priority a problem is assigned, and there should be no "perceived" priorities—only clearly defined, well-understood ones.

Well-defined procedures will increase the accuracy and consistency of the service you provide. The better defined your procedures are, the more correctly they will be performed. There will be fewer reasons for customers to call back. Procedures will help ensure that things get done properly the first time. The following sections discuss the use of priorities and procedures in more detail.

Priorities

A priority is a measurement that we assign to a call or a task to indicate its importance relative to all other calls and tasks. Calls that we can resolve at point of call are typically not assigned a priority. They are simply resolved in the order in which they are received. Tasks and calls that we cannot resolve at point of call, that we need to assign priority to, include the following:

Problems. Problems are interruptions in service to customers. Something is wrong with hardware, software, or procedures, and as a result the technology is not working as it should. Customers are prevented from achieving optimal productivity in their jobs.

Requests. Customers making requests are asking for services that are part of the Help Desk's advertised list of services. These might include training, ordering PCs, and so on.

Questions. Questions are queries about how to perform specific tasks using technology. Application questions are of the type, "How do I pull my spreadsheet into my word processing package?" Procedural questions are of the type, "How do I download a file from the mainframe?" or "How can I send this document to someone who is not on the LAN?" Consulting questions might include "What software should I use to create a newsletter?" or "Is there anything that can help me do this on a PC?"

Work. You need to make sure that work you have planned, such as call elimination initiatives or software and hardware upgrades, gets done. You may also have to ensure that some work you have not planned but has become necessary actually gets done. You have to be able to prioritize work, planned and unplanned, against everything else going on in your Help Desk. The danger of failing to prioritize necessary work is that you will find yourself constantly giving other things a higher priority and never getting around to achieving your objectives: to eliminate calls. Unachieved objectives are the first warning sign of an out-of-control problem cycle.

An effective priority structure for your Help Desk must address all four of these categories.

What's in a Priority?

Priorities measure the impact of the problem (or request, question, or work) on the profitability of the business. For example, if a cash register can't function, sales can't be entered and customers who are waiting impatiently may be lost forever. There is a direct and severe negative impact on the profitability of the business. If, however, the result of a problem is that performance reports will be a day late, the negative impact on the business will likely be negligible. The cash register problem should therefore get a much higher priority than the reporting problem. As these two examples show, in order to measure impact on the business we need to consider both the importance of the component involved, for example the cash register system, and how severe any impairment such as a malfunctioning program or hardware device is (see Figure 4.3).

Figure 4.3   Definition of impact on the business.

Importance of Component

A component can be software, hardware, specific projects, or even specific people:

> **Hardware and software.** Examples of important software and hardware components include most of the hardware and software in warehouses' shipping and receiving systems or in airlines' reservation systems.
>
> **Specific projects.** When organizations are in a highly competitive mode, as most today are, projects that have the potential to put them ahead of the competition become critical. Anything that stops these projects, such as technology problems, is really stopping the organization from getting ahead of the competition.
>
> **Specific people.** Organizations usually have people who are critical to the business, people who need high-priority problem resolution wherever they are or at whatever computer they happen to be using. An example of such a person might be the hands-on president of a small company who is constantly making critical business decisions and deals for new business.

Severity of Event

The severity of an event, such as a problem, can be measured by how much functionality the component in question has lost. Is the component completely shut down, unable to function at all, or is it still functioning but at a degraded rate? How widespread are the effects of the event? Is the impact localized, with only one person impacted, or is it widespread, with whole departments impacted?

A newspaper that sells ads considers its ad sales systems, which include workstations, the network, and ad sales software, as critical to the business. If the network goes down and no one can sell ads, that newspaper all of a sudden is not making money. It's losing significant revenue every minute the network is down. That problem gets the highest priority. If only one of the PCs on the network is down or if network response is degraded, the newspaper is still getting some revenue but not as much as it should be getting. The paper is still losing money. The business is impacted, so the problem must get a high priority. If, however, one of the people on the ad sales network wants a custom screen saver installed, that person may just have to wait. Although ad sales is a critical system, the severity of the event—the custom screen saver not being installed—is nil. Our priorities should be helping us ensure that we never spend time on minor problems or requests while severe ones are outstanding.

Priority Scales

Priority scales are scales that allow you to measure the priority of a Help Desk call or task. A commonly used scale is one whose values range from one to five, with one denoting the highest priority and five the lowest. Regardless of the values used, what is most important in a scale is the clarity of the definition. The definition should make it clear to the person assigning priorities what the priority should be. Often, the priority will be obvious. "The warehouse is down," "no one can take any ads," or "the mainframe is down" are pretty good indications that you have a serious, top-priority problem on your hands. On the other hand, "The colors on my screen look kind of washed out" probably won't have you pushing the panic button. Other times, the priority will not be as easy to determine, and this is when a clear definition will help. If the definition refers to critical or noncritical components, then a list of critical components should accompany it. Response times are often tied into priority definitions to further clarify what each priority means. SLAs use this kind of priority-response relationship to define and measure service levels. Table 4.1 shows a priority scale that covers problems, work, questions, and requests.

Priorities and You

I've described what priorities are, why we need them, and how they're constructed. I'd now like to discuss how priorities affect you, the Help Desk practitioner, and how they can help get you out of an out-of-control problem cycle and keep you out.

   If you are responsible for resolving those calls that do not get resolved at point of call, you should have a clear understanding of what

Table 4.1 Priority Scale

Priority	Problems	Work	Questions	Requests
1	Critical component(s) down. Business is impacted.	N/A	N/A	N/A
2	Critical component(s) degraded. Business is impacted.	N/A	Critical user can't get business done. Business is impacted.	Emergency requirement. Business is impacted.
3	Multiple, noncritical components down or degraded. Business not impacted.	Planned or unplanned work that is necessary to prevent serious problems or unplanned work that will resolve recurring problems that are putting a strain on Help Desk resources.	N/A	All other requests for services supported by the Help Desk.
4	Single, noncritical component down or degraded. Business not impacted.	N/A	N/A	N/A
5	Little or no impact. Problem could be cosmetic.	N/A	Everything else.	N/A

your priorities are. When things get busy you may have to drop certain calls or tasks, and you want to make sure that you drop the least important ones. Dropping less important calls or tasks will help keep you in control. You can then concentrate on getting the most important things completed. If you know the relative importance of calls and tasks, this will be easier for you to do. You should have a scale like the one shown in Table 4.1. If you are unclear about your priorities or if you don't have any kind of scale, talk to your manager. You may be dropping the wrong things.

If you do have a priority scale but it does not include work, then you are in danger of having your work, which should include call elimination initiatives, constantly pushed to the bottom of your in basket. You may never get to it if it doesn't get a priority assigned to it. The priority also needs to be high enough to ensure that work gets done before calls of lesser importance. Work such as call elimination initiatives will decrease the number of calls coming into the Help Desk, which will, in turn, help you get out and/or stay out of an out-of-control problem cycle.

Don't let an emotional customer tempt you from following established priorities. You must learn to respond to requests to bypass priorities with statements such as the following:

> "If we increase your priority on this problem, we will be decreasing the priority of several other customers on their problems. We can't do that."

> "I can't give your request for a new laptop a higher priority. Requests for laptops are handled on a first-come, first-served basis, and there are several requests in front of yours. All of those would have to be pushed back to accommodate your request. Those customers would certainly not agree to that. It just isn't possible."

Procedures

A senior manager once said to me, "I don't want my department to have to define rigorous procedures. I want things to flow naturally."

This just didn't make sense, and I told him so. "Rivers flow naturally.

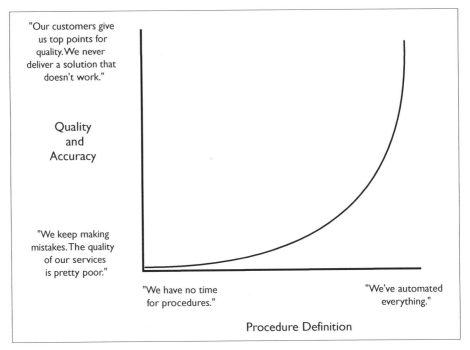

Figure 4.4 As procedure definition increases, quality and accuracy improve.

But they only flow naturally because the riverbed is solid, immovable, and often even cast in stone."

Showing much more savvy than that senior manager, a Help Desk practitioner taking one of my courses in Ottawa, Ontario, commented near the end of the course that "It sounds like you're saying that the best Help Desks are those that have the most well-established and highly defined procedures."

Bingo. It is no coincidence that the best Help Desks are those in which things run smoothly, in which everyone understands what to do and when—in other words, Help Desks with highly defined procedures. If you don't have a well-defined procedure for something, chances are it will be done incorrectly at least some of the time. Figure 4.4 shows how quality and accuracy improve as procedures are more sharply defined. Automation is considered to be the highest level of procedure definition.

Let's go back to the out-of-control problem cycle. If you have well-defined procedures you will have a greater rate of accuracy, which means fewer unnecessary calls. You will be able to handle calls quicker because you won't be scrambling for help when coping with a new situation. When you set up procedures you are in reality writing a script for automation. You may be able to automate some of the things you have procedures for. An example of this would be terminal resets. Interactive voice response (IVR) systems, which include hardware and software components, can be used to automate terminal resets. The automated system prompts the customer to enter the required information via a telephone keypad. The script that the IVR uses is simply a procedure coded into language that the IVR can understand, the same procedure that Help Desk practitioners used previously to perform the terminal resets manually.

How Do I Create Procedures?

I know that creating procedures rates about even with "push bamboo shoots under my fingernails" on your list of things you like to do. But think of it this way: You only have to create the procedure once and then revisit it every so often to make sure it's still valid. Once it's created, people will stop coming to you to ask how it's done. They'll go to the procedure instead. Even if you're not in—maybe vacationing in Hawaii—they'll still be able to follow the procedure.

If you are the one performing a function then you should create the procedure for it. You're the one who knows it; you're the one who will give it the highest level of accuracy. You don't need to go to town on procedures. You aren't writing a thesis, and you don't need to use language so sophisticated that even the spell checker gets confused. Here are a few tips to make creating procedures easier for you (and hopefully less painful):

- Keep things short and simple. Use a point or bullet-list format.
- Automate procedures wherever possible. For example, don't write a procedure on how to log a call. Instead, set up your Help Desk management software to prompt people through the process (if it isn't already set up to do that).
- Take ownership of the procedure. Pick a reasonable time frame in which to revisit the procedure and check it for accuracy. This is in the Help Desk's and your best interests. You don't want colleagues

coming to you for information and taking up your valuable time when they could be going to the procedure.

- Don't duplicate information that is stored and maintained elsewhere. Cross-reference instead. Otherwise, you're just creating more work for yourself as well as a maintenance nightmare.

- Don't try to train people how to use tools in your procedures. This is an ineffective training method and leads to ungainly procedures that are hard to maintain. The same applies to communication skills, customer skills, and the like. People should not be learning skills from procedures; they should be getting those skills from training programs, which offer much more effective ways—for example, practice and feedback—to learn a skill.

Where Do I Put Them?

Keep procedures in a central online site that is accessible by your entire Help Desk staff. An intranet site would be ideal. Never, ever, ever print procedures. The second a procedure is printed it becomes out of date. People never keep the most current copies of procedures. For some reason, the most current copies disappear, and when the time to use the procedure arrives, people can only find the severely out-of-date version from several years ago. Procedures should be developed online, stored online, and read online. There is no reason to print out a procedure or have a hard copy of a procedures manual.

What Procedures Do I Need?

You typically need to have procedures in place that describe how to deliver each of the services your Help Desk offers. Depending on the type of Help Desk you have, these might include some of the following areas:

Handling a call. Much of the information on handling a call can be automated by your Help Desk management system, for example, how to log a call, how to assign a priority, and so on. You may need to include information on when, how, and where to route or escalate a call.

Resolving a problem. Procedures might include details on how to pick up or take ownership of a problem, how and when to check for trends in a particular problem type, where to go for further help, and' what needs to be done at problem closure (for example, updating a problem resolution knowledge base or notifying a customer). Again, use your Help Desk management system to automate or prompt as much as possible.

Answering a question. You may have procedures that prompt you to check for trends so you can see whether a customer has called previously with questions and perhaps required some training. You might have procedures in place that prompt you through the process of making recommendations for training. You might want to set up procedures that explain where to look for further help or how to update any lists of frequently asked questions (FAQs) with new questions that keep recurring.

Servicing a request. For such Help Desk services as ordering and installing PCs, the procedures might include information on what the Help Desk must do and provide as well as what is required from the customer, such as certain forms and sign-offs. Procedures would also include information on specifying installation times so everyone can give the same information to customers.

Handling an emergency. The procedures for handling emergencies might include information on how to set escalation procedures into motion and on whom to keep informed at various stages of the emergency.

Informing customers of system problems. In the case of system problems, procedures would typically include information on whose responsibility it is to inform customers of such problems, what media to use to broadcast the information, and whom to broadcast it to.

Help Desk reporting. You should be generating reporting from your Help Desk management system. Procedures might spell out what reports to produce, what figures to look at, and what trends to watch for.

Disaster recovery. Procedures for disaster recovery are usually set up in conjunction with dedicated disaster recovery groups.

Communicating with other Help Desks. You want procedures in place for relaying information on major problems in each Help Desk's area of responsibility, for passing problems between Help Desks, and for relaying information on changes in each Help Desk's environment.

Communicating with other areas of support. You will want to have procedures for handing problems off to other areas of support and for defining the ownership of problems.

Specific processes internal to your Help Desk. You might have procedures for activities that need to be performed at the beginning and end of Help Desk shifts, such as work status reporting, time logging, and so on.

Information on marketing procedures and vehicles for communicating procedures can be found in Chapter 11.

A Cycle of Evaluation and Improvement

In Chapter 3, we talked about getting into an improvement cycle—looking for ways to improve the relationships between support levels. To keep your Help Desk out of an out-of-control problem cycle and to be an effective Help Desk practitioner you must go somewhat further. You must look beyond relationships and evaluate all aspects of your Help Desk environment to see where things need to be improved. This can't be a onetime event; it must be an ongoing activity. You need to be in a cycle of continual evaluation and improvement. This involves playing your role of problem eliminator to its fullest.

Where should you be looking for improvements? What do you need to be evaluating? You need to be looking at two things: your individual performance and the performance of the Help Desk.

Individual Performance

When it comes to individual performance you have a lot to review. If you're thinking, "Wow, that Czegel woman really expects a lot from a Help Desk practitioner," you're right: I do expect a lot from you, but so should you. A Help Desk will only be as effective as the practitioners who work on it. An out-of-control Help Desk can only be brought back into control by the practitioners who work on it. A manager can guide you, but a manager cannot do all the work. That's up to you.

If you want to be effective, if you want to make your Help Desk effective, you need to be constantly measuring yourself against the following benchmarks:

- Am I fulfilling the mission as well as I can?
- Am I working as effectively as I can to achieve our Help Desk's objectives?
- Am I providing the services that my Help Desk has defined, and am I staying within them?
- Am I playing the role of partner? Am I doing all I can to make my Help Desk effective?
- Am I playing all of the other Help Desk roles effectively?
- Am I doing all I can to make the structure of my Help Desk work? Am I trying to improve relationships with other areas?
- Do I have all the skills I need? Am I taking all the training I need?
- Am I keeping up to date on technology, methods, and ideas?

If you answer no to any of these questions you have identified an opportunity for improvement. The first three chapters of this book will help you identify ways to improve. They describe the base you need to be effective—to be a success.

Help Desk Performance

Now that you've had a chance to evaluate your own performance, take a look at the environment that you work in—your Help Desk. First, look at the five common support mistakes described earlier in this chapter. Are you guilty of making any of those mistakes? Is your Help Desk guilty of making them? If so, pick one that you'd like to put an end to. Look at why it is happening in your environment. Talk to your colleagues and your manager. You may not be able to eliminate the mistake on your own, but you can certainly get things moving toward that end. You should always have a call elimination project active. Getting rid of the support mistake could be one of those projects. Your project will involve finding all the causes and then getting rid of them one by one. Fortunately for you, you have access to a very nice step-by-step methodology for identifying the causes of problems and developing solutions for them. It is described in some detail in Chapter 7. So, before you run off and start solving support mistakes, read that chapter. It will help you divide your solutions into manageable chunks so you can get problems resolved and make improvements, even in your busy environment.

Next, look at the procedures that we talked about earlier in this chapter. Are you following them? Are your colleagues following them? Are they working? Are they up to date? Do they even exist? Could better procedures improve your Help Desk's performance? What about your priorities? Do you understand them? Are they working? Do your customers abide by them? Do you abide by them? Do your colleagues? Is your Help Desk interacting effectively with other Help Desks? With other support areas? Are there things you could be doing better? Are you getting the information you need and giving others the information they need?

Each time you find a problem area in which your Help Desk could be doing better you have identified an opportunity for improvement. Once you've identified it, you need to make the improvement and then go on to the next problem area (see Figure 4.5). I guarantee you that the evaluation portion of your evaluation and improvement cycle will never come up empty. You will always have something to improve.

In Chapter 9, we will look at more formal and comprehensive performance measurements.

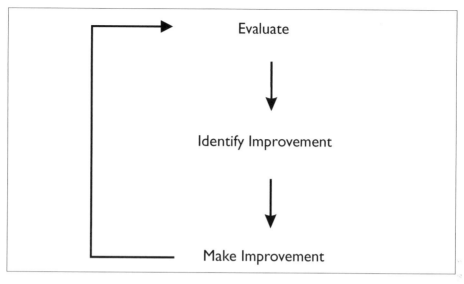

Figure 4.5   Ongoing cycle of evaluation and improvement.

Checklist

In this chapter we looked at situations where problems become dangerous. We looked at an out-of-control problem cycle and techniques for avoiding it. Ask yourself the following questions to check your understanding and retention of the concepts presented in this chapter and how well you are applying them. If you need to, go back to the appropriate section for a quick review.

- ✓ What are the symptoms of an out-of-control problem cycle?
- ✓ What are the most common support mistakes?
- ✓ Why do they happen?
- ✓ How can the common support mistakes lead to an out-of-control problem cycle?
- ✓ How can I avoid them?
- ✓ How can focus, structure, and tools help me stay out of an out-of-control problem cycle?

✓ How can priorities help me stay out of an out-of-control problem cycle?

✓ Do I know what the priorities on my Help Desk are? Do I follow them?

✓ How can procedures help me stay out of an out-of-control problem cycle?

✓ Do I know what the procedures on my Help Desk are? Do I follow them? Are there any that are missing or incorrect?

✓ Am I evaluating my own performance to identify areas for improvement that will keep me out of an out-of-control problem cycle? Am I acting on the opportunities for improvement I have identified?

✓ Am I evaluating my Help Desk's performance by identifying areas for improvement that will keep the Help Desk out of an out-of-control problem cycle? Am I acting on the opportunities for improvement I have identified?

✓ Am I playing the role of problem eliminator?

✓ Am I playing the role of partner?

Listening to Resolve and Prevent Problems

As we saw in Chapter 4, we can cause all kinds of problems when we don't listen effectively. On a Help Desk, the last thing any of us needs is more problems. It's worth taking the time to make sure that our listening skills are enhancing rather than impairing our ability to resolve and prevent problems.

In This Chapter

In this chapter I will discuss how we can use effective listening to improve our ability to resolve problems and to prevent problems caused by miscommunication. The topics I will cover are as follows:

- The communication process in problem solving
- What is listening?
- Negative filters
- The challenges of listening in a Help Desk environment
- Positive listening habits

The Communication Process in Problem Solving

When we are trying to solve a problem we gather information by listening and questioning. Similarly, when we are conveying information we communicate it and then check to see if the recipient has interpreted it correctly by, again, questioning and listening. The communication process is thus a two-part cycle of receiving and communicating information in which each part is a cycle of listening and questioning.

Listening is the foundation skill of communication in problem solving, so we will focus on it exclusively in this chapter. In Chapter 6, we'll look at the overall process of solving problems by receiving and conveying information.

What Is Listening?

You probably have not given much thought to the act of listening. It's just something that you do naturally—it comes easily. Words go into your ears and from your ears to your brain, right? Not quite. Listening is a lot more complicated than that. As Figure 5.1 shows, listening is a cycle composed of four activities that occur continuously:

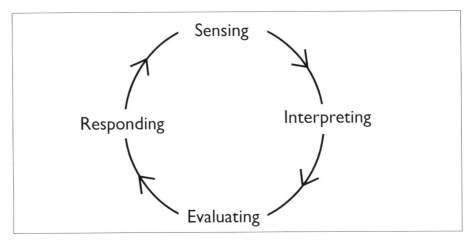

Figure 5.1   The listening cycle.

1. Sensing
2. Interpreting
3. Evaluating
4. Responding

Sensing

The sensing part of listening to a message is really just about gathering data about that message. You aren't yet trying to translate it. When someone is speaking to us, the message we get comes not only from the words that person is using but also from that person's tone and body language. Sensing involves taking in all of the things that make up the total message the person is trying to get across. Contrary to popular belief, we don't just use our ears when we listen—we use all of our senses. When we sense an incoming message we use our ears to hear words and tone and our eyes to see body language and expressions. Although on a Help Desk our senses of taste, smell, and touch typically don't come into play, in other aspects of our life they do. For example, if someone is telling you that your house is on fire, you would not only be sensing that person's hysterical tone and agitated body language, you would probably be sensing smoke and perhaps heat as well.

On a Help Desk you might not even have the sense of sight to give you information. You probably do most of your customer interactions on the phone, so you have a bit of a problem seeing the customer's body language. Your brain must rely primarily on spoken words and tone. Let's look a little more closely at the inputs our brains rely on most when sensing a message.

My students are always astounded to hear how little of a message's meaning actually comes from the words in the message. The percentages I use throughout this section come from an excellent book by Karen Leland and Keith Bailey called *Customer Service for Dummies* (IDG Books Worldwide, 1995). Their book also helped me develop my thoughts and ideas on negative filters (which we'll get to later in this chapter) as well as on getting beyond challenging behavior by focusing on the needs of the customer (which we'll look at in Chapter 7).

When you are on the phone with a customer, approximately 86 percent of what you hear comes from the customer's tone of voice, and only

14 percent from the words the customer uses. "What!" scream my students, when I give them these figures. "That's ridiculous!" "Is it?" I answer knowingly (I can be annoyingly smug at times). Then I look at one of the students in my class. "Meryl," I say in a jocular tone, "you are a complete idiot." Everyone laughs, including Meryl. "OK," I say. "I just told Meryl she was an idiot, and everyone in the class laughed, including Meryl. Meryl, how did you feel about being told you are an idiot?" "Well, you were just joking so it was kind of funny," Meryl replies. "How did you know I was joking? My words were 'you are a complete idiot.'" "Ah," the class says in unison as my point hits home. "It was your tone," Meryl says. "Your tone told me you were joking." "Yes," I add. "My tone totally negated the meaning of my words."

That anecdote was a good albeit very simple illustration of how much power tone has in affecting the meaning of a message. When we bring body language into the picture the percentages become even more astounding. When we can see a person who is speaking to us we get about 55 percent of the meaning of the message from that person's body language, 38 percent from his or her tone of voice, and only 7 percent from the words he or she uses. Let's say you're in a doctor's office. The doctor says to you, "I believe in giving each patient my full attention. I want to make sure I understand all of your symptoms." But as she speaks she looks anxiously at her watch. Do you believe the words she has just used? Probably not. Her body language, which she may be unaware of, has betrayed her and negated her words.

To sum up, when you are on the phone on a Help Desk, the sensing part of listening to the customer involves taking in the customer's tone as well as his or her words. If you are interacting with the customer face to face, sensing involves taking in tone, words, and body language.

Dangers

One of the dangers that can occur in the sensing stage is to miss some of the inputs. On a Help Desk we have to listen to a lot of information. Our customers spend a lot of time telling us about their problems. It is easy for us to drift off sometimes (at least it is for me), to start thinking about other problems, and to perhaps miss something of importance. We must learn to keep all of our senses focused on the person who is giving us the message, and sometimes that is not an easy task.

Interpreting

Once you have gathered all of the message inputs—"sensed" the message—your brain interprets it. Your brain takes all of the inputs, such as tone, words, and body language, and uses your knowledge and experiences to interpret the meaning of the message. Continuing the example from the previous section, it is in this stage of the listening process that Meryl would decide what the words *You are an idiot* really mean. She would consider my jocular tone against the actual words and interpret them as, "Barb is joking with me; she doesn't mean it; she knows I have a good sense of humor." Had I used a serious tone, on the other hand, Meryl's interpretation would have taken that tone into account and her conclusion might have been "Barb is incredibly rude. She does not think much of me; in fact, she thinks I'm an idiot."

On a Help Desk we typically have to interpret a lot of words as customers describe their problems to us. In the interpreting stage, we are unconsciously translating acronyms, for example, and trying to figure out what the customer is really saying. Let's look at Scenario 1 to see some of the challenges we can encounter in this stage.

SCENARIO 1

Gabor has been working on Surpec's Help Desk for two years. In the past 12 months or so the company has experienced incredible growth, and Gabor has seen his customer base double in size. He has also seen its profile change. He now gets at least half his calls from customers who are struggling to get used to using a PC after having spent the better part of their working lives in front of a dumb terminal.

Gabor takes a call from Tulla, one of his new customers. "Gabor, I have a problem." Tulla sounds very upset. "Well, let's see if we can get it cleared up for you. Why don't you describe your problem to me." Tulla is silent for a moment and then starts. Her voice is shaky. "I was putting the new pricing data into the computer. I was doing everything that the training woman told me to. I was doing everything she said. I got about halfway through, but when I put the last transaction in I did just what the training woman told me and pressed enter and now, poof!, no more transactions! The mouse is not moving and nothing is happening and I didn't mean to do it! I've broken everything!"

Discussion

Let's talk about how Gabor is sensing and interpreting Tulla's message. He is sensing her shaky and upset tone as well as the words she uses to describe how she entered her transactions, how she cannot enter any more transactions, and how her mouse has stopped moving. He has some knowledge and experience to help him make his interpretation. He knows that Tulla is a very inexperienced PC user and is used to dealing with mainframe terminals. She has never experienced anything like this. He uses this information to help him interpret her words, to temper her hysterical proclamation that "I've broken everything!" He also has enough experience with technology to know that Tulla's words mean that her PC has frozen up. Nothing has really been destroyed; nothing has disappeared.

Gabor's interpretation will dictate how he evaluates and responds to the message. If he interprets the message as described in the last paragraph, he can respond very calmly and explain to Tulla that this is not the end of the world, she has not lost everything, and her PC probably just needs to be rebooted. If Gabor had not had the knowledge and experience that he does, if he had not paid attention to Tulla's tone as well as her words, he might have interpreted the message incorrectly and responded inappropriately. He might have frightened Tulla so much that she refused to touch her PC, necessitating a visit from a PC technician. That technician would have to reboot her PC and convince her that the problem was not serious and that she could actually fix it herself. This would be an unnecessary waste of time with a definite negative impact on the profitability of the business.

Evaluating

Once we have sensed and interpreted the message we evaluate it. We form an opinion about it. Do we believe it? Do we agree? Do we disagree? Our knowledge, experiences, personality, preferences, prejudices, likes, and dislikes all come into play. It is here that we run into the danger of letting any of these factors cause us to incorrectly evaluate the message. Consider Scenario 2.

SCENARIO 2

Lena picks up the phone after the first ring. "Help Desk, Lena speaking. How can I help you?" "Lena, this is Robert." Oh no! Lena groans silently. She hadn't glanced at the call display so she hadn't prepared herself. Robert was her least favorite customer—always calling, always complaining about stupid insignificant things. "Yes, Robert," Lena responds, forcing a cheerful note into her voice.

"It's my screen again." Robert's voice is tentative. "Yes?" "I know that you people have adjusted it again and again, but I really think it is broken this time."

"Tell me what the problem is." Lena tries to sound nonjudgmental. "Well," Robert hesitates slightly. He is not sure that his explanation is welcome and not sure that it will be believed. "My monitor keeps flickering, and every once in a while a bunch of lines will show across it." "A bunch of lines you say?" "Yes. Thick black lines," Robert offers, hesitating again before continuing. "They stay for a minute and then they leave." "Right." "They come back, and they seem to get thicker when they come back." "OK. We'll send someone out to have a look at your PC. How is this afternoon?" "I guess that's OK." It really isn't, but Robert has given up being taken seriously. Unfortunately for Lena, the black lines turn out to be a very serious virus, and by the time someone visits Robert's PC the virus has done significant damage to several PCs within the department.

Discussion

Let's look at what happened here during the sensing, interpreting, and evaluating processes. Lena sensed the tentativeness in Robert's voice and listened to his words telling her that something was wrong with his PC. She interprets them using her technical knowledge and experience. Unfortunately, her previous prejudices and experiences lead her to a false evaluation. She has interpreted correctly that Robert is unsure of being taken seriously, but her evaluation of that is probably something like, "He realizes that we think he's a pain, and I'm not about to dissuade him of that." When she evaluates Robert's words she makes an even bigger mistake. Her prejudice against Robert as well as her and her colleagues' previous experiences with him lead her to dismiss the monitor lines as "not a serious problem." She chooses to ignore the fact that Robert said the lines were gradually getting thicker. Had she thought about this, she might have recognized Robert's problem as a potential virus and had someone look at it as soon as possible.

Responding

Once we have evaluated the message, it is time for us to respond, to acknowledge the message, and to react to the speaker. "But," you say, "responding involves speaking; how can that be part of listening?" Listening needs to be active if it is to be effective. You need to respond to speakers so as to clarify, to let them know that you are still there, still awake, and still listening. You need to encourage them to continue with their message and help them get the right message across. Let's look at Scenario 3.

SCENARIO 3

Wanda grimaces at the phone as it rings. "I have to finish this problem," she thinks dejectedly. "I can't possibly take another call!" Yet as the thought crosses her mind her hand is already reaching for the phone. "This is Eugene calling. I've got a problem on my computer here." "Yes, Eugene. Describe the problem to me." Eugene starts to describe the problem. In great detail. Wanda listens to about 20 seconds or so of Eugene's explanation, and then her mind drifts back to the problem she has been working on. It should have taken her just a few minutes to fix, but it turned out to be a real challenge. The number of calls she's been getting hasn't helped either. She'd just be starting to get somewhere when the phone would ring. She needs to fix the problem before the afternoon ends. Her mind starts working on the problem again, and she forgets about Eugene.

Eugene has been talking into the phone for what seems like a long time to him but has actually only been about a minute and a half. He starts to feel uncomfortable. He stops describing the problem. "Hello!" he shouts into the phone. "Hello! Is anybody there?" Wanda jumps guiltily."Yes. Yes, Eugene, I'm here. I'm listening," she lies. "Well, can you say something once in a while so I know you're there?" Eugene complains. "Sure I can. I'm sorry. I guess I'm just a bit tired. Please continue."

Discussion

As Eugene found, it is very unnerving to try to get information across to someone who is not responding. You start to feel like no one is listening, like you're talking to yourself. You either decide "why bother?" and stop talking or you try to get a response, as Eugene did. Even people who tend to talk a lot begin to be uncomfortable after about a minute of getting no response. In my classes, I sometimes use an exercise in which people talk to someone who doesn't respond. I've had diehard talkers who went on for almost a full two minutes without getting any kind of response, but they were very much the exception. Most people slow down and stop after about one minute. But responding to the speaker isn't only for the speaker's benefit. It can significantly affect the quality of information you get. Let's look at Scenario 4.

SCENARIO **4**

Wanda has finally managed to get some time off of the phones to work on her problem. August, a very quiet individual, takes her place, and as he sits down he gets a call. "Help Desk, August speaking. What can I do for you?" "Hi August, this is Mary from the president's office. I've got a problem with my printer. At least I think it's my printer." "Can you describe the problem?"

Mary starts to describe the trouble she has been having printing out a spreadsheet. August listens quietly, keying in a few notes as Mary speaks. She tells him what she did to try to get the spreadsheet to print.

As she continues, she notices August's lack of response and starts to wonder if he is even listening to her. She quickly finishes her explanation. Maybe she has gone on for too long. Maybe she has told him much more than he needs to know. She won't tell him that her word processing documents and her online day timer wouldn't print either. After Mary stops talking, August pauses and then replies, "OK, Mary, I'll have someone look at that problem. I've checked your access to the spreadsheet program from here and it looks fine. It's nothing that I can resolve from here." "Can you let me know when it's done?"

"Yes. I'll do that."

Discussion

By not responding, August has missed half of the problem. He may have sensed, interpreted, and evaluated what he heard correctly, but because he did not respond he did not hear the whole story. To hear everything that is being said you need to assure the speaker that you are listening. A speaker who believes he or she is being listened to is typically going to give out more information than a speaker who thinks no one is listening. If you're missing information when you're resolving a problem, then chances are you will take longer to fix the problem or you won't get it fixed. You will negatively impact the profitability of the business. Responding gives you a chance to clarify information and to make sure you "sensed" the whole message, interpreted it, and evaluated it correctly.

Continuing the Cycle

When you respond to the speaker you are encouraging him or her to continue, or you are inviting the speaker to speak again. When the speaker starts to speak, you start sensing, interpreting, and evaluating again. This process will continue until the conversation is finished.

Negative Filters

Before we go any further in our discussion of listening I want to spend some time talking about an aspect of listening that we all face. It is particularly dangerous on a Help Desk, and we most likely don't even know it is there. I'm talking about negative filters.

When we listen, interpret, and evaluate, we do so through filters, which are composed of our knowledge, life experiences, attitudes, prejudices, values, feelings about the speaker, and so on. Some of these filters are useful; they keep us from getting into trouble. For example, suppose someone calls me up and says, "Good morning, ma'am! You have won the World Famous Lottery, and we're coming by to deliver a check for *one million dollars* to your home! First, though, just as an act of good faith on your part, could you please deposit one thousand dollars into this account? As soon as you do, we'll be there with your check!" I probably would not run off to the bank to deposit that thousand-dollar check. I'd be more likely to say, "Thanks very much but I'm busy now." My life experiences, the things I've seen, read, and learned, have taught me that phone calls like the one I've just described are bogus 100 percent of the time. The filter that made me hear "Hi, I am a crook; would you like to be bilked out of one thousand dollars?" instead of the words the person was saying is a good filter.

Unfortunately, for every good filter we have, we also seem to have several negative filters. Negative filters are filters we have built up about our customers, our coworkers, or other people we know. These filters are negative in that they make us react negatively to someone so we do not hear what he or she is saying. As Figure 5.2 shows, when we use negative filters we do not listen to what the person actually says; we listen to a version of the person's message that has gone through and been distorted by our negative filter. As Help Desk practitioners, a large part of our job and our effectiveness revolves around getting correct and complete information from our customers and coworkers. Negative filters prevent us from doing this. Negative filters make us look at a call display and say, "Oh, no, not him again! I don't want to talk to him!" Negative filters can make us not want to help our customers.

Let's look at some examples of negative filters in action.

SCENARIO 5

Mike has been working on the Help Desk for about two years. He has become familiar with most of his customers and has even, together with his colleagues, created a set of categories for them. The three most popular of these are "Technologically Disabled" for those who just

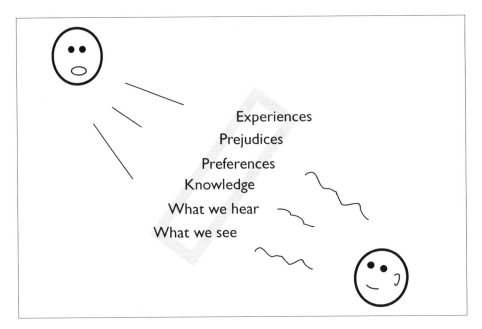

Figure 5.2   A negative filter.

can't seem to understand technology, "Know-It-All: Not" for those who think they know everything about technology but in reality are totally ignorant, and "Chronically Crabby" for those who always seem to be upset or in a bad mood. Arny from Marketing falls into the Technologically Disabled category, and it is Arny who is on the line when Mike picks up his next call.

"Hi. This is Arny from Marketing. I have a problem." "You *are* a problem," thinks Mike to himself as he starts to log the information Arny gives him.

"I can't seem to share files anymore." Arny goes on to explain his problem.

Mike shakes his head as he listens and mouths "Technologically Disabled" to Ken, a PC technician who is passing by. Ken smiles in return. Mike suspects that Arny doesn't have a problem at all; he was probably just trying to look at the wrong file. When Arny finishes, Mike asks him questions about the file he was trying to share. Arny's answers seem valid, but Mike doesn't believe them. Arny does not know anything and will never know anything about technology. Mike promises to send someone out to Arny's office and hangs up the phone. He'll give this call to Ken since Ken happens to be in the office.

"Ken! Call for you from Arny. I know he's your favorite. Says he can't access shared files." Ken rolls his eyes. "Good old Arny. He's our job security. I'm just off to grab a sandwich. I'll pop by his office this afternoon." When Ken drops into Arny's office later that afternoon, he gets a nasty surprise. The file-sharing violation is a symptom of a severe problem that has corrupted a set of very important files. After Arny talked to Mike he had tried to get the data from his backup files and had managed to corrupt them also. Ken becomes more and more worried as he works through the problem. It looks like all of the most recent backups are corrupt too. "Did you ever have this problem before?" Ken asks. "Yes, a couple of times. I called the Help Desk. They told me to make copies, shut down, and reboot, but this time that didn't work." Ken sighed. He knew exactly what the Help Desk would have thought when Arny called. They had all been very wrong. The problem had been very real. It looked like the files were not salvageable.

Discussion

Mike had such a complete set of negative filters that he had even categorized them. Unfortunately, his filter for Arny was so thick that he brushed aside a very real and serious problem. His filter distorted what Arny was saying to the point that he created and substituted his own message. His filter caused him to hear, "I can't share files, but I don't really know how to share files." Let's look at another scenario, this one involving negative filters toward colleagues.

SCENARIO 6

Mike is back on the Help Desk after a month of being away. He had been working on some call elimination initiatives with Marilyn from second-level support. The first agenda for this morning is a meeting with his colleagues to update them on the progress of the projects. Four of the six Help Desk practitioners gather in the meeting room. Mike updates them on what he and Marilyn did. Ken is going to be the next one rotating on to project work, so he briefs the group on the problems he's been handling. When Ken is done, the group spends a few minutes discussing who will take over Ken's outstanding calls and then the meeting ends.

As everyone is leaving the meeting room Mike asks Ken to stay behind.

Ken looks at him expectantly. "I wanted to warn you about Marilyn," Mike says, lowering his voice. "Why? What's the problem with Marilyn?" "When you ask her to do something she says she'll do it, but you can't count on her. I had to do a lot of the technical setup myself because she just wasn't doing it, and I didn't want to be late. I sure didn't want to have to take the blame for the stuff not going in." "Oh. Thanks for the warning." "No problem." A week later, Ken is working with Marilyn. Remembering Mike's warning, Ken does not give any of the technical setup tasks to Marilyn even when she asks him to pass the technical setup to her. As a result, he has to stay late each night to get his work done. On Friday, he has to get away early to get his daughter to a soccer game, so he works through his lunch to try to get everything done. As he is munching his sandwich at his desk Marilyn comes by. "Ken, what are you doing here? I thought you usually went out to lunch on Fridays." "Oh, I'm trying to get all of this technical setup done before I leave. Laura has soccer tonight." "Technical setup? Why the heck are you doing that? I'll do that for you. You go for lunch. I've got to take a late lunch anyway today because the others are off doing installations." Within a few minutes Marilyn had jotted down the details Ken gave her and disappeared.

Ken went off to lunch slightly surprised and slightly apprehensive. When he came back there was a note on his desk from Marilyn. "All done and tested. I did the install as well. I'll be back at 2:30 if you have any questions." Before Ken left for the day he dropped by Marilyn's desk. "Thanks for doing all the stuff for me. You made it a lot easier for me to leave early." "No problem. That's my job. I guess I should have told you to give the technical setup to me. I thought you knew. It's stuff I do every day so there's no need for you to get into it." "I thought Mike did the technical setup," replied Ken without thinking. "Well, he tried even though I did tell him that I'd do it. We were really busy when he was here so we had to do all of the setup in the evenings. We had to discard what he did. He just didn't know all of the environments, and it was too much to learn in the short time he was here." Ken thanked her again and left. He felt very foolish.

Discussion

Scenario 6 is an example of how easily we can pick up a negative filter and how damaging and false it can be when we do. Ken had never worked with Marilyn. He had no negative filters for her until Mike gave him one. Ken found out for himself that the filter was false. Using it had made him feel and look rather foolish: Marilyn had asked him to let her do the technical setup, but he had ignored her.

Beware of Friends Bearing Filters

Scenario 6 shows us how easily we pass negative filters around. We think we are doing people favors when in reality we are impairing their ability to listen. Consider how often we think we are "helping" someone by telling them something about a colleague or customer or friend, something that will help them "deal" with that person. Negative filters need to be contained and eliminated on the Help Desk. They will keep you from achieving maximum effectiveness. The following are some suggestions for containing and eliminating filters.

Keep Your Filters Clean

First—and this is not going to be easy—try to keep yourself from forming a negative filter in the first place. How do you do this? Empathy. Understanding. Remember how in Chapter 1 we talked about walking in your customers' shoes? If you do this you will become more understanding, more tolerant, and less critical of your customers.

A student in one of my classes had a very interesting way of doing this. He worked for a law firm and found that he was developing very thick negative filters against his most demanding customers. To get rid of the filters, when a call came in he pretended he had never dealt with that customer before. The history of interactions between him and his customer was a clean slate. He would look at the call display on his phone, see the name, and force himself to think, "I have no history of in teractions with this person. This is our first interaction." He told the class that it was very difficult to do this at first but that it did become a habit.

Keep Your Filters to Yourself

If you do develop a negative filter, do not pass it on to anyone. This can be difficult because you may not even recognize it as a negative filter. Sure, you are telling Mary that Bill is very difficult to get along with, but you are doing this for her own good, right? After all, Mary should know that Bill needs to be treated differently. Let's look at this from a different angle; let's listen to Bill talking to Mary. "Mary, that Help Desk practitioner person [that's you!] is really difficult to get along with. I wanted to warn you so you'd be prepared."

There are two sides to every interaction. Perhaps you don't get along with Bill. That doesn't mean Mary won't. Perhaps you couldn't get another Help Desk practitioner, Marilyn, to do anything for you, but perhaps your coworker Ken can. Perhaps you just didn't ask in the right way. Our negative filter is our problem, and before we pass it on to someone we have to take a really close look at that filter and reconsider it. Passing a filter on to someone can cause trouble for that person.

A student in one of my classes had an interesting example to relate regarding passing filters on. He worked in a networking area that had a lot of interactions with the local phone company. One of the women he worked with told him, "If you want people at that phone company to do something for you, you really have to step on them. Don't bother being nice; you really have to be firm and let them know you mean business. Otherwise, they just take forever." The fellow was rather worried about this because his project had a very tight deadline. As a result, when he called the phone company up he was somewhat less than polite. As he put it, "A very polite woman answered the phone, and I jumped down her throat. I demanded; I insisted; I was disbelieving. I was a rude son of a gun. She remained polite, asking me questions, reassuring me. She should have told me where to go and hung up the phone. After about five minutes of talking to this really polite and soft-spoken person I realized what I was doing. I felt like such a complete jerk. I called her back and apologized to her." He learned a hard lesson. He didn't pick negative filters up as readily after that.

Don't Pick Filters Up

The example of a negative filter that I closed the last section with brings us nicely to my final point. Don't pick up negative filters that are offered to you. My "son of a gun" student who was rude to the phone company employee could have gone back to the colleague who had given him the negative filter and told her off. He didn't. He realized that, yes, she was guilty for offering it to him, but he was just as guilty for taking it. When someone is offering you a negative filter, remember that the likelihood that that filter will do you any good is probably nil. The potential of that filter to do harm, however, is very high. The consequences of picking up a negative filter might include the following:

- You may end up treating someone in a way that is totally undeserved, perhaps even rude.

- You may damage or sever a relationship with someone for no good reason. You may discover that the person who gave you the filter is actually the person with the negative characteristic or trait he or she warned you about.

- You will be less effective at interacting with the target of the filter. You will not be able to hear what that person is saying with any degree of accuracy. This will impair your problem-solving ability when you are dealing with that person.

The Challenges of Listening in a Help Desk Environment

We've talked about the components of listening, and we've talked about how difficult it is to listen through negative filters. In this section, we're going to look at the challenges that you have to overcome when you are trying to listen in a Help Desk environment. Some of these challenges are as follows:

- You are always busy, always in a hurry, and often stressed.

- You face many environmental distractions.

- Your customers are often emotional.

- Your customers have varying styles of communication.
- Your customers have widely varying levels of expertise.
- The Help Desk is a breeding ground for negative filters.

Let's look at each of these factors more closely.

Hurry and Stress

As a Help Desk practitioner you are probably always in a hurry. There never seem to be enough people, and the calls just keep coming. Everyone wants everything yesterday. Even when you get time to work on projects, the projects have ridiculous deadlines. When you are in a hurry and you are listening to a customer, the danger that you have to deal with is rushing your listening. In other words, as the customer is speaking you are waiting for him or her to finish; you are not concentrating on the meaning of the message. Stress magnifies this problem.

Environmental Distractions

A Help Desk tends to be a noisy, hectic sort of environment. People speak loudly and interrupt you, phones are ringing and lights are flashing, and people are going in and out. All of these factors make it difficult to concentrate on what someone is saying, especially over the phone. You might be working beside someone who has a very loud voice. This makes it difficult for you to hear your customer. As a result, you have trouble "sensing" the message.

Interestingly enough, some of the most challenging distractions come from the people who are trying to help us and are working with us. I have heard several stories of supervisors or managers interrupting Help Desk practitioners who were on the phone with a customer trying to resolve a problem. One supervisor would come into the Help Desk area and make announcements to the group. The result was that, for the length of time the supervisor was speaking, the group could either listen to the announcement or listen to the customers. They could not do both. This meant that they each had to choose between missing the announcement and missing what the customer was saying.

Emotional Customers

By definition, customers are calling you with problems. Many times they are not cheerful about having problems. Many times they are downright upset about having problems. When someone has a tight deadline and a tool they rely on ceases to work the way they want, they get very upset. They are losing control of the task. They no longer have control over whether they can get it done on time or not. That can be a very helpless feeling, and one that generates a lot of emotion.

It is difficult to listen to someone who is being emotional. We tend to focus on the behavior of the person rather than the message itself. We hear the raised voices, the strain, the agitation, the tension. We don't hear the words.

Varying Styles of Communication

Your customers will have any number of interesting ways of getting their messages across. You need to hear what they are saying so you have the data to solve their problems. You might have customers who talk very slowly, customers who say very little, and customers who take forever to get to the point. When you are in a hurry, the slow talk of a customer may make you focus on getting them to finish rather than on solving the problem. Customers who say very little don't give you much data to solve their problem with. If you aren't effective in the responding phase of listening, you can miss significant parts of the problem. You need to constantly question and check with the customer to make sure you hear everything they are saying.

Varying Levels of Expertise

You may take calls from customers who are highly skilled and know more about their computers than you do. In these situations, you can spend ten minutes doing some intensive but successful problem solving, working with the customer as a team. Five minutes later, however, you might get a call from a complete novice, someone who is afraid of the PC. In these situations, you take on a teaching role and work at a much slower pace. It is sometimes difficult to switch into a different mode so quickly. When you go from a higher, more intense level to a lower, much slower level, you need time to decelerate. Your "sensing" ability may not make the adjustment quickly enough. Similarly, when you go from low to high, the customer might be ten sentences ahead of you before you realize that you are sensing too slowly, that you need to accelerate.

Negative Filters

You may work on a Help Desk with a high volume of interactions with customers, and a large percentage of these may involve customers with negative experiences with technology. This sort of environment is perfect for creating thick, negative filters that may deteriorate your ability to listen.

The Result

If we are not able to overcome these challenges to effective listening we may end up working against ourselves. The following are examples of the impact poor listening has on the Help Desk:

We end up working on the wrong problems. We waste our time and our customers' time. The profitability of the business is negatively impacted.

Our customers are unhappy. We are not hearing everything our customers are telling us, so they feel we are not interested, not listening. They do not feel valued or respected. These feelings might make them less cooperative in solving problems or during initiatives to improve the Help Desk. They may complain about us, which puts more pressure and more stress on us.

We miss opportunities for improvement. In Chapter 4 we talked about an ongoing cycle of evaluation and improvement. If we aren't hearing our customers, we are missing valuable input into this cycle.

We get more calls. When we don't hear things correctly, we make mistakes. Customers will call back, giving us extra work we don't need and negatively impacting the profitability of the business.

What Can We Do?

We as Help Desk practitioners do face a lot of challenges, but with each challenge comes the opportunity to become a more effective listener—to develop effective listening habits that will improve our problem-solving skills, improve our effectiveness as Help Desk practitioners, and improve our relationships with everyone around us. What can we do to become better listeners?

First, learn to control stress so you are at your most effective when you are listening. In Chapter 12 we present a different approach to managing stress. We discuss fostering a healthy Help Desk attitude and taking control of your life so you can overcome the challenges the Help Desk throws at you. Next, learn to look beyond challenging behavior to hear what it is that the customer needs. In Chapter 7 you'll find a method for interrupting politely that will help you refocus a customer and hear what the real problem is. Finally, pick up the positive listening habits described in the next section.

Positive Listening Habits

Positive listening habits are habits that improve your ability to hear the message your customer is trying to get across. They open your senses and remove barriers to effective interpretation and evaluation. They encourage effective responses. The eleven listening habits we will be discussing in this section are as follows:

1. Focus on the message, not on the delivery.
2. Ignore negative filters.
3. Ignore or eliminate distractions.
4. Do one thing at a time.
5. Listen actively.
6. Resist the urge to step on thoughts.
7. Keep a level head.
8. Empathize.
9. Foster an accepting attitude.
10. Take responsibility for the communication.
11. Improve with each interaction.

Focus on the Message

Customers have so many interesting ways of delivering messages that it is sometimes difficult to focus on the actual message they are trying to communicate. When we are interacting face to face with our customers this becomes even more difficult. As a simple but dramatic illustration, consider what would happen if you were taking one of my courses and I showed up wearing a housecoat. I'd get up in front of the class, start talking about Help Desks, and you wouldn't hear a word I was saying. You would be too busy thinking some—or all—of the following thoughts:

"Is she nuts?"

"Why is she wearing a housecoat?"

"Did she forget to get dressed?"

"Is this some kind of a trick?"

If I were sitting in a class watching someone try to teach in a housecoat, my reaction would be no different from yours, except I'd probably be more suspicious. I'd jump right to, "Is this some kind of a trick?" What if I used the washroom at break (I'm back in my normal clothes now) and came back with a piece of toilet paper hanging out the back of my pants. This would probably drive you crazy:

"Oh my god, look at that! Toilet paper!"

"Does she know?"

"Shouldn't someone tell her?"

"How embarrassing!"

I could be telling you that I was going to be hanged for murder the following day, and you wouldn't hear a word I was saying. Nothing I could say could compete with that piece of toilet paper.

The communication techniques of our customers are rarely as dramatic as those I've just described, and they probably never involve housecoats or toilet paper. But the effect they have on our listening is significant. Someone who says "um" after every second word can make you grind your teeth to powder. It's hard to listen effectively when you are grinding your teeth to powder. Grinding takes a lot of energy. A customer who beats around the bush for a long time, refusing to come to the point, can have the same effect on us. We don't really hear what the customer is saying because we're too busy thinking, "Why doesn't he just spit it out? Why can't he just get to the point? Why is he telling me all this other stuff?" When the customer finally does come to the point we have a hard time hearing because we are so tense.

We have to learn to ignore everything but the message. If the customer is smacking gum every few seconds it does not matter. We don't care about the gum; we care about the message. If the customer is saying "um" continuously, or jumping from topic to topic, this does not bother us because we are focused on getting at the message, not on improving our customer's communication skills at this specific moment in time. If we are listening effectively and our customer starts jumping from topic to topic, we use the responding phase in the listening cycle to steer that person where we want. The interaction might go something like the following:

Customer: "Something is wrong with my monitor."

You: "Please describe the problem to me."

Customer: "My CD-ROM drive is acting weird too. And I'd really like to upgrade my word processing software. This mouse is getting kind of slow too, and can I have one of the mouse pads with our logo on it?"

You: "Let's start with your monitor. What are the symptoms?"

And so on. We don't worry about why the person is acting in a specific way; we worry about hearing what the person is saying. To help yourself do this, you should consciously practice whenever you have the opportunity. This means that you should be pleased whenever you get a call from a customer who has interesting communication techniques. Consider it an opportunity to practice and improve your listening skills.

When you are listening to someone and find yourself thinking about his or her delivery rather than the message, pull yourself back and answer the following question: "What does this customer need, and what do I have to do to deliver it?" You aren't here to criticize or improve the customer's communication skills. You're here to help that customer, and the most effective thing you can do, the best thing for the profitability of the business, is to figure out what the customer needs and how you can deliver it. Chapter 7 provides some interesting ideas for refocusing customers and getting beyond challenging behavior.

Ignore Negative Filters

I could repeat here everything I said about negative filters earlier in this chapter. But hopefully you got the point: Don't use them.

Ignore or Eliminate Distractions

Your customers are your primary responsibility, your reason for existence on the Help Desk. You need to respect them and respect what they have to say. Respecting what your customer is saying means ignoring or eliminating distractions that make it hard for you to focus on him or her. Look at Scenario 7.

SCENARIO 7

You're listening to your customer. Your manager comes up to ask you a question. You cannot listen effectively to both your customer and your manager at the same time. You say to your customer, "Excuse me, I'm having trouble hearing you because there is a lot of noise at this end. Let me just get things quieted down so I can focus on what you're saying." To your manager you say, "I'm sorry, I could not hear the customer while you were talking. Can I just finish this call and then talk to you?" Your manager will probably blurt out a quick message and disappear or say "yes, of course."

Discussion

For some reason we often prefer to go on trying to listen to two people talking at once than to interrupt and explain the situation so we can hear one of the messages clearly. In Scenario 7, if you had gone on trying to listen to both the customer and your manager, several things would have resulted:

- You would not have heard the customer properly. This means you might not have heard all the information correctly. As a result, you might not fix the problem properly, and you might get another call back from that customer.

- The customer might have felt that you were not paying attention. The customer might have felt that you were not really listening. This could contribute to an image problem and to complaints against the Help Desk.

- You would have given your manager permission to keep interrupting you. Your manager probably does not realize the problem he or she is creating by talking to you while you are on the phone. He or she will not stop until you tell him or her about the problem.

As we saw in Scenario 7, if you don't eliminate distractions they will keep happening. People will keep interrupting you while you're on the phone, keep speaking very loudly near you so you can't hear the customer, and so on. Address the situation that is keeping you from hearing the customer. Talk to the person or people involved, but remember that the chances are they do not realize the effect their behavior is having on you. Focus on the problem, on the fact that you cannot hear the customer, not on the behavior that is causing the noise. People will be more willing to work with you to find a solution if you don't attack them.

There are some distractions that you cannot eliminate, that are simply part of being on a Help Desk, and that are not so loud that they drown out what your customer is saying. The constant activity of people going in and out of the Help Desk area is a prime example. You need to learn to ignore these distractions. You ignore them by focusing on the message, on what the customer is saying, not on what is going on around you. You answer the question, "What does this customer need, and how can I deliver it?" Getting the answer to that question will keep you focused on the customer and listening.

Do One Thing at a Time

By doing one thing at a time I do not mean you should be working on more than one project or more than one assignment at the same time. I mean at any one point in time you should be focused on only one thing, one activity. This means that when you are on the phone with a customer you should not be trying to look up help for another problem, filling in your time sheet, or deciding your picks for the football pool. You should be focusing on your customer and on what he or she is saying. If you are doing something else at the same time you won't hear everything the customer says. You simply cannot do two things that require any level of thought at the same time. I have tried to carry on phone conversations while I was balancing my online checkbook, and without exception the results were disastrous. I'd either end up agreeing to do something I had not wanted to do, or I'd get a very unpleasant surprise the next time I went back to my checkbook.

When I am deep in work I am very focused. I have an unusually strong ability to concentrate. I once thought that nothing could disturb that. As I was sitting in front of my computer writing this book, however, someone came up to me and asked, "Would you like some ice cream?" "No thanks," I said and continued working. When I stopped to read what I had keyed in, I laughed. Instead of "on the screen" I had keyed in "on the ice cream." My brain was not able to write and answer a question at the same time.

When you are listening to your customer, listen to your customer. Period. Don't try to do anything else at the same time.

Listen Actively

Listening is not a one-sided activity. In the responding phase of listening we need to respond to the customer, to clarify, to let him or her know that we are still alive and interested. Scenarios 3 and 4 earlier in this chapter are good examples of what happens when we don't listen actively: We simply don't hear the whole message. Active listening includes the use of phrases such as "uh-huh" or "I see" that acknowledge to the customer that we hear what is being said. Active listening also includes asking questions to clarify, paraphrasing, or making comments on the information being presented, for example, "That sounds reasonable" or "Monitor, model T210X. Is that correct?"

In face-to-face contact, active listening can also include nodding, eye contact, the use of facial expressions such as smiling, and body language such as leaning slightly toward the speaker. Many of us do these things automatically, but it does not hurt to take the occasional audit of your behavior. The next time you're listening, take a conscious inventory of your activities. Make sure you are responding to the customer.

Resist the Urge to Step on Thoughts

When people speak too slowly, we sometimes "help" them by finishing their sentences for them. When we think we know what customers are going to say we jump in and say it for them. In reality, we aren't being as helpful as we think we are being. Customers do not like having sentences or thoughts finished for them. I don't like it either. Neither do you. By interrupting our customers we are being disrespectful; we are stepping on their thoughts. We are saying, "I know better than you what you are about to say" or "I'm not really listening to you, I'm following my own path of thought."

Aside from being rude, interrupting customers in this way is not very effective. If you finish someone's sentence or thought "for" them they very often think, "I don't think that person understands what I'm trying to say," and they may start over again. If your goal was to hurry your customer, you accomplished the exact opposite. Or, much worse, they may stop trying to give you information or won't bother to correct your incorrect assumptions. You are left with little or no information. Listening effectively means letting customers finish their sentences and their thoughts. It means not making assumptions about what the customer is going to say. When we make assumptions, when we interrupt, we stop hearing what the customer is saying.

Keep a Level Head

When we are dealing with customers who are agitated, angry, or upset, we need to keep "grounded." In other words, we need to stay calm. Figure 5.3 shows what happens when we react with anger to a customer's anger. Our anger feeds the customer's anger, driving the customer further away from "the ground," that is, from calm. This is not what we want to do. We cannot hear the customer if we are tied up in emotion. We cannot help the customer. We are not doing what's best for the profitability of the business.

Figure 5.4 shows what happens when we react to a customer's anger

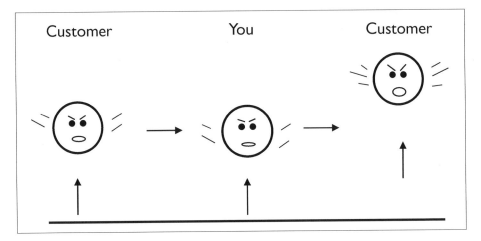

Figure 5.3   Reacting to anger feeds anger.

with calm. It is hard to stay angry at someone who is being calm and empathetic. The customer will gradually come back down, and his or her anger will lessen. We can then start working on fixing the customer's problem. How do we keep calm when our customers are not? We focus on what the customer is trying to say, not on the customer's behavior.

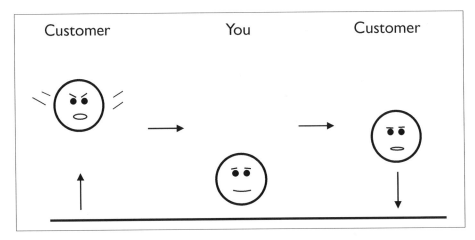

Figure 5.4   Keeping calm in the face of anger deflates anger.

We focus on answering the questions, "What does this customer need?" and "How can I deliver it?" Chapter 7 will give you ideas for getting beyond emotional behavior so you hear what the customer is saying and are able to help.

Empathize

When we empathize with a customer, that is, see things from his or her point of view, several good things happen. First, we get better information. Our customers open up to us, are more cooperative, and are less likely to hold things back. Our customers think, "This person understands how this is inconveniencing me. This person wants to help me." Second, when we empathize we can focus more easily on what the customer is saying, and we can hear more clearly. When we understand what the customer is going through and that he or she is under stresses we may not understand, we are less likely to focus on behavior and less likely to take anger or emotional behavior personally. We will find it easier to keep grounded.

Third, empathy helps us become more tolerant. Things about our customers that used to distract us from the message, that used to make it difficult for us to hear, do not bother us. We are more accepting of idiosyncrasies and of less than perfect communication techniques. Our ability to listen in trying circumstances improves. What does empathy look like? Some examples of empathetic phrases are as follows:

- "This has really inconvenienced you. Let me get you up and running as quickly as possible."
- "I want to make sure that you have the information you need for that meeting. Let me get that spreadsheet printed off for you on our department printer, and then I'll look at your printer problem."

In the section on customer service in Chapter 1, I talked about walking in your customer's shoes. Walking in your customer's shoes will help you become more empathetic by helping you understand what your customer's world is like. When you are listening to a customer, slip a pair of his or her shoes on—empathize.

Foster an Accepting Attitude

Fostering an accepting attitude is closely related to empathy. As I discussed in the last section, being empathetic will usually help you develop a more accepting attitude. Having an accepting attitude will make your life so much easier and your listening so much better—and not just on the Help Desk—that I felt it deserved a section of its own.

I know this may be hard to swallow, but we are not perfect. We never will be perfect. Our customers aren't perfect either. I sometimes hear Help Desk practitioners saying, "Oh, if only we had better customers." I suspect that their customers are probably saying, "Oh, if only we had better people on the Help Desk." We expect people to accept us as we are, to work with us, to listen to us. Don't our customers deserve the same? If we accept our customers as they are, with their quirks and imperfections, we stop worrying so much about their behavior. We will stop getting upset by behavior and poor communication techniques. We will stop focusing on the improvements that we feel people need and on the habits they need to lose. We can accept them as they are, and we can focus on the message they are trying to get across and help them. Consider Scenario 8.

SCENARIO 8

You go out on a Help Desk call to the graphics design office. Martin greets you with four earrings in each ear, a partly shaved head, orange hair, and an obnoxious attitude. His attitude says, "I am important, you are scum, fix my PC."

"I need this fixed right away," he says, waving a hand at his PC and looking at you only briefly. "What seems to be the problem," you say, sitting down in front of the PC and turning it on. "Well, that's your responsibility to figure out, isn't it?"

"Yes it is, but I can do it a lot faster and get your PC fixed more quickly if you point me in the right direction." "Oh. OK." Martin proceeds to give you a brief description of a PC whose configuration files have been tampered with. You find and fix the problem quickly, and let

Martin know that it's done. "It's about time. I can finally get some work done again." You leave the graphics design office, mentally shaking your head.

Discussion

Your accepting attitude made the interaction described in Scenario 8 very positive. What you probably said to yourself upon meeting Martin and his attitude was "Martin is obnoxious, but that's just the way he is. It's nothing personal, no reflection on me. Maybe he has to be like that to survive in this department." You did not get upset at Martin's comments; you were able to listen to what he told you. As a result, you fixed the problem quickly and gave Martin the ability to get back to work. You minimized the negative impact on the business. Also, you made the whole interaction more pleasant for yourself by accepting Martin the way he is. You didn't waste any time getting stressed, grinding your teeth, or planning his lobotomy. In fact, as you were leaving the department you were probably feeling a little sorry for Martin. You were thinking, "He must have a lot of trouble making friends. He probably gets a lot of people annoyed and makes a lot of enemies."

Take Responsibility for the Communication

Communication with our customers is two-way. On a Help Desk we need to take responsibility for both "ways." We cannot say, "The customer didn't tell me this therefore the trouble it caused is the customer's fault. I did my part. I listened to what the customer said." Listening in a Help Desk environment means making sure we get all of the information and going after information we need and that the customer may be holding back without even realizing it.

When we take responsibility for the communication we have the attitude, "It is my responsibility to make sure that I hear the whole story and get all of the facts." This attitude will make us much better listeners. We will listen more intensely and respond more demandingly. Our customers will feel more confident about our ability to help them. When we have the information we need we can fix problems more quickly and accurately. When Help Desk practitioners consistently take responsibility for communication, for minimizing resolution time, and for eliminating errors, there is a positive impact on the profitability scale of the business. Taking responsibility for the process of getting and giving information is discussed in more detail in Chapter 6.

Improve with Each Interaction

Here we are back again to evaluation and improvement. In Chapter 4 we talked about getting into a cycle of evaluation and improvement in order to keep control of problems. We talked about looking at our own performance and asking, "Do I have the skills I need? Am I playing all of my Help Desk roles effectively?" One of those roles is that of communicator, and one of the skills is communication. Listening is an important part of communication.

You are going to make mistakes as you try to improve your listening skills. Quite simply, there are times when you will fail. This doesn't matter as long as you are in an improvement cycle, looking at each interaction and asking, "Is there any way I could have improved my listening? What could I have done better?"—and then acting on the improvement you identified. If you do this you will have no alternative but to improve. You will become a more effective listener, a more effective communicator, and a more effective Help Desk practitioner.

Checklist

We covered a lot of material in this chapter. You have a lot to remember. Come back to this section once in a while and ask yourself the following questions to make sure you are being as effective a listener as you can be:

✓ Am I aware of the four phases of listening—sensing, interpreting, evaluating, and responding?

✓ Do I have any negative filters? How can I get rid of them?

✓ Am I passing any negative filters on?

✓ Am I picking any negative filters up?

✓ Do I understand the challenges I face in trying to listen in a Help Desk environment?

✓ When I listen do I focus on the message rather than the delivery?

✓ Do I eliminate distractions that prevent me from hearing?

✓ Can I ignore distractions that I have to live with?

✓ Do I focus solely on the customer while I am trying to resolve a problem and not try to do something else at the same time?

✓ Am I an active listener?

✓ Do I let customers finish thoughts and sentences without interrupting?

✓ Do I remain calm even when a customer gets emotional?

✓ Am I empathetic?

✓ Do I foster an accepting attitude toward my customers and their behavior?

✓ Do I take responsibility for the entire communication with a customer?

✓ Am I constantly improving my listening skills?

CHAPTER SIX

Getting and Giving Information

Problem solving on the Help Desk involves interacting with technology and with customers. Although interactions with technology can be complex, frustrating, and extremely challenging, it is the interactions with our customers that typically make or break our effectiveness as Help Desk practitioners. If we don't get the right information then we end up working on the wrong problem. This means extra calls into the Help Desk. If we don't get the right information across to the customer the customer may create more problems or not do what is required to resolve the problem—resulting in more calls into the Help Desk. The result is a negative impact on the profitability of the business.

The better we are at getting information from the customers and at getting information across to them, the more effective our problem solving will be. We will provide solutions faster and more accurately. We will be minimizing the negative impact on the profitability of the business we support.

In This Chapter

In Chapter 5, we looked at listening, the foundation skill of communication. In this chapter, we will step back and look at the whole cycle of getting and giving information in problem solving. We will also discuss how to become more effective at delivering a message and at getting information through questioning. The topics I will cover are as follows:

- The cycle of information exchange
- Delivering your message
- Questioning
- The impact of effective information exchange

The Cycle of Information Exchange

We start solving a problem the moment a customer calls and we pick up the phone. Figure 6.1 illustrates the information exchange process we go through to solve problems. Our first action is to listen to the customer. We may then confirm our understanding of the customer's words by asking questions and listening to see if we do indeed understand the problem correctly. As Figure 6.1 shows, checking our understanding is a cycle within the larger cycle of information exchange. When we are certain we understand the customer, we may then want to get more information about the problem by asking questions. We don't try to deliver a solution until we are really sure we understand what the customer has said and we have collected all the information we can. We then process the information, analyzing it to come up with a solution.

Let's look at Scenario 1 for an illustration of this information exchange cycle. The comments in italics relate the events in the scenario to the cycle of information exchange.

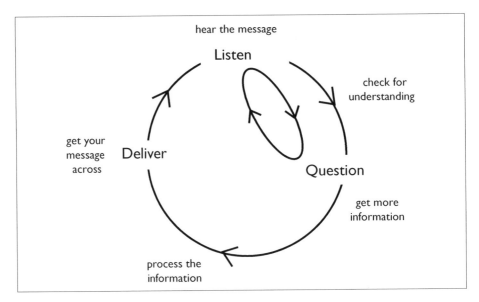

Figure 6.1   The cycle of information exchange.

SCENARIO 1

Jonathan, an experienced Help Desk practitioner, takes a call from Tracy, a fairly new technology user. "Help Desk, Jonathan speaking. What can I do for you this morning?"

"Hi, Jonathan, this is Tracy from Accounts Payable. I'm having trouble accessing the network." *Tracy is delivering a message; Jonathan is listening to hear it accurately.* "Can you describe the problem you're having?" *Jonathan is questioning to get more information.* "I try to log in, and it seems to accept my password, then something flashes on the screen, and I'm back where I started. I did manage to get through to the network once, but when I started to do something it immediately flashed something onto the screen and kicked me out." *Tracy is giving more information; Jonathan is listening again.*

"OK, let me make sure I understand. You log into the corporate network using your password, and you get some kind of message and you're put back into the log-in screen." *Jonathan is checking his understanding of the customer's problem.* "Yes, that's right." "And one time you actually did manage to get on to the network, but when you started trying to do something you got some kind of message again and you went back to the log-in screen." *Jonathan is checking his understanding further.* "Yes." *Jonathan now processes the information he has gathered. He is analyzing it, perhaps searching through the knowledge base, trying to decide what the problem is and what will fix it. Once he has figured out the problem and its solution he will have to get that information across to Tracy.*

"From what you've told me, I think you have a corrupt configuration file on your hard drive. I'm going to send you the correct file, and then I'm going to ask you to set up a few parameters for me. Is that OK with you?" *Jonathan knows what the problem is and how to fix it and has started delivering his message. He delivers part of his message then checks that he understands the problem by giving the customer a chance to ask questions and express concerns.* "Sure, but you'll tell me how to do it won't you?" "Absolutely," Jonathan continues. "Now, I've sent you the file. This is what I want you to do." *Jonathan gives Tracy some instructions.* "I think I can do that," Tracy responds. "I did something like that a few times where I used to work." "Good. Now, just explain to me what you'll be doing so we have the same understanding. I want to make sure we don't miss anything." *Jonathan is checking the customer's understanding even though Tracy says she can do the procedure. The fact that Tracy claims she's done something like this before is an added reason to check. She may assume the procedure is the same as the one she performed before rather than the one Jonathan has just given her.*

Discussion

Scenario 1 is an example of the cycle of information exchange that occurs during the communication phase of problem solving. Jonathan listened to Tracy's message, questioned to get more information, and checked to make sure he understood correctly. Once he had analyzed the problem, he delivered a set of instructions and then listened to Tracy's response to make sure she understood exactly what she had to do. Note the way Jonathan took responsibility for the communication. Even though Tracy told him she had done this before, he checked to make sure she understood, that she was not going to follow her memory rather than his instructions.

Scenario 1 is an example of a good cycle of information exchange. To illustrate how important this cycle is, let's look at Scenario 2 where a very different Tracy and Jonathan ignore the cycle.

SCENARIO 2

Jonathan takes a call from Tracy. "Help Desk, Jonathan speaking. What can I do for you this morning?" "Hi, Jonathan, this is Tracy from Accounts Payable. I'm having trouble accessing the network." *As before, Tracy is delivering a message; Jonathan is listening to hear it accurately.* "Can you describe the problem you're having?" *Jonathan is questioning to get more information.* "I try to log in, and it seems to accept my password, then something flashes on the screen, and I'm back where I started. I did manage to get through to the network once, but when I started to do something it immediately flashed something onto the screen and kicked me out." *Tracy is giving more information; Jonathan is listening again.* "OK, I've got the picture." Jonathan thinks to himself, "Tracy doesn't know very much about PCs. I think this is a password thing." *Oops. Jonathan is not bothering to check his own understanding. And was that a negative filter creeping in?*

Jonathan resets Tracy's password without telling her. "OK, I've done something on this end that I think will solve the problem. Want to try again?" Tracy tries again.

"That didn't work. I still can't get in, and that message flashed up again." Jonathan is annoyed. This Tracy is turning out to be more of a problem than he anticipated. *Notice how Jonathan is starting to put the blame on Tracy. He is definitely not taking responsibility for this communication.* "OK. Let me think for a minute." *Jonathan reprocesses the information Tracy gave him before and decides that the problem is a corrupt file.* "I think the problem is a corrupt file on your hard drive. I'm going to send you the correct file, and then I'm going to ask you to set up a few parameters for me." *Jonathan thinks he's found the problem and solution now. He starts delivering his message to Tracy. But he doesn't give her time to respond, express concerns, or ask questions.*

"I'm a bit nervous about this," Tracy starts. "You needn't be," Jonathan interrupts. "This is easy as pie. I've sent you the file you need. Now this is what I want you to do." Jonathan gives Tracy the instructions. "I think I can do that," Tracy says slowly. "I did something like that a few times where I used to work." "Good. Just give us a call if you have any more problems." Jonathan is off the phone before Tracy can say another word. *Jonathan does not bother to check Tracy's understanding. He's in too much of a hurry to get off the phone.* Tracy hangs up the phone and looks at her PC apprehensively. Well, she'd done this before. Sort of. Half an hour later Tracy is frustrated and no closer to getting on to the network. She calls the Help Desk back and gets someone who walks her through the procedure.

Discussion

The results of Scenario 2 are very different from Scenario 1. The cycle of information exchange was broken. Jonathan did not check his own understanding of Tracy's problem, did not try to get more information, and did not check that Tracy understood the procedure for correcting the problem. He took no responsibility for the communication. As soon as Tracy suggested that she might have had experience with this problem before, he was quite willing to drop responsibility for the communication into her lap. Jonathan also let a negative filter interfere when he was listening to Tracy explain her problem and thus assumed that the problem was Tracy forgetting her password. He ended up offering a solution for the wrong problem. When he did finally figure out what the problem was he did not bother to check that Tracy understood his instructions. Tracy did not understand, and the problem was not fixed. It took Tracy another half hour to get the problem resolved. The profitability of the business was negatively impacted.

Scenario 2 is a very simple but telling example of what happens when the information exchange cycle is interrupted: If the cycle does not take place the quality of problem solving deteriorates rapidly.

Delivering Your Message

While you are solving problems you constantly have to get messages across to the customer. These messages include explanations of why the problem happened and what you're going to do about it; instructions that the customer must follow to fix the problem; or information about the technological environment, such as service interruptions, upgrades, and so on. In this section, we're going to discuss how to get your message across more effectively—how to make sure that customers hear what you are saying. First, we are going to look at the challenges you face on the Help Desk. The better you understand the challenges, the more effectively you can meet them. Second, we will look at how to translate technical information into information the customer can understand. Third, we will look at some of the poor habits we need to avoid, and we will then finish up by looking at the steps you need to follow to ensure that you get your message across effectively.

Challenges to Getting Your Message Across

In Chapter 5 we saw that a Help Desk environment presents several challenges to effective listening. That same environment also presents challenges to getting your message across effectively. These include the following:

- Translating—putting technical information into terms the customer can understand.
- The varying skill and comfort levels of your customers.
- Customers who say they understand when they do not.
- Delivering bad news.
- Explaining the behavior of complicated and sometimes unpredictable technology.

Translating

The Help Desk environment is rife with technical jargon. Acronyms and technical terms are a part of our everyday lives, and we sometimes don't realize that people don't understand what we're talking about. If they don't understand, chances are they won't tell us because they don't want us to know they don't understand. We might think they're stupid. Before you say, "That's silly, they should say something," keep in mind that sometimes you and I do the exact same thing.

In fact, I think I'll give you a rest and use myself as an example. Say

I go out to dinner with someone who is in a business I know nothing about—the stock market, for example. This person really knows his stuff, and he talks on and on very enthusiastically. I do not understand a lot of what he is saying, and his enthusiasm and confident manner discourage me from asking him to explain. I nod and smile politely, and my eyes gradually glaze over. My friend hasn't a clue that anything is wrong until he hears a plop and looks over to see that my face has fallen forward into my cream of broccoli soup.

Customers can't really hear us when they don't understand us. To put it another way, in the interpretation phase of their listening process they cannot decode the words we are using. If we don't stop and check that they understand us we've lost them completely. The section titled "Effective Translation" later in this chapter contains some tips and examples to help you become an effective translator.

Varying Skill and Comfort Levels of Customers

In the previous section I talked about translating technical information to the level of your audience. Easy for me to say. One of the challenges you typically face as a Help Desk practitioner is that the skill levels of your customers vary widely. This means that when you give an explanation you need to gauge how much your customer knows, and design your communication accordingly. If you have to explain a technical problem to two customers, a novice and an expert, chances are the explanation you give to one will be very different from the explanation you give to the other. Not only do you have to translate the information, you have to translate it to the level that each understands and will not find insulting.

If you don't know the skill level of a customer you should gear your explanation to a middle level. You may even say something like, "I don't know how familiar you are with this technology, so I'm going to assume you've got a basic understanding and go from there." If they are experts they will let you know, and you can adjust your delivery accordingly. Some customers know very little about the technology they use but aren't intimidated by it. They're not afraid of it, they experiment, they occasionally get burned, and they don't mind talking to us about it. Other customers are very uncomfortable with their technology. They live in constant fear of "deleting everything." When we try to question them about a problem they clam up, fearing they may have caused the problem and that we might blame them.

Customers who are not comfortable with technology will not hear us very well when we try to get our message across and may withhold information when we try to get more details from them. If we are used to dealing with customers who are comfortable with technology then we may not realize when someone is uncomfortable. We may assume they understand us, and we may not realize that they are not telling us everything they know about the problem. If we do a good job checking for understanding we can be sure that these customers will understand what we are telling them. The section titled "Getting Your Message across Effectively" later in this chapter gives you ideas on how to check for understanding.

Customers Who Say They Understand When They Don't

People who say "I understand" when they don't can be a source of unnecessary calls to the Help Desk. You may take the time and care to explain something to a customer who says, "Yes, thank you, I understand" only to find that the customer did not understand at all, in fact, did not have a clue. This can't possibly be your fault, right? Wrong. You are responsible for the communication. Your customers may have what they feel are good reasons for saying "I understand" when they don't. They may be afraid of annoying the person giving the explanation, they may be afraid of appearing stupid, or they may simply be in a hurry.

In my last year of high school I took a physics class. I did not find physics very interesting, and I spent most of the classes daydreaming. Near the end of the year we were given an assignment with a series of fairly complex problems that I had no idea how to approach. My friend and I decided to go to the physics teacher for help. "Of course, I can help you," he said and proceeded to give us a detailed explanation of how to approach the problems. He wrote everything down on a notepad, illustrating his points and jotting down the important facts for us. We were very quickly lost but didn't want to tell him, fearful he'd be impatient or annoyed. But we weren't very worried because he was writing everything down for us; we'd have time to figure it out at our leisure. When he was finished he looked at us carefully. "Do you understand what I've done here?" We both nodded, afraid to admit that we were totally lost and unwilling to ask him to start over again. "Good, then you won't need this," he said, and tore up the notes he had written as my friend and I watched in horror.

That experience pretty much cured me of saying "I understand" when I don't, but many of your customers may not yet be cured. The responsibility for the communication is yours. You cannot take shortcuts when you are checking the customer's understanding. Accepting "I understand" as an indication of understanding is a shortcut. We can't do what my physics teacher did; we need to make sure our customers understand.

Delivering Bad News

If your job was to let lottery winners know they were now fabulously wealthy, you would probably not have any problem getting your messages across and ensuring understanding. People love to hear good news. Our challenge on the Help Desk is that much of what we communicate is not good news. In fact, some of it is terrible news. We may have to deal with emotional reactions, customers who are not cooperative because they are upset, customers who are worrying about their problems, or customers who have stopped listening. Chapter 7 presents some good ideas for getting beyond customers' challenging or emotional behavior to deliver a message.

Explaining the Behavior of Complicated and Unpredictable Technology

There isn't a lot we can do about the fact that what we support is complicated, often times unpredictable, and constantly changing. It is not easy to explain to your customer Chantal that the interrupt sequence on her network card is interfering with other devices in her PC and that's why she is experiencing problems. We need to translate the information into terms the customer can understand, and we need to take steps to ensure that understanding.

Effective Translation

In this section, I present some guidelines for communicating technical information to nontechnical people, illustrated with three examples.

Guidelines

The following are a few guidelines to help you translate technical information:

Avoid acronyms, unless they are an established part of your corporate culture. I suspect that most of your customers are quite comfortable with the terms *PC* and *LAN* but not with acronyms like *SCSI, BIOS, PCI, TCP/IP*, and so on. Even if a customer uses an acronym, he or she may not know what it means. For example, I often hear people speak very confidently about the amount of RAM they have in their computers when they are really talking about the size of their hard drives.

Avoid technical terms like *cache, controller,* **and so on.** Instead, use more general words that convey these concepts. Customers aren't interested in the details. When you call your telephone company about an interruption in your service you do not want to hear the technical names for the network equipment or cable that is causing the problem. You just want to know what the problem is in very general terms, that it will be fixed, and that it will be fixed quickly.

Use shorter sentences. This will allow you to check the customer's understanding more often. If you run on and on, spewing out technical information left and right, you will lose your audience.

Avoid oversimplifying and appearing condescending. For example, "Your computer is not feeling well at the moment" probably wouldn't work with even the most inexperienced user. In fact, it might get you throttled. Translate to the level of your audience but don't patronize.

Avoid a dictatorial tone, especially when you're giving instructions. Be encouraging. Our customers typically use technology to get their work done. They don't need to know much about *how* it works; they need to know *how to use it*. It's up to us to make sure that the technology works and that they're using it effectively. When we need to help them by giving them instructions, we will either intimidate them or annoy them if we come across as dictatorial. It's very easy to be dictatorial when you've given the same instructions hundreds of times, you know your stuff, and the customer on the other end of the phone is not very knowledgeable and obviously needs your help. But a customer who is annoyed or intimidated is a customer who will not be listening effectively. We can't do a good job getting our message across if the person we're talking to is not listening.

Examples

The following three examples illustrate a few of the guidelines for translating technical information effectively.

Example A

Translation needed: "The 3272 is down. The Ethernet network doesn't have mainframe access."

Translation: "We're having a problem on the network. We can't transmit information to or from the mainframe." Or, simply, "The network is down."

Example B

Translation needed: "The IVR (interactive voice response) scripts have been corrupted, so none of the options work."

Translation: "The terminal reset, password reset, and job status verification options on our phone menu are not working."

Example C

Translation needed: "The interrupt settings on your network card conflict with two other devices."

Translation: "There's an incompatibility between components in your PC," or "The device that connects your PC to the network needs to be reconfigured," or, if your customer knows what a network card is, "Your network card is not set up properly."

I think you get the idea. We don't want to crush our customers with technical information, but neither do we want to make them feel like idiots. We just want to make sure they understand.

Poor Habits to Avoid

I want to make you aware of some habits you could easily fall into because of your pressurized environment. A Help Desk is typically fast-paced, stressful, and demanding. The following habits (see Figure 6.2) can be picked up too easily:

Being a motormouth. We typically give the same explanations over and over, and we know them by heart. We may start to think that the faster we say them the sooner we will be finished. I have a horse that thinks like this. If I spend too much time practicing a specific sequence of movements she gets to know them so well that she tries to whip through them so we'll be finished faster and she can go back to

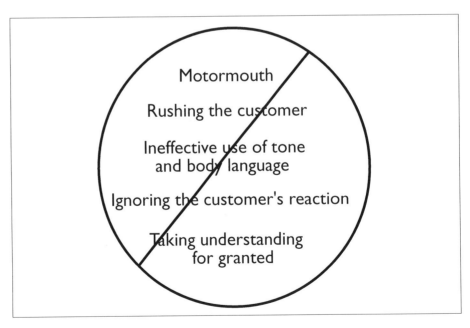

Figure 6.2   Habits to avoid.

her favorite activity, which is eating. On a Help Desk we sometimes get to know our routine explanations so well that we whip through them so we can get back to the rest of our calls, those flashing lights that are waiting for us.

Unfortunately, sometimes we speak faster than our customers can hear. We zip through an entire explanation, and they are still listening to the first few words. They cannot possibly understand what we are saying. Help Desk practitioners who suffer from motormouth may not be aware of their affliction. Ask your colleagues to gauge the speed of your delivery. Speaking quickly does not gain you anything if customers have to call back because they did not understand your very fast explanation. You will have a more positive impact on the profitability of the business if you slow your speech down so customers can get your message right the first time.

Rushing customers. Our doctors do this to us all the time, and we hate it. Our customers hate it too. They call us with a few problems or questions, and we rush them through the first one and don't give them a chance to tell us about anything else. The more we can resolve in one call, the fewer calls we will have. When you take a call from a customer, take the time to make sure you have addressed everything the customer was calling you about.

Not using tone and/or body language effectively. It takes the same amount of effort to sound cheerful and interested as it does to sound disgruntled, bored, or condescending. A customer who is listening to someone who is disgruntled, bored, or condescending will simply not listen as well as a customer who is listening to someone who sounds cheerful and interested. And a customer who is not listening well is bound to miss part of the explanation, which may result in more calls to the Help Desk. This is bound to have a negative impact on the profitability of the business.

In a Help Desk environment it is not always easy to be cheerful and interested, but you must always *sound* cheerful and interested. Don't let your tone of voice create extra calls. If this is a problem for you, do what many call center employees do: Stick a small mirror on your wall and whenever you pick up the phone, look into the mirror to make sure you are smiling. Smiling goes a long way toward ensuring a welcoming tone.

The same holds true for body language. When you are working with a customer face to face, make sure your body language is saying, "I am glad to be here. I want to help you." Don't glance at your watch every few minutes, and avoid tensing up. Give your customer your full attention; adopt a loose, friendly stance; and do not worry about what you have to do later in the day. Focus on the customer's problem.

Ignoring the customer's reaction. It is sometimes easier to ignore a customer's reaction than to acknowledge and handle it. If a customer is angry or annoyed, ending the conversation and getting off the phone quickly are an easy way to get out of having to face the customer's emotional response. However, when we evade a customer's reaction it does not go away; it often leads to another call or to a complaint. The image of the Help Desk suffers, and the customer will be more of a challenge to deal with in the future.

When you are getting your message across to customers, face the music. Acknowledge the customer's response, and do what you can to resolve the issue in question. Chapter 7 discusses some ways you can do this.

Not taking the time to ensure understanding. As we discussed in the section, "Challenges to Getting Your Message Across," customers won't always tell us when they don't understand our solutions. Because we are busy and have other calls waiting it is sometimes easier for us to assume our customers understand than to take the time to make sure of that understanding. If a customer says, "Yes, I understand," we think, "Great, I can finish this call and get on to the next one," even though our gut may be telling us, "This customer does not understand." When it comes to the profitability of the business, taking the time to ensure understanding is much less expensive than getting another call from that customer. The next section, "Getting Your Message across Effectively," discusses ways to check that the customer understands you.

You now understand the dangerous habits you can get into. Be on the lookout for them and avoid them at all costs.

Getting Your Message across Effectively

Figure 6.3 illustrates the steps involved in getting a message across to our customers. First, we prepare our message by assessing our customer, adjusting our delivery to a level that is appropriate for him or her, and translating any technical information. Second, we actually deliver our message. Finally, we check for understanding. If we find the customer does not understand, we try again by going back to our preparation stage, reassessing our customer, making any required adjustments, and then trying our delivery again.

In Chapter 5 we looked at eleven good listening habits. Getting your message across effectively involves a good deal of listening, so those eleven habits apply here as well. Now we'll look at each of the phases of getting your message across in more detail.

Preparation

The more effort you invest in preparing what you say the more likely your message will be understood the first time around. The preparation phase of getting your message across involves assessing your audience, adjusting your delivery mode accordingly, and translating your message into terms the customer will understand.

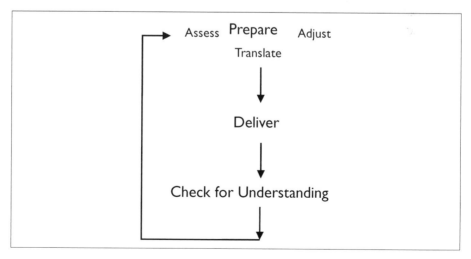

Figure 6.3   Getting your message across.

Assessing

When you are about to make an explanation, answer a question, or walk a customer through a procedure, you need to assess that customer to learn how technologically literate and knowledgeable he or she is, how emotional he or she is, and how slowly or quickly he or she speaks.

Adjusting

Once you've assessed your customer you need to adjust your delivery accordingly. You need to match your presentation to your audience, the customer. You need to speak at the customer's level of technological literacy and knowledge. If your customer speaks slowly, you need to be especially careful to avoid motormouth, or anything close to it. If your customer is upset or emotional, you must take care to stay grounded, to focus on what he or she needs and on how you can deliver it. You need to acknowledge the customer's feelings in your delivery and let him or her know that you empathize.

Translating

When you have assessed your audience and adjusted your delivery, you must look at the technical content of your solution to see if anything needs to be translated. If necessary, reword what you are about to say so the customer hears and understands it.

Delivery

When you actually start speaking, the first thing you should say is exactly what you plan to tell the customer. For example, if you are about to give the customer instructions on how to check a diskette for viruses, you might say, "I'm going to walk you through the virus checking procedure now. Is that okay?" This prepares the customer for what's coming. If you just jump into the procedure, the customer may miss the first part of your instructions while he or she tries to figure out what you are doing.

Check the customer's understanding at frequent intervals. Give the customer a piece of information and then check to see if it was understood. If it was, give the customer the next piece and so on.

Checking for Understanding

After you have finished your first delivery you must check for understanding. You can do this in several ways. First, encourage questions from the customer. Give the customer time to ask questions, and take the time to answer them fully. After each delivery ask questions like, "Do you understand what I mean?" "Is that OK with you?" "Is that clear?" "Do you have any questions about that?" "Anything unclear?" "Want me to go through that again?" and so on. Remember to keep your tone cheerful and interested. If customers feel you are getting impatient they may not admit that they do not understand.

If you have doubts about whether the customer understood your delivery, ask the customer to paraphrase what you told them. You can say something like, "Why don't you tell me what steps you're going to go through so I can make sure that I didn't miss anything." If you feel the customer may not want to ask questions, be reassuring. A statement like, "This can be pretty confusing, so I want to make sure I explain it properly. I want you to really understand this," can make the customer feel that it is OK to ask questions, that it is OK to not understand.

If you discover that the customer has not understood your delivery, you need to go back to the preparation phase. You need to reassess to see what went wrong. You may readjust your delivery and do some more translating. Then you can try your delivery again. Continue preparing, delivering, and checking for understanding, as shown in Figure 6.3, until the customer understands. Scenario 3 provides an example of the process of getting your message across.

SCENARIO 3

Ludwik calls the Help Desk with a problem. Eleanor takes the call. "My PC keeps stopping. I'll work for a while and things will be okay, kind of slow maybe, and then everything stops. I go to my supervisor, and she does something to make it go again. She told me to call you." Eleanor asks Ludwik a few questions and determines that the problem is a buildup of temporary files. She needs to walk him through the procedure for deleting the files. "Ludwik, sometimes the system creates temporary files. They're full of garbage, and they don't do anything, but they do take up space. Sometimes they take up so much space that there is no room to run the programs. I think that's what's happening to you."

"What can I do?" "That's what I'm going to help you with. What we have to do is to get rid of those temporary files. I'll walk you through the procedure." "You mean I'm going to have to do it?" Ludwik sounds concerned. "Yes, you're going to do it, but I'm going to be right here telling you what to do so you won't be on your own. And it's hardly any work. We've set up a procedure to do it, and it's right on your PC. Are you OK with that?" "Well . . . as long as you'll stay on the phone." "I'll be right here. Now I'm going to tell you what you have to do. I'll give you a chance to ask questions, and I'll make sure that you understand what I'm doing and feel comfortable with it. Are you ready to start?" "OK. Shoot."

Discussion

From Ludwik's explanation and her questioning, Eleanor correctly assesses that he has a low level of PC literacy and comfort. She also notes that he is nervous and afraid of doing something wrong. Eleanor adjusts her delivery accordingly. She is very reassuring and explains in simple terms what temporary files are and why they are a problem. She translates her explanation, removing all technical terms and jargon, such as "temp files." Some of her customers would know what a temp file is. She knows Ludwik does not.

Eleanor constantly checks Ludwik's level of comfort and understanding. She asks questions like "Are you OK with that?" and tells him, "I'll make sure that you understand what I'm doing and feel comfortable with it." Before she starts to deliver her instructions, Eleanor tells Ludwik what she will be doing and checks his comfort level by asking, "Are you ready to start?" When she does start giving instructions Ludwik will be well prepared and fairly comfortable. He will understand that she is there to support him, and he won't be afraid to ask questions. The whole interaction ensures that Ludwik will get his problem resolved on the phone and won't have to call back for more instructions. Eleanor's handling of the situation minimizes the negative impact of Ludwik's problem on the profitability of the business.

Questioning

Questioning should be an easy process. You ask a question, and the customer gives an answer. Simple, right? No, unfortunately not. Let's look at some of the challenges you encounter.

Challenges

The challenges you face when you ask your customers questions include the following:

- Customers who don't answer
- Customers who mislead us
- Complex technology

Customers Who Don't Answer

Why is it sometimes difficult to get information out of our customers even when we ask the right questions? Perhaps we are dealing with customers who do not have much respect for the Help Desk. "Don't ask *me* questions," they might say, "*you're* the one who is supposed to know what's going on. *You're* the one who's supposed to fix this." Another reason they may not want to answer us is fear. They're afraid that they've done something wrong, and they don't want us to find out. "I really don't know anything about this. I can't really answer any of your questions." It seems rather contrary, but they do expect us to resolve the problem even if they aren't willing to give us information.

Customers Who Mislead Us

Customers do not get up in the morning with the intention of coming into the office and misleading the Help Desk. In fact, they don't even realize they're doing it. Customers mislead us simply because they make assumptions about the information they have. Say you have a customer who is experiencing printer difficulties. You ask, "Have you changed anything on your system since the printer was last working?" Your customer might well answer "No" even if the customer installed new software that morning. To the customer, the installation wasn't a change that could have affected the printer; it was just new software. The customer's thought process might be something like, "I installed the software but that couldn't possibly have anything to do with the printer not working. I won't bother telling the Help Desk people that. It might just lead them down the wrong path."

Customers may also mislead us because they don't know the technology, and they use the wrong words to describe the problem. As a very simple example, a customer might say, "My screen is stopped." You might translate this to mean "My system has frozen" when it might really mean "My full motion video isn't working."

Complex Technology

The technology we work with is extremely complex in that a problem in one part of the system can cause symptoms in another, seemingly totally unrelated part of the system. As an example, several years ago I experienced a problem on my printed graphics. When I displayed the graphics on the screen, there were no lines. But when I printed them on my laser printer, two or three lines ran across the page. No lines appeared on pages containing text, only on the graphics. I tried everything. I played with system settings, software settings, printer drivers, printer settings, and so on. I finally called someone for help.

"Look at your whole system," my friend advised, "and see what you have changed since you last printed graphics correctly." I hung up the phone and thought about it. I hadn't printed graphics in a while, so I had to think carefully. The last thing I had changed was my processor, which I had upgraded. At the same time, I'd also gotten a new video card. I decided to check out the video card. I went onto the Internet, found an updated driver for my card, and installed it. The lines across my graphics disappeared. A faulty video card driver was the culprit.

If someone had asked me, "Have you changed anything?" I might well have said "No." If when I first had the problem someone had suggested to me that it might be the video card driver I might not have believed it. If we—who are supposed to be fairly familiar with technology—can have this much trouble convincing ourselves of the source of a problem how can we expect our customers to do any better? We may ask questions, but their answers will not always take into account the complexity of the technology.

Meeting the Challenges with Open- and Close-ended Questions

I sometimes do an exercise in my class in which the class tries to get information out of a fourteen-year-old. "Class," I say, "you are each the parent of a fourteen-year-old boy named Tim. He comes home from school very upset one day. I want you to ask him questions to try to find out what happened, why he is so upset." The class starts off very confidently (except for those of us who have experienced this exact situation):

"How was your day?" asks one person.

"Fine," answers Tim. (As you've probably already guessed, I play the role of Tim.)

"What did you do in school today?" asks another person.

"Nothing."

"What happened to upset you?" asks another brave soul.

"I'm not upset. Nothing happened."

This continues on indefinitely and usually ends when someone stands up and shouts "Go to your room!" Those of us who have seen our children through their teens laugh. Everyone else is just frustrated. The point of the exercise is to point out how much we rely on close-ended questions for the information we get. I have done this exercise many, many times, and I have yet to find a person who asks an open-ended question. (Now, realistically, Tim probably wouldn't answer even an open-ended question because he's fourteen, but that's irrelevant to the exercise.)

We are very used to asking close-ended questions, questions that can be answered with a word or phrase, questions that ask us for a specific piece of information. Some examples of close-ended questions we might use on the Help Desk include "Are you able to log on to the network?" or "When was the last time you used your printer?" Close-ended questions are very valuable, but they are not enough. We need questions that will open people up, that will encourage them to give more information. Open-ended questions do just that. They encourage the customer to think, to describe. They throw out a net to gather information from the customer. Open-ended questions are often not questions at all but statements. Some examples of the types of words used in open-ended questions are as follows:

"Describe . . ."

"Tell me . . ."

"Explain how . . ."

Examples of open-ended questions we might use are as follows:

"Describe everything that is on your screen."

"Tell me everything you did this morning."

"Explain how you log on to the network."

Open-ended questions are typically less leading than close-ended questions. For example, if we ask, "Do you see anything unusual on your screen?" we are assuming the customer's definition of *unusual* is the same as ours. We might be leading the customer to look for only some things. If we say, "Describe everything that is on your screen" or "Tell me everything you see on your screen," we are going to get answers that are more accurate, answers that are not skewed by what the customer thinks he or she should be looking for. Scenario 4 shows how we tend to use close-ended questions and the trouble they can get us into. Scenario 5 is the same scenario but using open-ended questions.

SCENARIO 4

Evi calls the Help Desk in a panic. "My PC won't do anything! I try to turn it on, and it won't boot up!" Harry takes the call. "Don't worry," he reassures her. "We'll find the problem. Now, you said your PC won't boot up?" "That's right, it won't start up!"

"Any messages on your screen?" "Yes. Just one. It says 'System failure, unable to boot.'" "Hmm. OK. When was the last time you booted up?" "This morning, when I came in." "And everything went fine?" "Yes, everything was fine." "When did your PC stop working?" "When I got back from lunch. I tried to turn it back on, and it wouldn't boot up." "What did you do this morning?" "Just editing." "Did you do anything unusual?"

"No." "Did anything unusual happen?" "No."

Discussion

Harry doesn't realize it, but his close-ended questions are limiting Evi's answers. He is asking for "unusual" things. Unusual things may not have caused the problem, and what is unusual to Harry may not be unusual to Evi. Let's look at what happens when Harry uses open-ended questions to widen the breadth of information he is getting.

SCENARIO 5

Evi calls the Help Desk in a panic. "My PC won't do anything! I try to turn it on and it won't boot up!" Harry takes the call. "Don't worry," he reassures her. "We'll find the problem. Now, describe the problem you are having." "When I turn on my PC, it does not boot up. It just gives me a message that says 'System failure, unable to boot.'" "When was the last time you booted up?" "This morning, when I came in." "When did you shut down your PC?" "When I went to lunch." "And when did you find the problem?" "When I got back from lunch. I tried to turn the PC on."

"Now, Evi, I'd like you to describe everything you did this morning." "Everything?" "Everything. No matter how unimportant it may seem to you." "OK. Well, I did some editing on a catalog I'm working on. Then one of the women from the graphics department brought me a diskette with our logo on it, and I loaded that into my catalog." "Is that diskette still in your PC?" "Yes. As a matter of fact it is." "OK. I want you to take the diskette out and try rebooting."

Evi does as Harry suggests, and her PC boots up without a problem.

Discussion

Harry's first open-ended question, "Describe the problem you are having," is a much better question than the one he used in Scenario 4, which was "Now, you said your PC won't boot up?" The open-ended question gives Evi a chance to describe the problem in her own words, without being led in any particular direction. In Scenario 5, it gets

Harry all of the information about the problem more quickly. Harry's next open-ended question cracks the case. He asks Evi to "describe everything you did this morning." He does not qualify the request by asking only for "unusual" information. He asks Evi to give him everything. Evi does not limit the information, does not give him only what she thinks is unusual. To Evi, getting a diskette from the graphics department is very usual. It happens very often. Harry, however, would have seen the diskette as something unusual, or at least something worth investigating.

Open- and Close-ended Questions in Combination

Using both open- and close-ended questions is a very powerful way of getting more and better information from your customers. It helps overcome some of the challenges we face in the questioning process we talked about earlier. We use close-ended questions when we want a specific piece of information. We use open-ended questions when we want a wider range of information or when we are looking for an unknown and don't want to limit ourselves. Customers will be less apt to mislead us when we use open-ended questions. They will make fewer assumptions, will not try to anticipate our leads, and won't filter the information they give us. We will get more unfiltered facts about the problem.

Open-ended questions help us overcome the challenge we face when coping with the complexity of technology during the questioning process. In my earlier example of the video card driver that caused lines in my printout, what finally got me thinking was the equivalent of the question, "Describe every change you've made to any component in your computer." I started thinking in wider terms, and my mind became more open. The question "Have you changed anything?" wouldn't have worked nearly as well. I would probably have said "No" because I was thinking only of changes that I felt could have caused my problem.

Effective Questioning

Questioning, like the other components of the information exchange cycle, is a process (see Figure 6.4). It involves asking questions, listening, evaluating the responses, and then asking more questions, perhaps in a direction dictated by the last response. All the good listening habits we

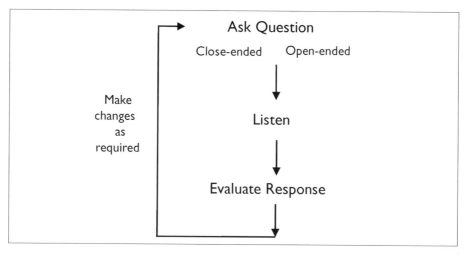

Figure 6.4 The questioning process.

discussed in Chapter 5 apply to questioning as well because listening is part of the questioning process. There are some habits that I haven't touched on yet and some I'd like to emphasize now. If we want our questions to get the kind of responses that get problems resolved we need to do the following:

Reassure. If people are afraid of answering, perhaps because they don't want to be blamed for something or they don't want us to think they're stupid, the more we can reassure them, the better answers we will get. For example, the phrases *"This happens all the time"* or *"We see a lot of this"* go a long way toward reassuring someone who is nervous about possibly having made a mistake. Knowing that others have experienced the exact same thing is very reassuring. If others have done it, it cannot be such a bad thing for us to have done it or experienced it.

Empathize. If people simply don't want to give us information we might say to them, "I could solve your problem faster if you told me a little more about it. I know you need to get working as soon as possible." Even tight-lipped customers will open up somewhat if they think you understand that they have been inconvenienced or if they think the information they give you can help solve their problem in less time.

Use both open- and close-ended questions. Get more and better information.

Try not to lead the customer. Don't give the customer a filter to put data through. Let the customer give you all the data.

Evaluate and change as necessary. If you are asking someone questions and you feel like you're getting nowhere, you probably are. You shouldn't just go on asking the same questions, for example, "Have you changed anything?" and then "Are you sure you haven't changed anything?" (I've even heard, "Are you *really* sure you haven't changed anything?") You need to evaluate, recognize when your questions aren't working and why, and then change them and try again.

The Impact of Effective Information Exchange

In the last two chapters we've talked about becoming effective at giving and getting information. What will this buy us? First, the more effective we are at getting information from customers, the better information we will have to help them. Their problems will be resolved faster and more accurately. This means fewer customers will call us back because we didn't solve the right problem. Second, when we are effective at getting information across to our customers they get the right information from us the first time. There is no need for them to call back to have us repeat the information. This also results in fewer calls to the Help Desk.

Third, we are less likely to get into the out-of-control problem cycle we saw in Chapter 4. We'll have better control of our problems because effective information exchange results in fewer calls, giving us more time to concentrate on each customer's problem. The quality of our resolutions will rise, and customers won't have to call us back with something that wasn't fixed right the first time. Fourth, our working environment will be more pleasant, and we will be less stressed. We will have fewer calls and fewer complaints, and our customers will be more pleasant. Customers who get their problems solved quickly and accurately, who feel Help Desk practitioners are listening to them and respect them, are simply going to be easier to deal with. Finally, the value of the Help Desk to the business will increase. The Help Desk will be minimizing the impact of technological problems on the profitability of the business.

Checklist

Information exchange is critical to your success as a Help Desk practitioner. Come back to this section often to check your effectiveness at getting your message across and at questioning—or just to review what you've learned so you don't forget it.

✓ Do I understand how the cycle of information exchange works?

✓ Do I translate technical information into terms the customer can understand?

✓ Do I check to see how technologically literate my customers are?

✓ Do I check to see how comfortable my customers are with technology?

✓ Do I adjust the level of the information I am delivering to the skill and comfort level of the customer?

✓ Do I suffer from motormouth?

✓ Do I rush my customers?

✓ Do I pay attention to my customers' reactions?

✓ Do I use tone of voice and body language effectively?

✓ Do I always take steps to ensure the customer's understanding?

✓ Do I understand the steps of preparation, delivery, and checking the customer's understanding, which are part of getting a message across?

✓ Do I know the difference between open- and close-ended questions?

✓ Do I use both open- and close-ended questions?

✓ Do I reassure my customers?

✓ Do I show my customers empathy?

✓ Do I make sure that my questions are not leading the customer?

✓ When I am questioning, do I constantly evaluate the success of my questions and change as necessary?

Proactive Problem Control

In Chapter 1 we spent a fair amount of time describing the skill of proaction. We're now going to put that skill to good use to help us control our Help Desk problems. Specifically, we're going to look at how we can be more proactive in eliminating calls coming into the Help Desk.

On a Help Desk, if you aren't eliminating calls, then you're not moving ahead and improving and you aren't freeing up space for the new calls that come in as the environment you support changes. You're getting into the out-of-control problem cycle that we saw in Chapter 4. When that happens, you will not be able to minimize the negative impact that problems involving the use of technology have on the profitability of the business. This chapter offers strategies to help you avoid this scenario.

In This Chapter

In this chapter we're going to look at four approaches for eliminating calls on the Help Desk. The topics we will cover are as follows:

- Understanding customer needs
- Early warning systems
- Dandelions and layered strategies for problem control
- Maintaining an improvement cycle

Understanding Customer Needs

If we understand what our customers need, we can work toward meeting that need before it becomes urgent, before it becomes a problem. Understanding what our customers need now and in the future involves the following skills:

- Listening with an ear toward improvement
- Understanding the current and future environment
- Getting beyond behavior to hear the need

Listening with an Ear toward Improvement

We spoke about listening at great length in Chapter 5. We're now going to talk about how to use what we hear to improve and how to find the places for improvement in what we hear. When we listen to our customers nonproactively, we sometimes fall into the trap of blaming them for their problems and accepting the situation, that is, accepting the fact that the customers' problems exist and assuming they will always exist. Figure 7.1 illustrates this nonproactive thinking, and Scenario 1 provides a nice example of blaming the customer.

SCENARIO 1

Perry calls the Help Desk. He's having trouble storing files on the shared network drive. Avery takes the call. "Help Desk, Avery speaking. What can I do for you this morning?" "It's Perry from Sales. I can't get my files on to the shared drive." Avery sighs to himself. He is very familiar with Perry and his problems—and his whining. Perry was good at whining. Avery straightens up and puts on his best Help Desk voice. "Perry, can you describe the whole problem to me?"

Figure 7.1 Blaming the customer.

"Sure I can, but you've heard it often enough that I shouldn't have to repeat it! I try to move my files to the shared drive, and I get some message telling me I'm not connected. I keep getting this again and again, and I'm really tired of it. Do you know how much time this is costing me? . . . "

Perry goes on and on. Avery listens quietly, checking the network to see if Perry's connection is valid. Finally Perry stops. Avery ignores all Perry's carrying-on and says, "I've reset your connections, so you should be able to move your files now." "Good!" Perry hangs up without another word. Avery lets out a sigh of relief. Thank goodness that was over with. Perry was a real pain, always complaining about everything. He would probably always be like that.

Discussion

Avery fixes Perry's problem quickly, but rather than doing something to ensure that it won't happen again he accepts it, dismissing the whole situation as being Perry's fault. The unfortunate thing here is that the situation will happen again and again unless Avery does something to stop it. The Help Desk will keep getting those calls, Perry will be inconvenienced, and the profitability of the business will be negatively impacted. Avery does have a choice, however. He can choose to blame Perry and accept the problem, or he can choose to listen to Perry and change the situation and get rid of the problem. Let's give Avery another chance. Scenario 2 shows a proactive Avery, determined to eliminate calls.

SCENARIO 2

Perry calls the Help Desk. Avery takes the call. "Help Desk, Avery speaking. What can I do for you this morning?" "It's Perry from Sales. I can't get my files on to the shared network drive." Avery takes a second to make sure he eliminates any negative filters he has toward Perry. "Perry, can you describe the whole problem to me?" "Sure I can, but you've heard it often enough that I shouldn't have to repeat it! I try to move my files to the shared drive, and I get some message telling me I'm not connected. I keep getting this again and again, and I'm really tired of it. Do you know how much time this is costing me? . . . "

Perry goes on and on. Avery listens quietly, checking the network to see if Perry's connection is valid. Finally Perry stops. Instead of blaming Perry, Avery makes sure he understands Perry's problem.

"Perry, you say this keeps happening. I've reset your network connection, but I want to put an end to this problem for you." Avery goes on to ask Perry several questions to try to nail down the cause of the problem. Avery has read Chapter 6, so he uses both open- and close-ended questions. Once Perry realizes that Avery wants to help him, he becomes less hostile and more cooperative. By the end of the conversation, Avery has determined that the operating system software on Perry's PC is somehow resetting Perry's network profile.

"Perry, I've found where the problem is originating; now I need to hunt down a solution for this. It might take me a few days, but as soon as I find something I will let you know." Later in the day Avery logs on to the Internet to investigate Perry's problem. He not only finds a record of Perry's problem, he is able to download an operating system patch for it. He passes it on to the second-level support people and discusses the problem with them. They agree to put the patch in at the end of the day. Avery calls Perry back and gives him an update. "I'm going to check back with you in two weeks," he tells Perry. "I want to make sure this problem is truly eliminated."

Discussion

In Scenario 2, Avery listened with an ear toward improvement. He discarded negative filters, he ignored the fact that Perry was whining, and he heard Perry's message. He heard how many times Perry had been unable to put files on to the network drive, and he understood how this was negatively impacting the profitability of the business. He knew he had to put a stop to this situation and change things to eliminate Perry's calls to the Help Desk. He did what he could to improve the situation and get rid of the problem (see Figure 7.2).

Whenever a customer calls the Help Desk, and especially when he or she is complaining as in Scenarios 1 and 2, you have a choice. You can choose to blame the customer and accept the situation, as Avery did in Scenario 1 and as illustrated in Figure 7.1. Or you can choose to listen to the customer with an ear toward improvement and change the situation for the better, as Avery did in Scenario 2 and as illustrated in Figure 7.2. If you choose to blame and accept, you are doing your Help Desk and the business you support a significant disservice. You are inviting more calls. If you choose to be proactive, to listen and change, you are eliminating calls to the Help Desk and minimizing the negative impact of technology problems on the profitability of the business. Your choice should be easy.

Understanding the Current and Future Environment

Our customers are impacted by the business environment in which they work. Changes in the business affect them, their needs, and what we need to do for them. As proactive Help Desk practitioners we need to know what is happening in the business so we can understand our customers' current and future requirements and do what we can to reduce their downtime. This will eliminate their need to call us. There are four areas we need to get involved in to keep a finger on the pulse of the business:

Figure 7.2   Listening to the customer.

The business itself. You know all those status reports that come by your desk, those company newsletters and minutes from the management meetings? They have valuable information in them. Instead of just passing them on to someone else or tossing them into the recycling bin, read them. Skim through them to see what is happening. If you aren't getting them, ask your manager for copies. You'll find out about upcoming initiatives, plans the business may have for growth, and other changes that could well impact you and your customers.

Other IT areas. Other areas in IT may have valuable information that you do not. They may know what implementations are coming up, what major projects are impending, and so on. They don't always remember to keep the Help Desk informed. The more you know about initiatives in other IT areas, the better you can prepare for them and lessen any negative impact they have on your customers.

Vendors. Vendors are a good source of information about what is going on in the technology industry. If you work with vendors make sure they understand your environment. Tap into their knowledge about improved hardware or software and solutions to known problems. Keep in touch with Help Desk vendors (or their Web sites) to see what new Help Desk software is available that might help you eliminate some of the problems in your environment or automate repetitive processes.

Your customer profile. In Chapter 2 we discussed understanding your customer profile. You need to be aware of changes in this profile that might affect your services to your customers and their requirements of you. Perhaps the number of customers you have is increasing, perhaps they are spreading to more locations, or perhaps their use of technology is changing. The sooner you know about these things the more you are likely to be able to lessen the impact on your customers and eliminate problems before they occur.

Once we understand our customers' current and future environment, we may need to go back to the focus and structure of our Help Desk. We may need to revisit our Help Desk's mission, our services, our objectives, and perhaps even our structure.

Getting beyond Behavior to Hear the Need

On the Help Desk we sometimes need to interact with customers who are emotional or exhibit challenging behavior. There are days when we wonder, "Why bother with these customers?" The answer is that if we take away the emotional or challenging behavior we will see a customer's real need. If we can meet that need then we are minimizing the negative impact of the customer's problem on the profitability of the business. If we can eliminate the reason for that customer calling in the first place, then we are minimizing the negative impact even more.

I define challenging behavior as behavior that makes it difficult for you to listen to the customer, to hear his or her problem, and thus to work with the customer to provide a solution. Examples of challenging behavior are as follows:

- Emotional behavior such as anger or crying
- Know-it-all, condescending behavior
- Going off topic, taking forever to get to the problem

The steps that are involved in getting beyond behavior to hear the customer's need are shown in Figure 7.3.

Listen to the Customers and Their Feelings

Everything I said about listening in Chapter 5 applies here. All our positive listening habits should be used even when our customers are ex-

> ✓ Listen to the customer, and to feelings
> ✓ Refocus the customer
> ✓ Work with the customer
>   to resolve the problem
> ✓ Do what is necessary to ensure
>   the problem will not recur

Figure 7.3   Getting beyond behavior to hear the need.

hibiting challenging behavior. The most important listening habits to use with customers who are angry or upset are to focus on the message rather than the delivery, ignore negative filters, empathize, and keep a level head. There is one more thing we can add to this list for emotional customers: Give them time to express their feelings. They need time to vent.

Several years ago, I was just starting a class in a hotel in Toronto when I got a message from a hotel services employee. One of my students had called to say she'd be late. I continued with the class, and sure enough, about fifteen minutes later my student showed up. She was completely frazzled and obviously upset. "I'm so sorry," she said and proceeded to explain what had happened. There had been an accident on the highway, and she had been stuck behind it for the past hour and a half. I let her talk and encouraged the class to get involved, ask her questions, and share their own anecdotes. After about ten minutes, she was calm and laughing and no longer stressed about being late. She helped herself to some coffee, and we restarted the class. I spent a few minutes bringing her up to date on where we were, and when we finally continued her mind was totally on the class.

The reason my student could control her stress so quickly and become an active participant in the class is because the rest of the class and I let her express her feelings—we let her vent. Once she had told everyone about her stressful experience she could let it go. If I had restarted the class right away and not given her an opportunity to vent, she would not have been able to let go of her stress. She probably wouldn't have heard a thing I said all during class because she would still be worrying about being late and focusing on her experience rather than what was going on around her. The class would have been affected as well. I teach a very interactive class, and the interactions are affected by the degree to which all the students participate. The woman who was late would not have been able to participate fully because her mind would have been elsewhere.

When we are upset, we need to vent and express our feelings. Our customers are the same. To listen to our customers vent without getting ourselves upset we have to understand two things. First, expressing feelings is a human need. The customer cannot begin describing the problem until he or she expresses some feelings. Second, the customer is not really angry at you. The customer is angry at the fact that there is a problem and frustrated that important work cannot get done. You should not take emotional behavior personally. It is not personal. If we are able to understand these two things we will be able to listen to our customers express their feelings without getting upset. Our calm will go a long way toward ensuring the success of the interaction. When we are calm we can listen. We can see past the behavior to hear the message the customer is getting across. We can focus on the question, "What does my customer need, and what do I have to do to deliver it?"

We cannot let our customers go on forever, whether they are venting or just talking a lot. We need to get their problems resolved so they can get on with their work. We need to refocus them on their problem.

Refocus the Customer

Inevitably, we will one day find ourselves dealing with a customer who is venting, running on and on about something without getting anywhere near the point, or condescending to the point of not allowing us to help. In these cases, we need to refocus that customer so we can start solving his or her problem. The key to refocusing the customer is to learn the art of the polite interruption. My students have a hard time with this at first. They really do not like interrupting people. After a few practice sessions though, there's no stopping them. They become very effective at temporarily halting the flow of words so both they and their customers can focus on the problem at hand.

The polite interruption relies heavily on human physiology in that at some point the customer simply has to breathe. "No!" my students tell me, "We have customers who don't breathe!" Well, unless you can prove to me that your customers are aliens I simply will not believe that. Everyone has to breathe sometime. It is the point at which the customer takes a breath that we interrupt them. It is an entry point into a conversation that has, up to this point, been only theirs. The polite interruption works like this:

- Wait for the customer to take a breath.
- Interrupt with a phrase that focuses them back on the problem and at the same time shows empathy.

Let's go to Scenario 3 for an example.

SCENARIO 3

Jenna is livid. She called the Help Desk this morning about a problem with her monitor, and she was told that someone would be at her office at 1 P.M. It is now 4:20 P.M. and still no Help Desk person. She called at 2 and at 3 and had been told that "someone is on the way." She has not been able to do any work since noon, and she can't wait much longer because she has two children to pick up at day care. She is just about to leave when Carla walks into her office.

"Hi, I'm Carla from the Help Desk. I understand you have a problem with your monitor," says Carla unsuspectingly.

Jenna explodes. "Well, you finally decided to show up, did you? I have been waiting here since one o'clock. I haven't been able to get anything done, and, unlike you people, I do have a very critical deadline to meet. I called twice, and each time they told me you were on your way. Which route did you take? Around the whole city and back? Do you know how much time this has cost me? And you are too late! I have to leave by 4:30 to pick up my kids from day care! What took you so long?"

At this point Jenna takes a breath, and Carla jumps in. "Jenna, I don't want to inconvenience you any further. Let's get you out of here quickly so you can pick your kids up. Can you describe the problem you're having with your monitor?" Jenna stops for a moment, slightly disoriented. The interruption has broken her flow of anger, and she answers Carla's question. She has been refocused on the problem.

Discussion

When Jenna first explodes, Carla is probably somewhat taken aback. It takes her a few seconds to gather her thoughts, and after letting Jenna have a bit of time to vent she waits for Jenna to breathe and interrupts. She focuses completely on Jenna's requirements, not on her behavior. She does not get flustered or angry. Carla uses the following statements to express empathy and to interrupt the flow of Jenna's anger: "I don't want to inconvenience you any further. Let's get you out of here quickly so you can pick your kids up." The statements show that Carla understands that Jenna has been inconvenienced and wants to help her. Carla then refocuses Jenna by asking her for some information. After your customer has been refocused in this way it is very difficult for him or her to continue being emotional. If, however, your customer does manage to continue venting, use the polite interruption again. The second time it will be even harder for your customer to continue. Continue trying to politely interrupt until your customer stops. Usually, your customer will stop venting after only one interruption.

The Phrase That Empathizes and Refocuses

I'd like to spend some time talking about the kinds of phrases you can use to politely interrupt customers and get them focused back on the business. First, I'll talk about apologizing, which is what almost all of my students try to do at first. I've discussed this with class after class and tried various exercises. What I and my students have found is that when I forbid them to apologize or use the words *I'm sorry*, they come up with much more effective phrases to interrupt with. Here are a few problems I've seen with saying "I'm sorry":

- Often you are apologizing for something you have no control over. Some customers will use this kind of apology to fuel their anger. It's almost as if for them apologizing is too trite, too easy.

- When you apologize you are sometimes tempted into giving excuses. For example, "I'm sorry I was late. I got held up." This will give some customers something else to get upset about. "You got held up? So why didn't you call me? Hasn't anyone ever taught you manners? And didn't anyone tell you how important my problem is? It's probably a lot more important than the one you were held up by!"

- When you apologize you may be tempted into becoming defensive. You could get into a "Yes you did, No I didn't" kind of argument. For example, you might say "I'm sorry, I was held up." The customer responds with "Why didn't you call? Haven't you any manners?" You get defensive and reply, "Well, I wasn't anywhere near a phone." The customer says, "You weren't near a phone? Where were you, Africa?"

In each of these examples, apologizing has taken the focus of the interaction far away from the problem and put it onto the behavior of the

Help Desk practitioner. This is not productive in any way; in fact, it is very destructive. You need to get these customers focused back on the problem as quickly as possible so it can get resolved. What phrases work best to show empathy and refocus the customer? The following types of phrases work well:

- Phrases that stay away from the Help Desk practitioner's behavior
- Phrases that acknowledge inconvenience to the customer
- Phrases that involve the customer in solving the problem

Examples of these kinds of phrases are as follows:

"Tell me exactly what's happening when you try to log on, so we can get you up and running as quickly as possible." This phrase involves the customer and also acknowledges that he or she needs to be up and running as soon as possible.

"I don't want you to be down any longer; you have some pretty heavy deadlines to meet. Tell me what happens when you initiate the software." This phrase tells the customer that you realize the customer has been down a long time and that he or she has important work to do. It asks for involvement from the customer.

Let's look at one more example of the polite interruption in Scenario 4.

SCENARIO **4**

John looks at the PC on his desk and shakes his head in anger. How could the Help Desk have done this? He had gone to a lot of trouble to get the 20-inch monitor approved, and here was a 17-inch monitor sitting on his desk with a note saying that a new monitor had been installed as he instructed. His instructions? They had specified a 20-inch monitor. He had been counting on the larger monitor to help him do the layout for the flyer graphics. With the 17-inch the process would take much longer, and he'd have to work a significant amount of overtime to meet his deadline. John calls the Help Desk.

"Help Desk, Margaret speaking. What can I do for you?"

"You can get this damned monitor off my desk and give me the one I asked for, for a start! I ordered a 20-inch monitor three weeks ago, and I got all the paperwork signed. And what do I find on my desk? A 17-inch monitor! Don't you guys know what the hell you're doing? I went to a lot of trouble getting authorization for the 20-inch. And I've got a major flyer due in two weeks, and I will not be able to meet that deadline with the monitor you've given me! Why did this happen? Can't you people read? I cannot believe that such a simple order got screwed up!"

As John took a breath, Margaret interrupted. "Sir, you obviously need that 20-inch monitor as soon as possible, so let's see what we can do about resolving this situation quickly. Can you please give me your name and the ID from the tag on the monitor that's on your desk?"

Discussion

If Margaret had not used the polite interruption so effectively, this interaction could have dissolved into an argument about who was to blame for the error and why it had happened. The focus would have been taken completely off of the problem and put onto laying blame. Margaret showed empathy by acknowledging that John needed that monitor quickly. She then got John involved by asking him for information. She focused by thinking, "John obviously needs a 20-inch monitor. Let's see what I can do to get it to him."

Work with the Customer to Resolve the Problem

After you have refocused the customer, you will work with him or her to resolve the problem. If your customer is the type who rambles on and on, you may have to use the polite interruption again to refocus him or her on the resolution. In resolving the problem you want to make sure that both you and your customer have the same understanding of the resolution. Check for understanding often. If you cannot come up with a resolution that satisfies your customer, ask him or her what would.

Do What Is Necessary to Ensure the Problem Will Not Recur

Dealing with challenging behavior is draining. You want to do what you can to ensure that you eliminate the reasons for this kind of behavior wherever possible. When you are finished with a call that involved dealing with challenging behavior, as in Scenario 4, take some time to analyze what you need to do to ensure that the problem that caused the behavior will never recur. The section titled "Dandelions and Layered Strategies for Problem Control" later in this chapter will help you do this.

Early Warning Systems

We've looked at understanding your customers' needs in order to eliminate calls to the Help Desk. Another way we can eliminate or prevent calls to the Help Desk is through our "early warning systems" (EWS). EWSs can warn us about potential problems before they happen so we can do something about them, which eliminates any negative impact those problems would have had on the profitability of the business. Our EWSs also help keep us away from the out-of-control problem cycle we talked about in Chapter 4.

Four EWSs are typically available to us on the Help Desk. They are the sensory, the statistical, the internal, and the external.

Sensory

Our sensory EWS is made up of feelings, and it comes from three sources: ourselves, our colleagues, and our customers. Our sensory EWS tells us when we're too stressed or when our morale starts to drop. Both of these symptoms could be indications that something is very wrong with the way the Help Desk is running. The symptoms might be caused by the fact that we aren't able to help our customers, that we aren't able to eliminate calls, that we have more work than we can handle, or that we are losing control.

Gut feelings are also part of our sensory EWS. People talk about gut feelings, but they don't think about what the term means. It's often brushed aside or put in the same category as extrasensory perception (ESP). Gut feelings have nothing to do with ESP, and it should not be brushed aside because it is based on very real data. Gut feelings are built out of our experiences, from what we've seen and learned. It's like the search engine in a knowledge base. We encounter a situation, and our gut feelings search our brain for similar situations in the past, for media articles our brain might remember, or for any bad or good experiences we might have had that are connected to situations similar to the one we're looking at now. If our gut feelings find something negative, they send us a warning that says, "I don't think you want to do this" or "Something is not quite right here."

Our colleagues also have input into our EWS. Their stress, morale, and gossip all feed into our EWS, telling us there's something wrong. For example, we might hear them gossiping about how the marketing department was changing completely and how rumor had it the department would be doubling its staff and getting state-of-the art graphics workstations. Unfortunately, sometimes this is the way news comes to us. As a proactive Help Desk practitioner who is out to eliminate calls, you would hear this rumor and think, "I'd better check this out. It could have a big impact on the Help Desk." You would find out if the rumor was true, and if it was you and your manager could start planning for the equipment you would have to set up or the extra support you would have to provide.

We also look to our customers for input into our EWS. We listen to their tone of voice and their words, and we sense their moods. We might find out from them that something is changing in their area that they are excited or upset about. Our customers can be a very good unofficial source of early warning for things that are happening in the business.

Statistical

Our statistical EWS comes from all the statistics we are bombarded with on the Help Desk. If we pay attention to them we will be able to pick up negative trends or unusual fluctuations or behaviors, all of which could indicate problems that need to be averted. If we look at the number and breakdown of the calls we're getting, we get an early warning about situations such as a steadily increasing volume of calls, increases in a particular type of call such as training-type calls, or calls that are related to a specific piece of software. We can then look at tools like automation, consider any training initiatives that may be required, or get patches for software—all before serious problems can hit.

There are several key statistics you should be looking at as a Help Desk practitioner interested in eliminating calls. We'll look at these in detail in Chapter 9.

Internal and External

Internal EWSs come from the business and from other IT areas. External EWSs also come from our vendors and the whole IT industry. As we saw in the section titled "Understanding the Current and Future Environ-ment" earlier in this chapter, the more we know about what is happen-ing in these areas, the greater the likelihood that we will be able to avoid the problems caused by upcoming events or changes.

What to Do with EWSs

Whether you know it or not, you are currently getting a lot of informa-tion from all your EWSs. You may be ignoring it or just letting it be ab-sorbed by all the noise around you and the Help Desk. You do have the option of doing nothing with the data you get from your EWSs. You can wait for things to hit you, as in Scenario 13 in Chapter 1. In that scenario, Ray's Ties waited until tie trends changed and then reacted. As we saw, this was not a very profitable way for Ray's Ties to operate.

If you are proactive, however, you will use the data from your EWSs to prevent the problem situations your sensory, statistical, and inter-nal/external EWSs are forecasting. When Ray's Ties became proactive (see Scenario 14 in Chapter 1) and started taking advantage of its EWS by using a tie market analyst, it stopped getting hit by decreases in rev-enue every time tie styles changed. It was able to prepare for changes, to be ready when they came, and to continue to offer its customers the lat-est in tie styles. Scenario 5 is an example of EWSs being used effectively.

SCENARIO 5

Lara works on the Help Desk. Each week her manager sends out e-mail summaries of the minutes from management meetings. Lara makes time to scan through these. She likes to know what is going on in the business. On this particular afternoon, Lara is scanning through the minutes before leaving for home when she notices an entry that says the logistics department is ramping up for a reengineering project. The project was initially targeted for the following year but was being pushed forward.

"Reengineering," Lara thinks. "That probably means they'll need more PCs, and those PCs might need to be moved." Lara calls up some of her customers in the logistics department, and they tell her what they know. As Lara leaves for home, she is worried. Her customers told her that, yes, the logistics department was very shortly going to embark on a reengineering initiative. They would be getting all kinds of new equipment, and they had hired some consultants, ABC Consulting, to set everything up. Lara realizes that the initiative is going to mean a significant amount of extra work for the Help Desk, but her gut feelings tell her that something else is not right, something about the consultants. The next morning Lara goes to see her manager, Toni. Toni hasn't read the minutes, but she pulls them up on her screen quickly as Lara tells her about the logistics project. "I hadn't had time to read these yet," Toni says as she skims through them. "Holy smokes, this is going to be a lot of work. I'd better go see Howard about this." Howard is the department head for logistics.

"There's something else," Lara tells her. "They've hired ABC Consulting to do the equipment installation."

"ABC?" Toni looks upset. "They're the ones who absolutely refused to work with us when they did the equipment for the warehouse. They basically said we were only the Help Desk and that it was none of our business. We had a hell of a time maintaining that stuff. The warehouse finally hired some on-site maintenance people to look after it. I wonder if Howard realizes that."

Now Lara remembered. Because the consultants had worked without any communication with the Help Desk, the Help Desk had been pulled into a—fortunately temporary—out-of-control problem cycle. She had been on the Help Desk at the time, and it had not been fun, to say the least. Toni goes to see Howard who in turn calls ABC Consulting. The next morning a consultant from ABC calls Lara. "Hi, I'm from ABC Consulting. I'm supposed to work with you to plan all of the equipment for the logistics project."

Since Toni had early warning about the upcoming logistics project she was able to outsource some temporary help to deal with the extra technology and support work entailed by the project. She actually had enough time to put together an estimate on the impact the project would have on the Help Desk and use that to justify the cost of the outsourced help. Lara worked with ABC Consulting to ensure that standards were adhered to, support was available for all equipment, and all customers were trained. As a result, when the logistics reengineering project started up, there was no negative impact. Other Help Desk customers did not notice any degradation in service because the outsourced help was looking after the extra load of requests coming from the logistics project.

The logistics department in turn had very few problems with its equipment because it all followed company standards and interfaced well with the architecture of the existing technology. Lara had put the technology architecture team in touch with ABC Consulting. Logistics staff members were trained before they got their equipment, and the logistics department had contracted with a trainer who came in for two hours each morning to address any problems people were having with the new technology.

Discussion

In Scenario 5 Lara averted what could have been a major disaster by using her internal and sensory EWSs. I would like to say that this scenario is the exception, that Help Desks do not usually find out about projects in such unofficial ways, but I would be lying. The unfortunate truth is that businesses often forget to get the Help Desk involved, they forget how critical a role it plays in new initiatives, and they don't take into account the impact of new initiatives on it. This makes our EWSs more critical than ever.

Dandelions and Layered Strategies for Problem Control

I've talked at length about the need to constantly look for ways to improve and eliminate problems and calls, but I haven't yet discussed an approach for resolving the problems and carrying out the improvements. In this section I'll do just that.

On the Help Desk, time is the one thing that hampers us most in our efforts to be proactive, get rid of problems, and eliminate calls. We want to get at the root causes of problems so they don't ever come back, but this usually involves a lot of time and resources that we don't always have available to us. We recognize that we don't want fixes. Fixes are cheap today, but the problems are back tomorrow. We want solutions that keep the problems away forever. But solutions are expensive. So what do we do?

First, we make sure we have a way of looking at problems, a methodology that helps us see all the levels of causes, not just the surface causes. Then we address these causes in a series of individual steps. Each step is a manageable chunk of time and resources, so we are not hit with a huge time and resource requirement all at once.

Levels of Causes

A simple strategy for identifying the layers of causes for a problem is based on the dandelion. Just about everyone is familiar with the lowly dandelion. All you have to do is to go outside in the spring or summer and look at your lawn or your neighbor's lawn. There will be dandelions somewhere. Everyone is always trying to get rid of them. You can resort to poison (which I hate to do because of the three dogs, two cats, and assorted people who live in my house) or you can pull them out. I have a lot of experience trying to pull dandelions out. As a result, I've learned a few interesting facts about them.

If you grab the dandelion by its flower and leaves, you can pull out the part of the dandelion that is above the surface quite easily. The problem is that the dandelion comes back almost the next day. If you use a large screwdriver, along with the flower and leaves you can get part of the root out as well. The dandelion stays away for a little longer, maybe a week. If, however, you pull out the dandelion's whole root it does not come back. Millions of other dandelions may come back but not that one. Several years ago, when my very innovative father was still alive and strong, he made me a tool that digs down and pulls dandelions out by the root. I still have it and I still use it. It's a good feeling to get rid of the whole dandelion and know it won't be back.

The causes of Help Desk problems aren't much different than dandelions. Like dandelions, we can divide the causes of problems into three layers or levels, as shown in Figure 7.4. If you address only the surface causes, which are equivalent to the flower and leaves of the dandelion, the problem you're trying to get rid of will come back very quickly. If you address the mid-level causes, the equivalent of the upper part of the dandelion root, your problem might stay away a little longer, but it

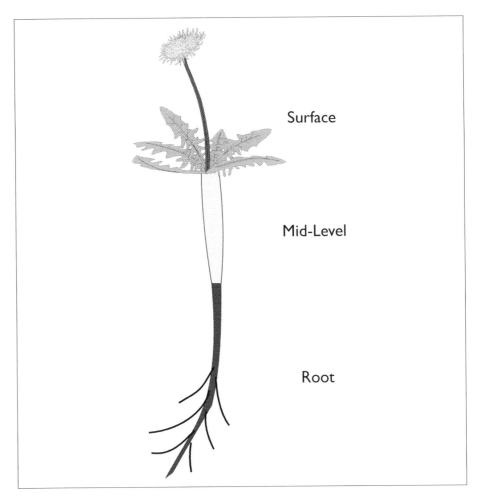

Figure 7.4   Levels of causes.

will be back. It is only if you address the "root" causes, like the root of the dandelion, that the problem will truly be solved. If you divide problem causes into three levels, it becomes easier to identify them. You won't be fooled as easily into looking only at surface causes—you will be looking for all the levels of causes.

Identifying the Levels of Causes

When you identify the causes of a problem, think about them in terms of surface, mid-level, and root:

Surface-level causes are superficial, "at-first-glance" causes. Unfortunately, surface causes are often attributed to the Help Desk practitioner. Surface-level causes might include poor service quality skills, poor customer service attitude, poor testing skills, and so on.

Mid-level causes involve looking a little deeper. For example, if a surface-level cause is a Help Desk practitioner's poor customer service attitude, some corresponding mid-level causes might be no customer service training, management's failure to establish expectations, or its failure to give effective feedback.

Root-level causes are the heart of the problem. Root-level causes typically involve procedures or the lack thereof: structural inadequacies, poor practices, and so on. The corresponding root-level causes for the surface level cause of poor customer service attitude might include poor hiring practices and no IT standards for customer service.

Example A: A Small Problem

Before we get too complicated, let's look at a simple example that illustrates the process of identifying the three levels of causes.

The problem: The customer's PC keeps freezing.

Surface-level cause: Too many temp files.

Mid-level cause: The customer is not cleaning up temp files as they build up.

Root-level cause: The application is generating too many temp files.

If we only address the surface-level cause—the fact that there are too many temp files—we might end up putting in a fix, such as deleting the temp files for the customer, rather than a real solution. The following week that customer would be calling back complaining about the same thing. Other customers would probably be calling about it as well. If we address the mid-level cause—the customer not cleaning the temp files up—we would get rid of the problem for a little longer. We might decide to teach the customer how to get rid of temp files. That customer wouldn't call us back about the problem, but others would. And if someone else took over that customer's position, we would be back where we started. However, if we address the root-level cause—the application is generating too many temp files—we could modify the application so it doesn't generate temp files in the first place. That would take care of the problem forever.

Example B: A Bigger Problem

Let's look at something a little more complicated now.

> **The problem:** The Help Desk is not meeting promised delivery dates. PC installations are constantly late. The three levels of causes for this problem are shown in Table 7.1.

If we address only the surface causes shown in Table 7.1, we wouldn't get rid of the PC delivery problem because such issues as no agreed-upon delivery and response times, high call load, and the absence of service level agreements (SLAs) would still be there to cause the problem. If we address the mid-level causes, the problem would still come back to haunt us because we wouldn't really know what our customer requirements for PC delivery were; we wouldn't have SLAs in place; we wouldn't have good priorities; and so on. In other words, the root would still be there to cause the problem again and again. The problem will be solved only when we address the root-level causes, that is, when we determine the customer's requirements, put SLAs in place, redefine priorities, implement a cycle of evaluation and improvement, market to customers, and establish a good hiring and training plan.

Guidelines for Identifying Levels of Causes

When you identify causes you'll find things go much easier if you follow a few guidelines:

Table 7.1 Example of Three Layers of Causes

Surface-level Causes	Mid-level Causes	Root-level Causes
Help Desk staff are unfamiliar with true delivery and response times.	No agreed-upon delivery and response times with vendors.	Don't know what the true customer requirements are for delivery times for new PCs.
Help Desk staff don't have control over all of the people involved in setting a delivery date (e.g., vendors).	Manager not ensuring that staff have the information they need to do the job.	No service level agreements (SLAs) in place with customers and vendors.
Help Desk staff have poor estimating skills.	Manager not setting clear expectations.	Existing priorities are ineffective. No one uses them.
Help Desk staff are not sure of expectations.	Manager not ensuring a clear understanding of roles/authority.	No ongoing Help Desk evaluation and improvement (call reduction initiatives) are taking place.
Help Desk staff are not sure they have the authority to refuse unreasonable requests.	No planned training for Help Desk staff.	No marketing of services to customers.
Help Desk staff are intimidated by customers, afraid to say no.	No skills assessment for Help Desk staff.	Hiring practices do not include skills requirements.
Help Desk staff are poor communicators, don't keep customers informed.	Call load too high.	Recommended or available training has not been identified for all skills.

- Several people should be involved in identifying causes. This is a group activity. The more brains you have in the room, the more causes you can identify. Ideally, the Help Desk team, or a subset thereof, should be identifying causes. When I do this activity with an entire Help Desk team I inevitably find that there will be one person who will come up with critical causes that no one else thought of. The more Help Desk practitioners you have in the room, the wider range of causes you will identify. If you are dealing with a higher-level problem you may have to get your manager involved.

- Start off by drawing an empty chart with three columns, as in Table 7.1.

- Brainstorm possible causes for the problem. As each cause is brought up, categorize it as either surface-level, mid-level, or root-level and enter it into the appropriate column. You need to be careful here that you identify only possible causes; people have a tendency to list solutions rather than focus on causes. You cannot implement an effective solution until you understand all the causes. So make sure there are no solutions in your chart of causes.

- Revisit all the causes to make sure they are in the appropriate columns.

- Weed out any solutions that have been inadvertently entered. Again, you are not interested in solutions just yet.

Layered Strategies for Problem Control

Once you have identified the causes of your problem, you can then go on to look at solutions. You approach solutions through a series of small steps, each of which is a short, manageable chunk of time and effort. You can group these steps into a series of three strategies: short-term, mid-term, and long-term.

A short-term strategy addresses the surface-level causes. It will temporarily remove the problem and give you time to get something more permanent in place. If we use the analogy of a dam that has sprung a leak, a short-term strategy is like sticking your finger into the hole to temporarily stop the flow while someone goes for help.

A mid-term strategy starts to evaluate, to analyze, to measure. Initiatives in a mid-term strategy might start addressing root-level causes as well as mid-level causes. In our dam analogy, a mid-term strategy would be to shore the dam up with pieces of wood.

A long-term strategy addresses the root causes of the problem. Initiatives in a long-term strategy would be aimed at eliminating the problem altogether. In our dam analogy, a long-term strategy would be to rebuild the dam.

Example C: A Small Problem

Again, we'll start with a very simple example. The problem is the same as Example A: *The customer's PC keeps freezing.* The causes are also the same. The strategies for addressing the causes are as follows:

> **Short-term strategy:** Clean up the temp files.
>
> **Mid-term strategy:** Teach all customers how to clean up temp files.
>
> **Long-term strategy:** Investigate and implement the changes necessary to ensure that applications don't generate so many temp files.

First, we clean up the temp files so our customer can start working again. This will give us time to put together a training strategy for teaching as many customers as possible how to clean up temp files. We might send out a note or actually have one person in each department teach the procedure to everyone else in the department. This will decrease the number of calls we get for this problem and give us some time to start investigating what we need to do to stop the applications from generating so many temp files in the first place.

Example D: A Bigger Problem

Let's go back to our more complicated example. The problem is the same as in Example B: *The Help Desk is not meeting promised delivery dates. PC installations are constantly late.* The three strategies developed to address the causes of this problem are shown in Table 7.2. Note that each strategy is composed of several tasks; each one is a manageable chunk of work; none is overwhelming. Much of the analysis required for the tasks in the long-term strategy, for example creation of SLAs, will be done while carrying out tasks in the mid-term strategy, for example, "Monitor actual service delivery and response times. Start getting customer feedback."

The short-term strategy in Table 7.2 includes initiatives that will almost immediately minimize the problem of PCs being delivered later than promised. It focuses on consistency. The Help Desk will do some initial investigation and come up with delivery times it can meet. These

Table 7.2 Three Strategies for Addressing Causes

Short-term Strategy	*Mid-term Strategy*	*Long-term Strategy*
Create a preliminary definition of services, including delivery and response times. Work with vendors and other departments to come up with dates that people can meet. Don't try to optimize these yet. You are only interested in coming up with dates that can actually be met.	Monitor actual service delivery and response times. Start getting customer feedback.	Clarify the customers' expectations on delivery times. Change procedures as required to meet these times (you now understand the procedures involved and the timing behind each procedure) or negotiate with customers.
Create a preliminary, temporary definition of priorities.	Analyze the procedures involved in delivery and response and work with all the parties involved to optimize these and ensure a mutual understanding.	Clarify priorities.
Market the service delivery and response times you created to customers. Make sure all Help Desk practitioners understand these times.	Create a training plan to address the requirements of each Help Desk practitioner.	Put SLAs in place with customers and vendors.
Make sure all Help Desk practitioners understand what authority they have.	The manager and practitioners need to set up an ongoing process for setting expectations, giving feedback, and clarifying authority.	Market to customers. Include a marketing plan as a subset of your manager's quarterly plan.
Investigate sources that provide communication training, and start getting people trained.	Plan improvements based on individual and team feedback and your monitoring of delivery and response times.	Start a cycle of ongoing evaluation and improvement.
		Build a skills requirement grid for the Help Desk. Change hiring practices to include the use of this grid.
		Investigate sources of training for each skill. Develop a grid of recommended training for each skill.

will probably be longer than customers like, but they are the times the Help Desk will actually be able to meet. The Help Desk will also market these times to customers by explaining that the process of PC delivery is being improved. This may make customers more cooperative.

The mid-term strategy in Table 7.2 starts to analyze processes and make more long-lasting improvements. Much of the work performed in the mid-term strategy can be used as the inputs for the tasks performed in the long-term strategy. The long-term strategy addresses root causes, core issues such as customer requirements, SLAs, and hiring practices. Each initiative within the strategies presented in Table 7.2 is a manageable unit of work in terms of time and effort.

Guidelines for Putting Strategies Together

When you put strategies together your goal is to end up with a series of tasks, each of which is manageable in terms of time and resources. You don't want any one task to be overwhelming. If it is, chances are it won't get done. Here are some guidelines to help you develop your strategies:

Involve several people when developing strategies. Ideally, strategies will be developed by the Help Desk team and the manager, or a subset of that group. The people who will actually be doing the work should be in the room while the strategies are being developed. If your manager was not involved in identifying causes, make sure he or she has had a chance to see your table of causes and to provide input before you start developing strategies.

Work from the chart of causes. Have it handy and use it as a guideline for putting strategies together. If you don't have it in front of you, you may overlook something.

Go through the chart of causes and determine the activities you can carry out to address each of the causes in the chart. Don't worry yet about whether they are short-, mid-, or long-term. Just identify the activities. Also, don't spend time worrying about who will do them or about the details of their implementation. You'll get to that later.

Make sure each cause is addressed and that each activity is a manageable chunk of work. If activities are too big you are setting yourself up for failure.

Once activities have been identified, start putting them into columns. Once you have identified all the activities you need to carry out to address the causes, start classifying them as either short-, mid-, or long-term.

Review your classification for feasibility. Go through each of the activities to make sure each is feasible, is a manageable chunk of work, and has been classified correctly.

You now have a high-level work plan for getting rid of your problem. Your next step is to look at implementation.

Implementing Strategies

You have identified causes and put together short-, mid-, and long-term strategies. Now you need to go through the tasks within each strategy and decide on initial timing estimates and resourcing. If you are a first-level Help Desk practitioner, these tasks may become the project work you do while you're off the phones. When you are implementing strategies you should keep in mind that you want to finish all the tasks that address the short-term causes as quickly as possible. You want some breathing room. You want to stop the calls while you get rid of the problem. The tasks in your short-term strategy typically have a very short duration. They are things you can implement quickly.

The key to finishing all three strategies is to work through the tasks one by one if necessary but to work continuously. If you try to work on too much at once you are setting yourself up for failure. If you keep working on small chunks you will finish everything. This is not the fastest method for getting rid of problems. To be fast, however, you need dedicated time and resources, which, being on a Help Desk, you probably don't have. This method divides your problem resolution process into manageable tasks that you can accomplish as part of your Help Desk project work.

Once you have completed the work for all of your strategies for a particular problem you may notice that other problems disappear too. Problems often share root causes. When you address these causes in the course of getting rid of one of the problems, the rest may well be eliminated. Managing the creation and implementation of the strategies can be done in several ways. An approach I have seen work extremely well is to have the entire team take the project on, take ownership of it, and work through all the tasks with minimal involvement from the manager. In other teams it may be necessary for one Help Desk practitioner to take charge of the project. You will know what works best in your environment.

Maintaining an Improvement Cycle

When you are working on your strategies you may be thinking, "Hooray, once we finish these we're done!" Not so. When you're finished with one problem you will simply move on to the next problem and repeat the whole process. Your goal is to eliminate calls. You will always be working on getting rid of problems so as to fulfill this goal. You may even start working on the strategies for another problem before you have completely finished with the first one. However, if you do this you need to be very careful not to bite off more than you can chew. If you try to do too much at once you will fail.

In Chapter 4 we talked about an ongoing cycle of evaluation and improvement. The evaluation process we discussed there will identify many of the problems that you can find solutions for using the layered strategy approach to problem solving outlined here. You take one of these identified problems, get rid of it using the layered strategy, then take another problem, and so on. You will never run out of problems to feed this improvement cycle, which is shown in Figure 7.5. The cycle will ensure that you are always working on eliminating calls, and it will help you maintain control of your problems.

Checklist

This chapter has given you, the proactive Help Desk practitioner, several approaches for eliminating calls and the problems associated with that challenge. Use the following checklist to check that you understand the

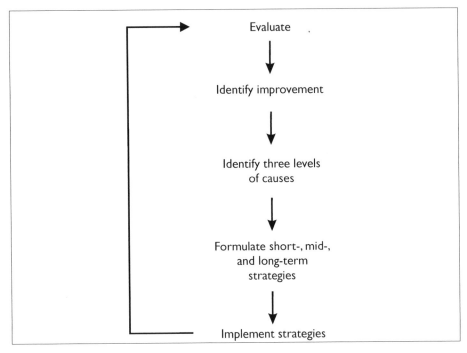

Figure 7.5   Improvement cycle using layered strategies for problem control.

concepts presented in this chapter and to jog your memory about the approaches you have learned:

✓ Do I listen to my customers with an ear toward improvement? Do I listen and change rather than blame and accept?

✓ Do I understand my customers' current and future environment?

✓ Am I able to get beyond challenging behavior to hear the customer's need?

✓ Do I listen to the customer and to his or her feelings?

✓ Am I able to refocus the customer? Am I able to express empathy and get the customer involved in the problem solving?

✓ Do I go on to resolve the problem and do what I can to make sure it does not recur?

✓ Do I use my early warning systems (EWSs)?

✓ Do I understand how dandelions and Help Desk problems are similar?

✓ Am I able to take a problem and identify the surface-, mid-, and root-level causes for it?

✓ Once I have identified three levels of causes for a problem, am I able to describe the tasks that will address each of the causes in each of the three levels?

✓ Do I understand the differences between short-, mid-, and long-term strategies?

✓ Am I able to create short-, mid-, and long-term strategies from the list of tasks I have put together to address the three levels of causes?

✓ Do I understand that getting rid of calls is an ongoing cycle? Do I make sure I am always evaluating myself and my Help Desk to find problems that I can feed into this cycle?

Using Tools

In Chapter 7 we discussed proactive problem solving and, specifically, eliminating calls. In this chapter we're going to look at what tools are available to resolve problems and eliminate calls and how we can make effective use of them.

Tools don't do much on their own. If you have a hammer, it won't do much if it's just lying there. It's when you pick it up and start banging nails back into fences (because, for example, horses believe the grass is greener on the other side of the fence and so must dismantle the fence) or building things that it becomes useful. It's the way we use tools that makes them valuable. Help Desk tools are no different. It's very sad to visit a Help Desk that has some of the most sophisticated Help Desk software available, only to find that no one seems to know how to use it properly and only 1 percent of it is actually being used, and badly at that. When I ask, "What happened?" I am inevitably told that there was money in the budget for purchasing software but not for training. People leave the tool lying there because they don't know how to use it. If you too have tools you're not trained on, get proactive about going after training. Chapter 10 will give you some ideas for creating a cost justification for training.

In This Chapter

I can't train you on the tools you're using at your Help Desk. What I can do is give you an overview of the tools that are available and a few ideas on using the tools you do have to eliminate calls and resolve problems more effectively. The topics I will cover are as follows:

- An overview of tools
- Getting the most out of the Internet
- Getting the most out of your Help Desk management system
- Getting the most out of knowledge bases
- Communication made easy
- Making customers self-sufficient

An Overview of Tools

Help Desk tools are becoming more and more integrated, and the range of available tools has increased dramatically over the past few years. You can buy a very simple, stand-alone Help Desk call-tracking system. You can also buy an enterprise system that might include a full-function Help Desk management system as well as such features as a knowledge base, asset management, Internet integration, remote control, change management, work order management, performance analysis, network management, and so on.

The tools I'm going to describe in this section include the basic Help Desk management system, asset management systems, knowledge bases, remote control software, and telephone-related technologies. I will leave the Internet for the next section. I will describe knowledge bases and tips for using the Help Desk management system more effectively in later sections as well. In Chapter 11, on marketing, I will also talk about how to set up an Internet or intranet Web site.

Help Desk Management Systems

At its most basic level, a Help Desk management system usually includes the following features:

- A function for capturing and logging call information
- A function for routing and/or escalating calls to the appropriate person or area
- A central database where all logged calls are stored
- Capabilities for reporting and querying against logged data

The system may also have plug-in units for other functions such as managing assets, forecasting and scheduling, knowledge base and expert systems, Internet access, and remote diagnostics. Help Desk management systems can also have connections to e-mail systems, automatic call distribution systems, automated attendants, interactive voice response (IVR) systems, pagers, and fax machines.

When a call is logged into a Help Desk management system, some form of customer identification, such as a user ID, is keyed in, and the system fills in as much information as it knows about that customer—for example, name, phone number, location, department, time of call, and hardware and software configurations. The system also assigns the call a unique identifier, often called a call ticket or incident number. The Help Desk practitioner can then enter the details of the call. These might include a description of the problem, the components involved, and an indication of its priority. A logged call contains all the details of the call, its status, and any progress that has been made on it. Notes are entered on the logged call by the person working on it. The progress made on calls can be monitored from call initiation to call close. Calls can be prioritized automatically based on several predefined variables.

Help Desk management systems allow practitioners to route calls to specific people or areas. The calls are actually routed into queues where practitioners can take ownership of a call by picking it off the queue; that practitioner's ID is automatically recorded against the call. The practitioner fills in notes on the logged call as he or she works on it to indicate what is being done and then enters a description of the resolution he or she provided when the call is completed. Completed calls are marked as closed, and some systems even automatically send an e-mail message to the customer to tell him or her that the call has been completed. Call management systems also typically have a function for escalating calls automatically. A predefined set of criteria is established, and when an outstanding call meets these criteria it is automatically escalated to the next level. The methods automatic escalation uses to notify the Help Desk practitioner can include messages, pagers, phones, alarms, or simply a flag against the call.

Logged calls, and all the notes surrounding them from beginning to end, are stored in a central database from which queries and reports can be run. Customers might be given access to this database so they can check on the progress of their calls. This database provides information that can point out problem areas or tell Help Desk managers if their Help Desks are working as they should. The data can be queried to find calls that have been outstanding for too long, calls that are receiving too high a priority, and calls that had to be reopened because they were not resolved properly the first time. The Help Desk management software can usually be set up so these kinds of queries run automatically and initiate some alarms or notifications if certain predefined situations are encountered. Managers can use reports and queries to get information, such as call volumes, by type of call or reason for call, and they can also use them to sort data by Help Desk practitioner. This data can tell the Help Desk manager if priorities are being used properly and are properly balanced, if procedures are correct and are being followed, and if there are practitioners who appear to be having trouble getting calls resolved. It can also alert the Help Desk to trends, such as problems with specific makes and models of hardware or recurring problems, and it can identify the customers or groups who need training in a specific product.

Asset Management Systems

An asset management system automatically tracks the hardware and software that is connected to a network. It collects extensive information, including details on applications and system software, hardware configurations, memory, hard drives, boards, hard drive utilization, setup options, and configuration files. The information collected is stored in an asset database. The system can remove illegal software and keep track of software usage to help ensure that adequate (but not excessive) licensing is maintained. Warranty information and current ownership information can also be maintained. Asset management systems may also include a financial component that does some book and tax value calculations against the database of asset information. Some asset software allows users to access online vendor catalogs to order new equipment or check prices. Even details on users' rights or spare parts can be tracked.

Reports from the asset database can be issued by node, customer, or type of equipment and can usually be heavily customized. Reports can be used to help solve network problems related to hardware and software configurations, plan upgrades, track warranties, and manage maintenance contracts and software licensing compliance. Asset management software can be set up to run at predetermined times and can inventory the assets of all or some part of a network at any one time. Some types have the ability to inventory portions of a PC each time the user of the PC logs onto the network. The system remembers where it was last time and continues from there. This means the customer does not have to wait while the software does a complete inventory. The software can also be used to give the same information on individual workstations that are not part of a network.

Knowledge Bases

A Help Desk knowledge base is a database of diagnostic information that helps the Help Desk practitioner solve problems. You query a knowledge base to find a solution to a problem you are having. A knowledge base may be a custom database built by the people using it for their specific environment. Prepackaged knowledge bases are also available for the most popular operating systems and software packages. Knowledge bases typically plug into a Help Desk management system so you can quickly check the knowledge base while you are on the phone with a customer to see if the solution you need is there.

Several approaches to problem solving use knowledge bases. Nick Straguzzi of Advantagekbs, Inc. offers a very interesting discussion of these various approaches in a white paper titled *Models, Cases, and Trees, Oh My . . . Which One to Use?* (it can be found at www.akbs.com). The paper defines four approaches to knowledge representation that I find very useful, so I will use the same (or a similar) categorization here: I will discuss text retrieval systems; decision tree systems; case-based systems; and systems based on symptoms, causes, and corrections (often called troubleshooting systems).

In text retrieval systems, a search engine is used against a database of information, which may include common problems and solutions, documentation, or procedures. Help Desks typically build their own problem/solution knowledge bases by adding a new problem and solution to the knowledge base when a successful resolution is found (if it is not already there). It is very easy to add or remove information from a text retrieval knowledge base. Numerous prepackaged knowledge bases are available for text retrieval systems. They provide solutions or technical information. Help Desks can plug them into their Help Desk management system and include them in their knowledge-base searches when solving a problem. The limitations of the text retrieval technology lie in the time required to perform searches. The performance of the Help Desk system can deteriorate rapidly as more text is added to the knowledge base. Speed of use naturally has a huge impact on how quickly Help Desk practitioners can solve customers' problems.

Decision trees work on the IF-THEN-ELSE principle. Gradually, through the process of elimination, this principle works down to the node of the tree that contains the problem. These systems are often implemented as hypertext documents. Presented with a multiple choice, the customers select a choice and are instantly taken to the next level in the tree. Decision trees are useful for common, well-understood problems in a fairly simple area of knowledge. If the area of knowledge becomes more complex, the tree becomes cumbersome and difficult to maintain. Design is also critical. If, for example, a key question has been missed or omitted, the poor Help Desk practitioner may end up with a solution that has nothing to do with the original problem.

Case-based problem solving involves matching the current problem with one that has occurred previously and for which the solution is known. In such a system, the practitioner typically enters the problem in free-form text, although the emergence of some standards for keywords would make this process easier. If the problem is not found, when its solution is known the problem is added to the database so the next time it occurs the solution will be there. The advantage to this type of expert system is that the practitioner does not need expert knowledge to use it. Fairly new practitioners can become productive using this system almost immediately. However, the practitioner must know enough to make the final decision on the solution by choosing between solutions and testing them.

The symptoms-causes-corrections approach focuses on identifying symptoms and causes. The system gathers symptoms, and when it has enough it suggests causes and tests them by asking questions. When it has gathered enough information, it suggests a specific solution. If the solution doesn't work, the system goes back to testing. This approach is not worthwhile for simple problems and does not work if the problem area is not well understood or the troubleshooting knowledge is not complete.

Remote Control Software

Remote diagnostic software products allow Help Desk practitioners to take over a customer's local or remote PC session from their own workstations so they can help resolve any problems the customer is experiencing. Help Desk practitioners can thus see exactly what the customer was doing at the time the problem occurred as well as what the customer's PC environment looks like, including configuration files. With remote diagnostic software, practitioners can watch the screens and operate the keyboards and mouses of any node on the local area network (LAN). The privacy concerns of Help Desk customers are addressed by including varying levels of security, such as requiring the end customer to allow entry.

Remote diagnostic tools are a time and resource saver and should be part of the tool kit of all but the smallest Help Desks. They give the Help Desk practitioner the ability to diagnose problems quickly and accurately from his or her own workstation without having to ask too many technical questions that the customer may not be able to answer or having to rely on the customer's version of what happened.

Telephone Technologies

The telephone technologies that are available for the Help Desk can manage phone traffic into the Help Desk, route calls, accept customer input that is entered via the telephone keypad, and interact with other technology based on the customer's input. Examples of these are automatic call distributors (ACD), automated attendants, and interactive voice response (IVR). The sophistication of these tools is increasing constantly, and their functionality can overlap to the point that one tool will often include another.

Computer Telephony Integration

Computer telephony integration (CTI) is the integration of computer and telephone technology to allow greater and easier communication between the two. An example of a CTI application is an interactive voice response (IVR) application that allows the customer to perform a computerized function, such as information retrieval or terminal reset, by pressing keys on the telephone keypad. With CTI, when a call comes into the Help Desk the telephone switch can identify the caller and pass the calling number to a caller ID database. Information from the database can be sent to the practitioner taking the call so when he or she picks up the phone the information for that caller is displayed on the practitioner's screen.

Other popular CTI applications include fax on demand and intelligent call routing, in which an auto attendant answers the call and routes it to a specific extension. Help Desk practitioners can also initiate faxes from their PCs. If a practitioner finds that explaining a solution is too complex or time-consuming, it may be easier for him or her to simply fax the information to the customer using a fax server on the LAN. CTI can also provide call conferencing; call transfer via computer, which is as simple as dragging names onto a phone icon; multiple message types (voice, fax, e-mail) in the same mailbox; and intelligent call forwarding, an application that can find you and forward your calls to you.

Automatic Call Distributor

At its simplest, an automatic call distributor (ACD) is a phone system, or software within a phone system, that manages the flow of calls coming into the Help Desk. An ACD typically routes calls on a first-come, first-served basis to the first available Help Desk practitioner. If all the practitioners are busy, callers are put into a queue and played a recorded message, such as "All Help Desk staff are currently busy; your call will be answered as soon as a Help Desk practitioner becomes available." The ACD monitors the queue and sends the caller who has been in the queue longest to the next available operator. Some ACDs allow the routing algorithm to be programmed so it can be customized to the requirements of each specific Help Desk and can vary according to traffic and time of day. The ACD monitors routed calls to make sure they are being distributed evenly among practitioners. More sophisticated ACDs ask customers to select from a list of options depending on the nature of their problem so their calls can be routed to the appropriate area. The ACD also provides statistics for calls, such as number of calls coming in, number of calls abandoned (unanswered), time on hold, and time per call. If the statistics provided by the ACD are not satisfactory—that is, they are not in the format required or do not give the required information—separate ACD reporting packages are available that will do the job. Some packages allow managers to pull ACD information up on their PCs and get the information in real time and in the desired form.

Automated Attendant

A basic automated attendant for Help Desks answers a customer's call with an automated greeting that offers a selection of options, then routes the call depending on the option the customer selects. These options usually include transferring the customer to a human operator. Automated attendants can also be much more sophisticated. They can anticipate a caller's needs—by determining where the caller is calling from, for example—and can be integrated with other technologies so networking and voice response features can be used to route calls and give out information. Such integration can give customers the ability to check on the status of their Help Desk calls by entering their call ticket numbers. It can also give them the ability to select an option and get prerecorded responses to frequently asked questions (FAQs). While customers are on hold, the automated attendant can play prerecorded messages. Some automated attendants can identify incoming phone numbers automatically so calls can be passed on to Help Desk practitioners who are servicing specific areas. Companies frequently use automated attendants to provide a reduced level of after-hours support.

Interactive Voice Response (IVR)

Interactive voice response (IVR) is a combination of hardware and software that allows a customer to interface with other technology, such as a mainframe, LAN, or fax machine, to get information or to perform a specific function. The customer typically makes a selection from a menu of options and then enters any required data via the telephone keypad. The IVR takes that data and acts upon it depending on the function requested. An IVR can fax selected documents back to the caller, provide prerecorded information on a specific topic, give the status of a job, reset terminals and printers, and reboot LAN file servers. The IVR can also be set up to interface with a call management system to allow customers to report problems, make requests, check on problems, or request status.

Getting the Most out of the Internet

The Internet offers incredible opportunities for the proactive Help Desk practitioner who is looking to reduce calls. This section will discuss the opportunities and challenges offered by the Internet as well as some ways you can use it proactively to improve your Help Desk's performance.

A Net of Opportunity

The Internet gives you access to a huge knowledge base of support information and a wealth of industry reference material and product information from around the world. This information can be referenced any time, anywhere. Vendor sites offer self-help information for specific products, and numerous technical sites offer suggestions, problem resolutions, and answers to frequently asked questions (FAQs). Through the Internet, you can talk to your counterparts in organizations all over the world. Discussion groups and news servers make it much easier to find someone who is in a similar situation or using a specific product. This means that everyone now has the opportunity to exchange ideas and experiences—not only those few fortunate enough to be able to attend conferences.

The Internet gives you the ability to transmit and download new software, updates, and fixes electronically. If a problem requires a software update or patch, they can be downloaded from the vendor's site almost instantly. Similarly, if a remote customer requires an update or patch, it can be transmitted quickly via the Internet. The Internet also gives your customers online access to self-help options and a central repository of information. Moreover, the World Wide Web is a great publishing tool. You can now make it easy for customers to access up-to-date standards, policies, procedures (e.g., steps to go through to order a PC), hints and tips, and lists of FAQs. Organizations such as educational institutions find this feature a tremendous help in their ability to provide a widely distributed and large customer base (e.g., students and faculty) with the information and help it needs to make the best use of technology.

The Internet facilitates two-way communication with your customers. Customer surveys or other feedback mechanisms can be put on a Web page, and when customers fill in the information and transmit it to you you can gather and analyze their input. Surveys can be included on any Web page to gather valuable customer feedback. Many Help Desk management systems are now Web-enabled to allow users to access them over the Internet. Remote Help Desk practitioners, working virtually anywhere, can access the software to log, track, assign, or escalate calls. Customers can also access call databases via the Internet to check on the status of their calls. Finally, using the Internet, customers and Help Desk practitioners can access knowledge bases to resolve problems. All these opportunities translate into reduced calls to the Help Desk, improved service for the calls that do come in, and more information for improvement initiatives.

A Net of Challenges

The Internet, however, not only offers the proactive Help Desk practitioner opportunities; it presents new challenges that must be addressed in order to take full advantage of this new medium. For example, anything that travels across the Internet is in danger of being tampered with. Anything you make available via the Internet must therefore have a security component. In fact, your organization in all likelihood probably already uses firewalls and encryption.

Information taken from the Internet is strictly "use at your own risk." Just as you can't believe everything you read on paper, you can't believe everything you read on the Internet. Opinions are often hard to differentiate from facts. Finding what you want on the Internet can also be difficult. The information is there but getting at it can be frustrating. No nice indexing system (as in a library) exists, at least not yet. Moreover, it is so easy to download software from the Internet that people often forget that some of it may not be legal, either because it may be a pirated or evaluation copy or because it may be shareware that needs to be paid for. As a result, Help Desks that handle software licensing have more to do now than ever before.

Viruses are also getting cleverer and harder to detect, some even hiding in macros. Because the Internet makes it easy for people to download software and exchange documents, they are doing so in incredible numbers, and the risk of exposure to viruses rises with each downloaded file. Just because a file is from a reliable source does not mean it does not have a virus. Extra precautions must be taken to prevent Internet users from accidentally accepting a virus.

Because the Internet is another technology component that must be supported, it has added a level of complexity to the Help Desk environment. It has in turn spawned new software that also needs to be supported, and the quality of service of the Internet service provider (ISP) represents a new source of worry. Help Desks that support a Web site are finding that they have a whole new set of customer service issues to deal with, many of them involving unexpected demand. For example, if you offer customers access to your Help Desk via the Web and you are suddenly inundated with e-mail—all requesting immediate responses—many of your customers are going to be disappointed.

Getting Proactive with the Internet

We've looked at the opportunities and challenges of the Internet. Now we're going to look at how to take advantage of those opportunities, overcome the challenges, and use the Internet to be proactive—to eliminate calls to the Help Desk.

If You Support Internet Use

Your customers use the Internet. As with every other product you support, it is in your best interests to make sure they know how to use the Internet, are aware of the unique dangers that surround it, and observe any organizational rules that govern its use. Your challenges are to ensure that customers have the information they need to make the best use of the Internet and to make them aware of the potential for security infringements, virus contamination, and copyright violations. You also need to try to reduce the number of calls generated by customers' use of the Internet. What can you do?

First, create standards or champion the process of standards creation for Web browser software. The more standardized the Internet software your customers use, the easier they will be to support. Treat Internet software as you would any other. Track its use, keep it up to date, and offer training for it. If you can't offer training, outsource it to someone who can or let people know where to get it. You may be able to purchase online, computer-based tutorials for the topics you want to train in. Your customers could even download these from your Web site.

Second, help your customers to help themselves. Start one or more Internet focus groups so customers can share information about using the Internet with their colleagues. Offer them self-help options via your Help Desk's Internet/intranet Web site. This site could include FAQs, how-to articles or tutorials, and links to sites your customers would find useful. Chapter 11 contains useful information on how to set such a site up. Third, make your customers aware of your policies for security and Internet use, your procedures for virus checking, the dangers of data exposure, and potential copyright infringements. You could put all this information on your Web site.

If You Support an Internet Web Site

Suppose your organization has a Web site, your Help Desk supports some of the products that your company offers through the site, and your customers contact you via e-mail. The challenges to you include estimating the number of problems/requests you are going to have to answer, meeting any support response times you have marketed, and keeping up with the changing business. You want to make sure that customer expectations are in line with your service; otherwise, you may end up with irate customers, and your organization's business may suffer. The following paragraphs discuss some things you can do to manage these challenges.

If possible, set up an automated reply for each customer request that lets customers know you got their request and gives them an estimated response time. This will really help keep customer expectations in line with reality. Of course, your response had better be within the time promised on the automated reply message or you will be back to having irate customers. Offer as much self-help as possible. Provide whatever support you can. Offer valuable links to other Web sites (if you don't have the answer online, maybe someone else does), FAQs, hints and tips, procedures for specific tasks, even access to a knowledge base if this makes sense. You might even offer a library of tutorials that customers can download. The tutorials can be text only; text and voice; or text, voice, and video, depending on what kind of equipment you and your customers have. You can develop simple how-to tutorials yourself or purchase prepackaged ones.

Whenever your organization wants to add a new service to its Web site, get involved. If the service involves the Help Desk, suggest that you pilot it first to see what volume of responses you can expect. You can offer the service to a select group of customers by giving them a special password and/or customer ID that they need to enter to gain access. They would then simply click on some kind of pilot service icon and be prompted for their password and/or ID. This approach would give you a good idea of the response you can expect so your Help Desk can prepare for it before releasing the service to all your customers.

Do not promise what you cannot deliver. Take time to research the customer traffic you should expect and the load you can handle so you do not set unrealistic customer expectations. If you have a heavy workload, let any response times you promise reflect that workload. A poor reputation, once earned, is hard to get rid of. (See the section "Avoiding Common Support Mistakes" in Chapter 4.) Make sure you are trained in all the products you support. Don't let training lapse because of time constraints.

If You Support an Internet Service Provider

You are the Help Desk for an Internet service provider (ISP), and your customers are all external. If this describes your Help Desk, you face some pretty significant challenges. First, as an ISP your organization is always looking to increase the number of subscribers. Chances are you're going to hear from a large percentage of them. Volume of calls is therefore going to be a challenge. Second, some of your customers will know nothing beyond how to turn a PC on, while others will know a lot more about the technology than you do. You must service both extremes. Chapters 5 and 6 described ways to improve communication and can help you deal with these challenges.

Third, when customers call, their problems may not be with their access setup or software. It could be a problem with their modem or modem setup, it could be a problem with their PCs' configuration, it could be a compatibility issue—it could be just about anything. As a result, you are sometimes going to be left trying to solve a problem that really belongs to another vendor. Fourth, an ISP's customers are external, and you therefore have absolutely no control over what kind of computers they have and what software, such as Web browsers, they are using. Your customers have no single standard.

The best thing you can do to manage these challenges and keep your customers satisfied is to eliminate, as much as possible, the need for them to call you. First, give your customers as many self-help options as possible. Your customer base is probably growing, so you want to eliminate as many calls as you can. Offer a support area for customers on your organization's Web site. This area could include information such as how and what to do to get Internet access up and running, FAQs about Internet access, links to sites with information your customers are interested in, and instructions or procedures for performing tasks such as downloading software, setting up a Web site, registering a domain name, and so on. There are many good examples of these on the Internet. (For example, try Interlog's Web site at www.interlog.com.)

Second, offer training courses. If your Help Desk doesn't want to be in the training business, outsource this function or arrange some kind of deal with training providers that already have the kind of training you need. You may be able to have them offer your customers training at special prices. The more your customers know how to do, the less they will need to call you. Third, offer an electronic newsletter that lets customers know about new services. Don't expect them to keep checking your Web site. E-mail it to them. Explain any service interruptions. If they think you understand what caused an interruption, they will be more confident that it won't happen again. If they know about upcoming service interruptions they may not call about them when they do happen.

Fourth, don't skimp on training for yourself. Keep up to date on all new Web technology. Fifth, don't promise what you cannot deliver. If you've just had an unexpected influx of customers (e.g., another provider has gone out of business and you have received some of their abandoned customers) adjust your promised response times accordingly. Keep a close eye on the business, use your early warning systems (EWSs) so that, wherever possible, you do not make promises that you just cannot keep. Finally, be on constant lookout for ideas. Check out your competitors' Web sites to see what they're offering their customers, especially those services that will reduce calls. You may not have control over implementing those services, but as a proactive Help Desk practitioner you can always suggest them to your manager and start the ball rolling.

If You Use the Internet as a Knowledge Base

Suppose your Help Desk uses the Internet as a knowledge base to search for problem resolutions and information on new products. In this case, your challenges include the sheer volume of information available (i.e., how do you find what you need?) and discerning between fact and opinion. This section provides some tips to help you make the best use of the information available on the Internet.

First, check out the Web sites of the vendors who make the products you use. Most vendors have online knowledge bases that are available for searching. For example, two sites that contain a large network of technical magazines and information you might find useful are www.pcweek.com and www.zdnet.com. Second, register with discussion groups that deal with topics of interest to you. If the volume of mail they generate proves to be too great, look for other ways to get the information, for example, news servers, digest versions of the newsgroup discussions, or searchable archives.

Third, register with Web sites that provide information of interest to you so you get regular updates or newsletters. Fourth, gather together all the sites you find most useful and make them part of your team's reference site (see Figure 8.1) so they are retained and are easily accessible. You can organize them in any way that makes sense to you. You can even set your browser software to make your reference site your home page so you start off each Internet session with your most useful links. Formalize and rotate the responsibility for gathering information and updating this site. Fifth, check out the "new and interesting sites" that are listed in the various online and paper computer journals you read. Sixth, make sure you are well trained in using the Internet, specifically, how to use search engines, what common search tools are available, and

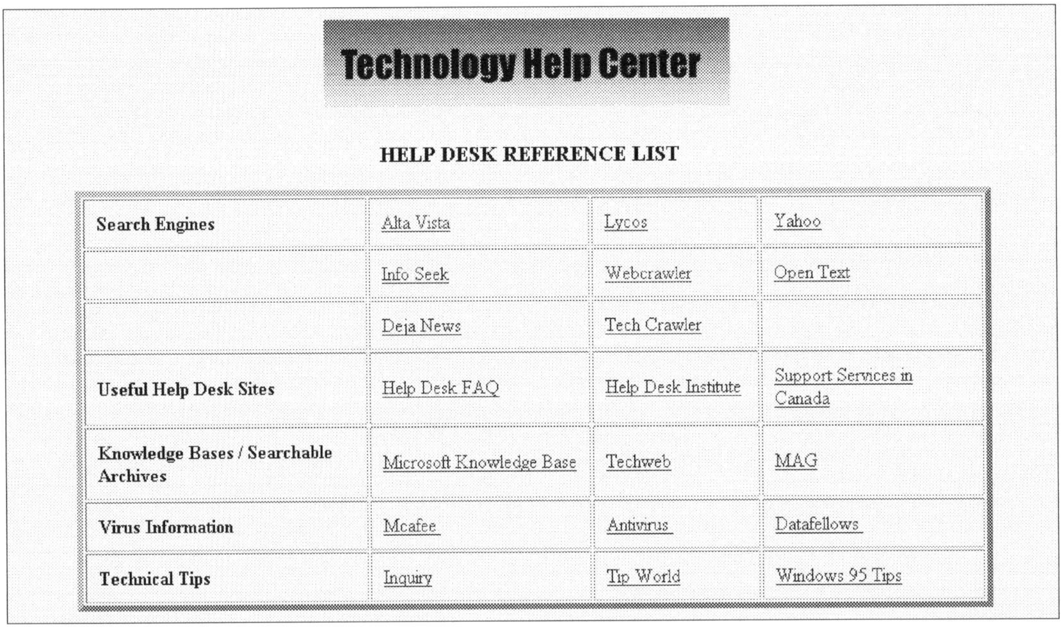

Technology Help Center

HELP DESK REFERENCE LIST

Search Engines	Alta Vista	Lycos	Yahoo
	Info Seek	Webcrawler	Open Text
	Deja News	Tech Crawler	
Useful Help Desk Sites	Help Desk FAQ	Help Desk Institute	Support Services in Canada
Knowledge Bases / Searchable Archives	Microsoft Knowledge Base	Techweb	MAG
Virus Information	Mcafee	Antivirus	Datafellows
Technical Tips	Inquiry	Tip World	Windows 95 Tips

Figure 8.1   A team reference site.

what they are capable of (strengths and weaknesses). This will be a small investment of time with a large payback.

Seventh, set up guidelines for using information based on how credible it is. Don't completely discount sources that are opinion-based only; you might get some great ideas from these, but make sure your favorite sources are marked as either factual or opinion. Finally, do what you can to help your customers make the best use of the information available on the Internet. Create a list of useful Web sites (based on input from customers) and put it on your Help Desk's Web site. Encourage customers to contribute to this list. Offer short tutorials on how to search for information, what search engines are available, where they are, and how to use them. This might be as simple as providing downloadable documents that customers can access from your Web site.

If You Use the Internet as a Distribution Tool

Your Help Desk regularly receives and/or sends software updates. You may download information or software from other sites to use on the Help Desk, and you may pass information on to customers. This instant accessibility is a big plus for your Help Desk, making it possible to reduce the time it takes to resolve problems. Your customers may also have this capability. Your challenges in this environment include the security of confidential data, the licensing of downloaded software, copyright infringement, and viruses. To ensure that you are getting/sending what you need without getting into trouble with bugs, hackers, or the law, you may want to act on the following suggestions.

First, understand the security measures and infrastructures your organization has in place for information coming in from the Internet. Follow all rules and procedures. Second, set up policies on your Help Desk so that virus checkers are used consistently. Make them easy to access. You might even set up a download area and have the virus checker run off of that automatically. Third, keep virus checking software up to date. Some vendors of virus detecting software allow you to register at their Web sites to be notified automatically of new virus information and any software updates that are available. Check to see if the vendor of the software you are using offers any of these services.

Fourth, set up policies regarding licensing. Treat downloaded software as purchased software. If you need to buy a license, do so. You should be setting an example for your customers, and getting caught with licensing violations is embarrassing for the whole company. Fifth, don't indiscriminately publish information you find on the Internet. Clear any copyright concerns with your legal department. Rather than publish the document yourself, give its location on the Web instead or simply include a link to the location if you are publishing online.

Do what you can to make sure your customers follow these precautions, or champion an initiative to ensure that they do. If your customers have the ability to download information and software from the Internet, get and use asset management software if you don't already have it. It will find (and eliminate, if you wish) occurrences of illegal software. If you need to cost justify this software, see Chapter 10. Work with your organization to set up policies for your customers regarding downloading information from the Internet, or encourage your manager to do so. You don't want to take potential benefits away from customers but neither do you want to expose your organization to legal action resulting from unlicensed software, copyright infringement, or data destruction caused by viruses. Work with your organization (or encourage your manager to do so) to set up policies governing the kinds of information that can be shared with other organizations and the kinds that are confidential and need to be kept within the organization. If your customers have Internet access, they can share documents or information with anyone else on the Internet. They need to be made aware of what they can and cannot share so they don't inadvertently give away confidential data.

Publish a "getting started on the Internet" package for your customers. Include it on your Help Desk's Web site. The package could include security policies; rules for downloading information; and information on viruses and virus checking, licensing issues, data confidentiality, and so on.

If You Use the Internet to Access Help Desk Management Software

Several Help Desk management software vendors offer options that will allow you to access that software via the Internet. This means you can access that software from virtually anywhere. If you are a remote Help

Desk practitioner who travels from site to site, you can now update your call information as you go and make use of all the tools the Help Desk management system offers. Customers can also access this software to log their own calls, to check on calls, and to use the knowledge base to try to solve their own problems. This means fewer calls to the Help Desk. The challenges to your Help Desk of allowing Internet access to your Help Desk management software stem from the fact that you are giving customers access to your Help Desk's management information. You need to do what you can to help them make the best use of it.

First, ensure customers know how to use the software, especially the knowledge base. Have them attend training classes or send them simple tutorials via e-mail. Second, ensure that your customers understand security restrictions, password usage, and the potential for exposure of the information they're passing on. Third, set up some kind of automated response to acknowledge your receipt of a log or an e-mail from the customer. The customer will then be sure the information was received. The more your customers understand how to use the system, the more confidence they will have in it and the better use they will make of it—which means fewer calls for you.

If You Use the Internet as a Publishing Tool

Information publishing is probably the biggest benefit of the Internet. People simply become more productive when they know more about what they're doing. Internet publishing can also be used for your Help Desk's marketing efforts, which involve communicating your Help Desk's performance, teaching customers about their technology, and keeping them informed about what is going on in the technological environment. The challenges you face in publishing information are understanding what customers need, organizing information, and keeping that information current. The following suggestions will help you meet these challenges.

First, create a Help Desk Web site as a central source for information. It doesn't matter where on the Web the information is actually stored; you can simply include a link to it. Chapter 11 contains a section on creating a Web site. Second, for information such as hints and tips or FAQs, have a "New this month" section (or whatever time period makes sense for you) so people can see what you have added most recently. Third, organize information in the ways people naturally access it. Go to your customers to get this information. For example, if you are building a FAQs list, don't just build one huge FAQ; break it down by subject. Analyze the distribution of your calls, or ask your customers to learn what these subjects should be.

Fourth, if you need to publish a very important and/or time-sensitive piece of information, don't just wait for people to come to your site and read it. Send them an e-mail letting them know an important update has been made. Fifth, wherever you have control over the content of information, be concise. Just because the information is online doesn't mean that people should be forced to wade through pages of garbage or fluff just to get to the key information. Sixth, keep the information up to date. Don't leave the responsibility for updating open (for example, "Update the FAQ whenever you run across an interesting question") or it won't happen. No one will have time. Work the responsibility out with your fellow Help Desk practitioners so you each take a turn. Have the assigned person collect data from Help Desk statistics, from customers, and from other practitioners. They should then organize it and perform the Web site update.

The Web is full of examples of Help Desks that have published information. A good starting point is the Help Desk FAQ, which is a source for Help Desk resources and references. It's at www.duke.edu/~pverghis/hdeskfaq.htm.

Getting the Most out of Your Help Desk Management System

To make improvements on the Help Desk so you can eliminate calls, you first need to understand where you need to improve. You need to evaluate yourself and analyze trends and statistics. You also need to be able to cost justify improvements. Perhaps your Help Desk needs some extra temporary help while you focus on eliminating calls. You aren't going to get funding for that help unless you can prove you need it. Chapter 10 discusses cost justification at some length. To do that, you need the data that goes into your Help Desk Management system. Without it, you simply don't know where you are.

Why am I telling you all this? Because you are the person who enters call data into your Help Desk management system. You are the person who determines the quality of the data—the statistics—that come out of it. The more accurate that data is the more useful it will be to you in eliminating calls and in justifying improvements. The first thing you can do to ensure you are getting the most out of your Help Desk management system, whether it is very simple or very complex, is to log every call you get. "Even the really simple ones that take two seconds to resolve?" I hear you ask. Yes, even the really simple ones that take two seconds to resolve. "But we get so many of them!" That's more reason for you to log them. You get so many of them, but you have no record that they even happened. If someone looked at your call statistics they might conclude you have free time. Similarly, if the number of two-second calls starts to increase for some reason, you won't know. Chapter 10, which deals with cost justification, offers examples that illustrate why you should log everything.

Second, log quality information. Make sure the information you enter is correct and complete. You can assign those short, two-second calls a specific call type so they can be filled in automatically. When you enter a solution, write it as if you were using it to try to resolve a problem. "Done" isn't going to be much help to you as a solution, yet that seems to be a favorite solution to use when logging a call. If you have any call type codes, use them, and make sure you are accurate. Being able to see trends in specific types of calls is very valuable when you are trying to eliminate calls or run a Help Desk.

Third, make sure you know how to use your Help Desk management system. Campaign for proper training. Understand what the system is capable of and know how to use all of its functions. If you have to pass a call on to someone and you don't do it properly, that call is going to take much longer than necessary to get resolved. The profitability of the business will be negatively impacted. Some Help Desk management systems have very useful communications tools such as notepads or whiteboards where you can put important notices that the rest of your team will want to know about, for example, "Suspected virus found on the fourth floor." If your Help Desk is small you probably won't need such a feature, but if it's larger, or distributed, such a feature could be very useful—but only if you know it's there and actually use it.

Fourth, when you see something that could be done better, do something about it. It's up to you, as a proactive Help Desk practitioner, to identify areas for improvement in the processes and tools of the system. It's not up to your manager; he or she probably isn't logging calls with the tool in question and would not necessarily see what you do with it. You might notice, for example, that the queues you put calls into for second-level support have not been set up quite right. If you do nothing about the problem you are making life difficult for second-level support and increasing the chance that calls will get lost. This is not the way to eliminate calls. You need to do something to get the queues set up properly so there will be less chance that customers will have to call back about misplaced calls.

Finally, constantly work to make the data as accurate as possible. When you bring customer data up on your Help Desk management screen and you notice that something doesn't look quite right, check it out and fix it. If you see that someone is filling in fields incorrectly, address the problem and get the data cleaned up.

Getting the Most out of Knowledge Bases

Knowledge bases can be bought or built. A Help Desk will typically buy some knowledge bases and build others. There are numerous knowledge bases available for the most common operating systems and applications, and these can provide an extremely valuable reference for problem resolution at your Help Desk. However, there are situations in your environment that may not be covered by prepackaged knowledge bases. You may want to build a knowledge base to cover those situations. The following section looks at how to get the most out of a knowledge base you are building.

What Goes in Comes Out

Knowledge bases are only as good as the information that goes into them. Consider the following scenario. You're searching your knowledge base for a solution to a problem, and you're in a hurry. All of a sudden you find a match. You've found the exact problem your customer is experiencing. With great excitement you open the record, and as suddenly as it came your excitement dissipates. The solution reads, "Same fix as usual." Unfortunately, you don't know what that is. You can't help your customer; you can't solve the customer's problem at point of call.

The solutions you log every day are probably going to be used in knowledge bases. You may have a sophisticated knowledge authoring system that is actually maintained by someone who goes through the Help Desk's problem logs, or you may have a system that you update yourself as you work. In the former case, there is someone checking the usefulness of the solutions Help Desk practitioners key in. That person will probably reformat the solutions into a standard format, with standard keywords, to maximize their value. In the latter case, you may be the only one involved in getting that solution into the knowledge base. Whatever you put in is what will come out for other practitioners. You went through the exercise of determining what the solution is. Why not maximize the value of your work by making it available to everyone? Why not help increase the number of calls that can be resolved at point of call?

Figure 8.2 illustrates how a simple knowledge base is used and updated. For example, say a call comes in. If you can resolve it, you do so and update the knowledge base with the solution. If the solution is already in the knowledge base you may want to check it for accuracy and update it as necessary. If you don't know the solution, you go to the knowledge base. If the solution is there (and if it isn't "Same fix as usual" or "Done") you use it to resolve the problem, still at point of call. If you find that the solution needs updating, then you do so. If you can't find the solution in the knowledge base, you pass it on to the next level of support. That level will resolve the problem and update the knowledge base as necessary. The next time a call comes in for that problem, the person who takes the call will be able to resolve it by going to the knowledge base.

That is how things should work. Unfortunately, the process breaks down when the participants don't understand, or have not bought into, their role in using and maintaining the knowledge base. If Help Desk practitioners are not updating the knowledge base with useful solutions—the process breaks down. If Help Desk practitioners are not going to the knowledge base for help—the process breaks down. And if sec-

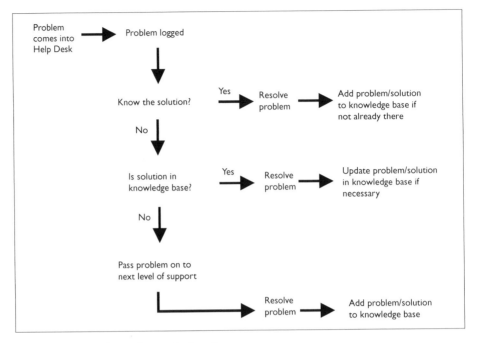

Figure 8.2   Using a knowledge base.

ond-level support has not bought into the knowledge base process and is not updating it with their solutions—the process breaks down. To make knowledge bases work, some processes simply need to be put into place.

Making Your Knowledge Base Work

First, make sure you and your colleagues understand how the knowledge base is set up and how it should be updated. Typically, you need to agree on a set of keywords that will help you classify problems and make searching easier. Once you have decided what the keywords are, your whole team needs to play the role of partner and use them. If even one practitioner decides not to use the keywords as they were set up, the process is in danger of failing. The solutions that person enters are less useful than they could be. People who search for those solutions are discouraged by what they find and are less likely to go to the knowledge base for help the next time. Updating a knowledge base according to standards should be a responsibility you are measured on. Encourage your manager to make this responsibility part of the performance appraisal process. Many Help Desk teams are doing peer appraisals, in which each team member is appraised by all the others. Team appraisals are an excellent time to bring up opportunities for improving the quality of knowledge base updates.

Second, make sure the solutions you enter are detailed enough to be implemented by another person who may not know the solution you found. In Figure 8.2, we saw that checking solutions is an ongoing process. Every time a solution is used, it should be checked for accuracy. Not only do you have to put in a good solution for your own problem, you also have to check solutions that other people have entered and change them as required to make them more effective. In Chapter 4 we talked about setting up procedures. Setting up procedures for entering and checking solutions may be a good idea for your Help Desk to consider. In fact, you might consider setting up a set of procedures that follow the flow shown in Figure 8.2.

Third, work on getting other levels of support to update and use the knowledge base according to your standards and procedures. In Chapter 3 we talked about relationships between levels of support and commitment to ongoing improvement. Getting another level of support to use your knowledge base tool is a good place to begin your improvement efforts. Work with your manager to get other support levels to buy in. You may need to do some selling, and a good selling point you can use is that the more solutions other support levels put into the knowledge base, the fewer problems you'll have to pass onto them. You may want to put a service level agreement (SLA) into place.

Fourth, you need to ensure that everyone using the knowledge base, both within and outside the Help Desk, knows how to use it to update and access the knowledge. If you could get or create a small online tutorial (it could just be a single document) or a Help file, people could access it any time they needed a reminder. On it, you could include your procedures and standards for the whole process of updating and using the knowledge base. Finally, if you notice that some part of the process is not working, do something about it. Don't just give up. I'm asking you to be proactive, to play the role of partner and problem eliminator. You can either let someone (i.e., your manager) know, address the team as a whole, or address the individual. How you handle this will depend on your environment. Self-managing teams tend to have forums for discussing issues such as a breakdown in processes. Other environments are less open and require a more formal approach.

Simpler Cases

If your environment is fortunate enough to have people dedicated to checking and/or entering the knowledge for you, you may not have to worry about some of the points we've been talking about here. However, you will still have to discipline yourself to make sure that you use the knowledge base and that you let people know when the knowledge is wrong. If you are using only prepackaged knowledge bases, then you still have some work to do. Spend some time learning what is in the knowledge base and how its search engines work. Some search engines are very sophisticated and will take into account factors such as how many times a solution has been used previously. The more you know about the knowledge bases, the more effectively you can use them.

Communication Made Easy

In Chapters 5 and 6 we talked extensively about communication. There, we dealt with in-person and over-the-phone communication. Help desk tools offer us two other means of communication: voice mail and e-mail.

Voice Mail

Voice mail can be an excellent communication tool, or it can be an annoyance. Your customers will love it or hate it depending on how you use it. If your customers leave voice mail messages for the Help Desk, encourage them to describe as much of the problem as possible so you can perhaps even resolve it before calling them back. You can use any of your existing marketing vehicles to try to get this idea across to your customers (see Chapter 11). When you call a customer back who did not leave a detailed message, encourage him or her to leave a more detailed message next time.

When you leave voice messages, make sure you identify yourself, leave a phone number, and give as much information as possible. Do what you can to give the customer enough information so he or she does not have to call the Help Desk back. Encourage your Help Desk to set up a time limit for returning voice mail messages, and then stick to it. Market that time to your customers so when they leave a voice mail message they will know when to expect a return call. You might want to state that time in your Help Desk's phone system message so customers will hear it before they leave a message. For example, "We will return your call within 30 minutes. . . . "

If you leave voice mail messages for someone, second-level support for example, do not then drop responsibility for that communication. As we saw in Chapters 5 and 6, your roles as communicator and problem eliminator dictate that you take responsibility for the communication until it is resolved. If you don't hear back within a certain time, call again. Be persistent. Other people may not use voice mail as effectively as you do. Voice mail can be helpful in communicating interruptions in service when you cannot use e-mail. You can set up voice mail lists that consist of a few individuals from each customer department who then have the responsibility to pass the information on to their departments. When you have a problem you just need to send the one message to everyone on the list.

E-mail

For the most part, the same usage guidelines apply to e-mail as to voice mail. If your customers are sending you problems via e-mail, encourage them to give you as much information as possible. Market the information that must be included in such e-mail on your Web site or in any other marketing vehicles you use (see Chapter 11). If customers are sending you e-mail through your Web site, set the e-mail up as a form and ask for specific information that will help you resolve their problems.

Establish and then market a time limit for returning customers' e-mail messages. If customers know when to expect a response they won't phone you in the meantime. Make sure you meet the time limit you advertise or customers will stop using e-mail. When you send someone an e-mail and don't hear back from them, try another means of communication. Call them, for example. Retain responsibility for the communication.

When you compose an e-mail message, remember that you are creating a permanent record. You can't take the words in an e-mail message back. Most of the communication ideas presented in Chapters 5 and 6 apply to e-mail as well. The rules that govern getting your message across effectively in person or over the phone also apply to written communications. If you have problems communicating in writing, do something about it. Take a business writing seminar. The more effective you are as a communicator, the more effective you can be as a problem eliminator.

Making Customers Self-Sufficient

The more customers can do for themselves, the less you, the very busy Help Desk practitioner, have to do for them. Some Help Desk management systems include interactive, computer-based tutorials that can be sent to customers via e-mail when a Help Desk practitioner detects a potential need for training in a call. Customers can view the tutorials at their own pace and keep them for future reference. Interactive, computer-based tutorials are available for many popular software products in bundled packages and can also be purchased individually. The possibilities for incorporating these tutorials into self-help applications are endless. For example, training could be incorporated into knowledge bases by including an option that lets customers download a tutorial on a specific topic they would like more information on.

You can make call databases accessible to customers so they can find out the status of their problems. You can also set up FAQs for customers on your Internet or intranet site or give them access to your knowledge base so they can do some of their own problem solving. You can set up interactive voice response (IVR) systems to let customers perform common requests like resetting terminals, resetting passwords, or initiating fax-backs of problem resolutions or specific procedures. If your organization does not have an IVR you may be able to justify one if you have enough requests that could be automated. Chapter 10 will help you with your cost justification strategy.

Checklist

In this chapter we looked at tools that can help us be proactive and eliminate calls. We also looked at specific suggestions for making better use of the Internet, of your Help Desk management systems, and of your knowledge bases. Use the following list to check that your knowledge and use of tools is effective:

✓ Do I understand what tools are available to facilitate problem elimination on the Help Desk?

✓ Do I understand how to make the best use of the Internet on my Help Desk?

✓ Am I logging every call?

✓ Is the quality of the information I am logging high?

✓ Do I understand all the functions my Help Desk management system is capable of?

✓ Am I constantly evaluating the use of the Help Desk management system and suggesting improvements when I see something that could be done better?

✓ Does my team have standards for categorizing the information we put into our knowledge base?

✓ Are the solutions I enter into the knowledge base thorough and easy to understand?

✓ Do other support levels use our knowledge base effectively?

✓ Do I understand how to use our knowledge base effectively?

✓ When I see something that needs correcting on the knowledge base do I correct it?

✓ When I see someone using the knowledge base incorrectly do I do something about it?

✓ Do I understand what information is contained in the prepackaged knowledge bases my Help Desk uses?

✓ Do I know how to use the prepackaged knowledge bases? Do I understand how the search engine works?

✓ Do I encourage customers to leave as much information as possible in their voice mail messages to the Help Desk?

✓ Do I leave my customers good information in my voice mail messages?

✓ Do I return all my voice mail messages within the promised time?

✓ Do I take responsibility for the communication even when customers don't respond to my voice mail messages?

✓ Do I encourage customers to provide complete information in their e-mail messages?

✓ Do I provide complete information in my e-mail messages to customers? Do I prevent unnecessary calls to the Help Desk?

✓ Do I answer all my e-mail messages within the promised time?

✓ Do I take responsibility for the communication even when my e-mail is not answered?

✓ Do I know how to make my customers more self-sufficient?

✓ Am I doing anything to make my customers more self-sufficient?

Understanding the Business of Help Desks

Everything You Need to Know about Performance

When it comes to measuring your Help Desk's performance, perhaps you are thinking, "Worrying about Help Desk performance is a manager's job." Not so: Worrying about Help Desk performance is *your* job. As a proactive Help Desk practitioner you are looking to eliminate calls and make improvements. Analyzing how your Help Desk is performing will tell you where you need to improve. The more you understand what defines good performance, the easier it will be for you to identify which improvements are the most critical to the business.

In This Chapter

In this chapter we're going to look at each of the components of performance, how you measure them, and what you should look for when evaluating your results. The topics we will cover include the following:

- Components of performance
- A moving picture
- Different perspectives
- Why is everyone so interested in ROI?
- Measuring how effectively you handle calls
- How proactive are you?

Components of Performance

If you want to get a true picture of performance you need to consider all three of its components:

Return on investment (ROI). This is a measure of the dollar value of what the Help Desk is delivering to the business balanced against the dollar value of what the Help Desk is costing the business.

Effectiveness of call load management. This describes how well the Help Desk is handling its call load within the changing environment it is supporting.

Level of proaction. This looks at the use of improvement and planning initiatives and their effectiveness in meeting current and future business demands.

These three items are not the same. A Help Desk may be doing a great job managing call load, but if a Help Desk outsourcing company can do the same job for less money, the Help Desk does not have a good ROI. A Help Desk may be doing a good job managing call load and may be doing it more cheaply than an outsourcer and yet still be doing almost nothing to plan for the future and make sure it is prepared to handle changes in the organization it supports. This Help Desk is heading for a fall. If things are left as they are, all three aspects of performance will be negatively impacted.

A Moving Picture

Performance is more than a snapshot of the how the Help Desk is doing now. A snapshot tells you only where the Help Desk is at one instant in time. It does not tell you where a Help Desk is going or where it is coming from. Look at Figures 9.1 and 9.2. As you can see, they are dramatically different. Yet if we just looked at just one point in time, Month 3, we would not see this difference; the downward spiral that is taking place in Figure 9.1 would be invisible to us. But when we look at the moving picture, that is, performance over a three-month period, we see the truth. We see the dramatic negative trend that the Help Desk in Figure 9.1 is following. Similarly, when we look at performance over time we see the dramatic improvement of the Help Desk in Figure 9.2. The snapshot of performance at Month 3 told us none of this.

An even more dramatic illustration of the need to look at performance over time is the Help Desk that is condemned for poor perfor-

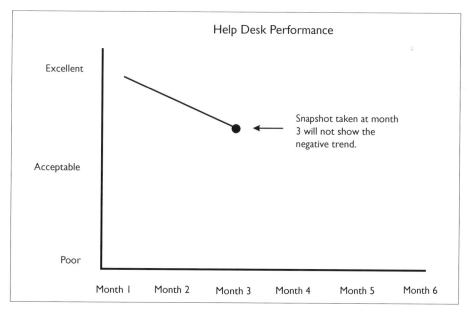

Figure 9.1   A performance snapshot hides this downward spiral.

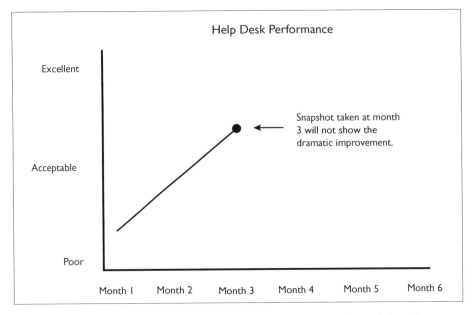

Figure 9.2   A performance snapshot can hide dramatic positive changes.

mance on the basis of its mediocre performance at one point in time. In Figure 9.3, if we look only at the performance at Month 3 we see a Help Desk that is dying because its average performance is just acceptable, at best. But when we look at its performance over three months, however, we see a Help Desk that is just coming alive and is trending upward toward excellence. Performance is a moving picture and must always be considered in terms of change, trends, and comparisons with previous data. We must look at where performance is coming from and where it is headed.

Different Perspectives

Performance also means different things to different people. For example, if you ask your customers how your Help Desk is performing they might think you're doing a fabulous job. You're answering all of their word processing questions quickly and correctly. They've started calling

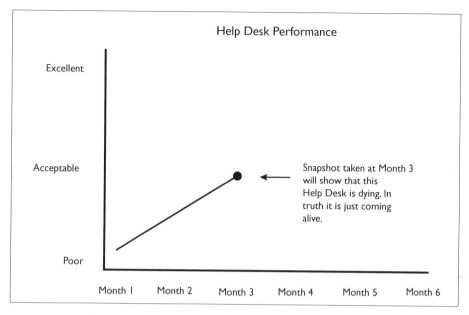

Figure 9.3 A performance snapshot can make an awakening Help Desk look like it is dying.

you more and more because your answers are so reliable. In fact, your call volumes are increasing because you are so good at answering these questions. If all you looked at was customer satisfaction, you'd think you were doing a pretty good job as a Help Desk. But that's just one point of view.

For example, as one of the Help Desk's practitioners you might be totally fed up. You are sick and tired of answering word processing questions. You have been so busy answering these kinds of questions that you haven't had time to work on any performance improvement initiatives. You do not think your Help Desk is doing a great job. It is focusing on the wrong things. Your manager is probably not very happy either. Rave reviews from customers might be pouring in, but objectives are not being met and improvement is not taking place. Senior management, on the other hand, may be happy with your Help Desk's performance. Perhaps all senior management is looking at is cost per call to the Help Desk. Your calls have gone up, but your Help Desk's costs have not, so the cost per call has dropped. However, as we'll see later, cost per call has little to do with value per call, and the business value per call on your Help Desk has fallen. Word processing questions are clogging up the lines and preventing you from focusing on the problems and improvements that offer the highest business value, that positively impact the profitability of the business.

These different perspectives on performance are a good reason why performance should be measured. It is very easy for people to get a false picture of Help Desk performance if they are only looking at it from one perspective and not at all of its components. For example, if your Help Desk starts encouraging customers to take training and turn to various self-help options for their word processing questions, some of them may see this as a dramatic degradation in Help Desk performance. In reality, it would be an improvement in performance. The change in service would allow you to start focusing on eliminating calls and on problems that are more important to the business. If you were measuring performance, you would soon have proof that your performance had improved. The number of how-to calls would go down, and your resolution times would decrease because you would be handling fewer word processing calls so other, more important calls could get through and be resolved at point of call. Even if customers complained to senior management about how poorly your Help Desk was meeting their needs, senior management would have your actual performance to look at. They could see that you were indeed doing what was best for the business.

If you're measuring all components of performance you have proof of your performance, proof of your value, and proof of your positive impact on the profitability of the business. Your Help Desk will have concrete performance data to market to customers and give to senior management. Decisions that impact the fate of the Help Desk could then be based on fact rather than perception.

Why Is Everyone So Interested in ROI?

Help Desk ROI can be defined as the dollar value of the gains, advantages, and services the Help Desk is bringing to the business (the return) divided by the Help Desk's operating cost (the investment). Why is everyone, senior management in particular, interested in ROI? For a business to be profitable it cannot afford to waste anything. It needs to know what it is getting for every dollar it spends. That includes the Help Desk. Senior management wants to know that if it is spending $1 million per year on its Help Desk, it is getting $1 million dollars' worth of services.

Calculating the investment in or cost of a Help Desk is fairly easy. Putting a dollar value on return is more difficult because the services and benefits of the Help Desk are not always obvious.

How Return Is Calculated

Perhaps the easiest way to calculate return is to base it on replacement value, or the market value of the services the Help Desk is providing. In other words, what would it cost someone else to do what your Help Desk is doing in today's market? To get this figure, managers and practitioners turn to Help Desk outsourcers. You ask a few outsourcers what they would charge for the services you perform. This isn't quite as easy as it sounds. You need to make sure that the fees they quote include exactly what your own Help Desk is delivering, including service levels. You'll have to define for them all the responsibilities you have, the services you perform and the levels required, and the hours and locations you cover (if your Help Desk has gone through the process of becoming focused, as described in Chapter 2, this will be much easier). You also have to include some consideration of the fact that someone will have to manage the outsourcing. To help keep the outsourcers you contact honest, during this process you also cannot divulge to them any information about your current Help Desk costs.

If, for example, the cost of running your Help Desk is $1 million per year and the outsourcers quote you costs of $900,000 to do the same things for you, then even if your Help Desk is meeting or surpassing all service levels its ROI does not look very good. It would appear that your organization is paying $1 million for $900,000 worth of services. If your Help Desk is performing poorly (e.g., poor response times, low customer satisfaction) then the ROI is even lower. At this point, senior management would be very tempted to outsource your Help Desk.

How Investment Is Calculated

For a Help Desk, the "investment" in "return on investment" is its operating cost. This will include factors such as staffing costs, cost of outsourced contracts, training costs for Help Desk practitioners and managers, the cost of any training material distributed or made available to Help Desk customers, the cost of office supplies, the cost of Help Desk hardware and software and associated maintenance, and facilities overhead (e.g., rent). An example of a Help Desk's operating cost over one year is shown in Table 9.1.

Investment, or the Help Desk's operating cost, is most useful when it is expressed on a cost-per-unit basis, for example, "cost per workstation." You cannot expect your Help Desk costs to remain the same if you add many workstations, for example. If the cost per workstation decreases, then even if your overall Help Desk costs increase you know you are more cost-effective than you were before, when the overall Help Desk cost was lower. A Help Desk in startup mode will typically have a very high cost-per-workstation figure. As more workstations are added and the Help Desk's services are stabilized, economies of scale will be realized and the cost per workstation will go down.

Although a popular measure, operating cost expressed as cost per

Table 9.1 Example of Yearly Operating Cost, or Investment

Item	Yearly Cost
Help Desk salaries and benefits	$880,000
Contract for outsourced hardware maintenance	210,000
Contract for leasing computer-based training for customers	110,000
Training for Help Desk practitioners and manager	40,000
Office supplies	5,000
Yearly Help Desk software maintenance costs	5,000
Help Desk hardware leasing costs	30,000
Yearly IVR hardware and software maintenance costs	50,000
Facilities overhead	18,000
TOTAL	$1,348,000
Number of workstations supported	2,000
OPERATING COST PER WORKSTATION	$674

call is a much less useful figure than cost per workstation, as we saw when we were discussing ways to view performance. The cost-per-call approach starts out with the premise that the lower your cost per call, the more successful your Help Desk is. This is a false premise. Consider the example of a software firm that manufactures complex engineering software and hires expensive, highly skilled professionals to staff its Help Desk. Customers' calls involve questions about how to apply the software to complicated engineering techniques. The cost per call might be $200 or higher. Each call can take from one hour to half a day to resolve. Then consider the other extreme: a Help Desk that costs only $10 per call but spends its time answering questions caused by customers who don't bother to take training. This Help Desk is unable to do any proactive work because it spends all its time answering repetitive, mundane questions. Customers with more complex problems must fend for themselves because the Help Desk is not staffed to answer them, and they probably couldn't get through to the Help Desk anyway.

Which Help Desk offers better value? The answer: the $200 per call Help Desk. It is supporting its business. The $10 per call Help Desk is a gross misuse of resources.

ROI Is Not Enough

ROI by itself is not an adequate measurement of Help Desk performance because it does not accurately reflect how well you are meeting the needs of the business, how well you are handling your call load, or how well you are preparing for the future. To really understand how your Help Desk is performing, you need to understand the other two components of performance: how effectively you are handling your call load and how proactive you are.

Measuring How Effectively You Handle Calls

To measure how effectively you are managing your calls within your changing environment, you're going to have to consider both qualitative and quantitative measures.

Qualitative versus Quantitative

Quantitative measures give you actual quantities or numbers, while qualitative measures give you the characteristics or qualities of the thing you are measuring—the attributes you can't put a number to. For example, say your Help Desk is measuring itself against a service level agreement (SLA). Your Help Desk manager looks at the numbers and thinks things look pretty good. Response times are being met 100 percent of the time. Your manager then decides to get some qualitative measures as well and goes to customers and to you, the Help Desk practitioner, for feedback. Customers think the Help Desk is doing a great job and is meeting all aspects of the agreement. You, on the other hand, think it's failing. The response times aren't reasonable, and you are working yourself to exhaustion trying to meet them. Having heard your comments, your Help Desk manager now has a very different picture of the Help Desk's performance and can address the situation before service is degraded or you drop from fatigue.

Another example of qualitative measures is a Help Desk that has a problem resolution time that looks good on paper but is completely unacceptable to a specific group of customers who need a faster resolution time. These customers are doing critical work that the Help Desk might not know about, and the existing resolution times are therefore negatively affecting the business. A third, and somewhat more drastic, example of qualitative measures is the Help Desk that is quite pleased to see the quantitative measure "number of calls" decreasing. Customers, however, are simply fed up with inadequate service and have found another source of support. In each of these three examples, looking only at the numbers would give a false impression.

The opposite holds true as well: just looking at qualitative measures would not give you the whole story either. For example, customers and Help Desk staff might be quite happy with the way the Help Desk is working, but the numbers might show that a large percentage of calls could have been prevented if the customers had been trained properly. This would indicate that customers are not using the technology properly or to its full potential. They are thus wasting their own time and the Help Desk's time with problems and questions that could be eliminated with the appropriate training.

Measures to Use

To understand how effectively you are managing Help Desk calls and to see where you can improve, you need to look at several measures:

- Objectives
- Service level agreements (SLAs)
- Customer evaluations (for example, surveys)
- Your own evaluations
- Statistics from your Help Desk management system. The most important of these include the following:

  Change in environment and in call load—for example, number of calls, by type of call; number of supported workstations; number of calls per workstation

  Change in resolution times—the percentage of calls resolved at point of call and for the remaining calls the resolution times broken down into percentages per interval of time

  Change in customer wait times—abandonment rate; customer wait times by percentage per interval of time

Objectives

When you're measuring your Help Desk against your objectives, you might be measuring the effectiveness of the changes or improvements you have made or the stability of existing service levels. For example, one of your objectives might be to reduce calls to the Help Desk by 20 percent. To achieve this reduction, you need to make some kind of change, such as installing an interactive voice response (IVR) application to handle specific types of calls or eliminating recurring problems that are causing extra calls. Another of your objectives might be to maintain an average problem resolution time of four hours. You're already at the four-hour level, but you want to ensure that you stay there.

You need to measure how well you are meeting your Help Desk objectives because this tells you how well your call elimination or improvement initiatives are working, and missed objectives are one of the first indications that you are sliding into an out-of-control problem cycle. As a proactive Help Desk practitioner, your performance against objectives is part of your early warning systems (EWSs). Measuring performance against objectives isn't always as simple as "Yes, we achieved this" or "No, we didn't." Your achievements might look different from your objectives for a number of reasons. Circumstances can change quickly, as can the demands of the business. You may have had to shift your focus to something of greater business value. You may have underestimated the time required to achieve the objective, or the objective may not have been realistic.

Even if you don't meet your objectives, you do learn where and how you need to improve. You can improve your knowledge of what is required to make a good performance estimate, for example, so future objectives will be more reasonable. You can find and correct what went wrong in your call elimination initiative and avoid the same mistakes in the future. In short, you can turn any failures you have into learning experiences. Table 9.2 is an example of a set of objectives and a Help Desk's performance against them. You would typically be involved in only one or two of them.

In the example in Table 9.2, not all objectives were achieved. The reasons for this included a problem with the support load, unrealistic objectives, and the way in which a specific tool was implemented. There are (at least) three ways in which you and your Help Desk can improve using this information. First, even though an 85 percent first-level call resolution was reached in your first objective, customers are fearful of the remote control technology. This could cause problems in the near future. You have learned that before you roll a new tool out, you need to take time to ensure that customers understand and are comfortable with what you are doing, why you are doing it, and how it will affect them.

Second, you've learned that it takes longer to do PC upgrades than you thought. Your future estimates will therefore be more accurate. Third, your EWS has been alerted to the fact that an improvement, specifically, the installation of asset management software, could not be made because of a high call load. You need to look at what is causing this high call load and how you can decrease it. One objective that your Help Desk did not meet, the installation of the word processing upgrade, was precluded by the emergence of something much more important to the business at this time, a network operating system upgrade. This upgrade can be considered a successful accomplishment.

Table 9.2 Example of Performance Against Objectives

Objective	Accomplished	Problems (if any)	What you learned
Increase number of calls resolved at point of call to 85% by using remote control software.	Achieved 85%.	Customer survey indicated that some customers are afraid that Help Desk staff can monitor their sessions at any time.	*Need to communicate the fact that the software requires that users allow access. A marketing effort is needed here.*
Upgrade all machines with less than 64 megabytes of memory to prepare for client/server.	85 of 110 machines upgraded.	Taking longer per machine than planned. Ran into scheduling difficulties with customers.	*Next time, need to take this into account. This was an unrealistic objective.*
Install 15 PCs in the sales area for the new sales promotion project.	Done on time. No major problems.		
Install new release of word processing software.	Network operating system required an emergency upgrade to fix response problems that occurred when the 950th user came online. This was successfully completed. Word processing upgrade was postponed.		
Research and select asset management package.	Not done.	Support load was too high.	*Have to get this done. Need to reduce the load or get help.*

Service Level Agreements

Service level agreements (SLAs) are two-way agreements between a service provider and a service receiver. On a Help Desk, you might have SLAs between the Help Desk (as a service receiver) and other levels of support (as service providers), between the Help Desk (as a service receiver) and vendors (as service providers), and between the Help Desk (as a service provider) and a group of customers (as service receivers). The agreements typically specify what services the provider provides and what targets it must meet. They also specify the responsibilities of the "receivers" who are using the services.

When you measure the performance of your Help Desk, other levels of support, or vendors against an SLA you are measuring the performance of those other levels of support and vendors as well as your compliance with any agreed-upon responsibilities. For example, you may have to put calls into specific queues when you pass them on to other levels of support, and you may have to restrict any paging to emergencies only. When you measure the performance of your Help Desk and your customers against an SLA you are measuring both your Help Desk's performance and the customer's compliance with the agreed-upon responsibilities. For example, customers may be required to get service by calling or e-mailing the Help Desk rather than by dragging a passing Help Desk practitioner back to the source of the problem.

If you are ever involved in actually setting an SLA up, here are a few things to remember:

- If you are establishing an SLA with your customers, don't forget about the people you rely on for support. Their performance affects your ability to meet performance measures. Spend time defining and agreeing on who is responsible for what. Don't expect this to be a trivial process; it will be time-consuming. This may result in the creation of SLAs with other levels of support.

- Each item in the SLA must be measurable. If you can't measure it, don't include it.

- Each item in the SLA should be very specific. For example, if performance reports are required, you should include a sample layout of the report and the report's frequency and recipients should be stated. The more specific each item is the less chance there is of misunderstandings and unfulfilled expectations.

- Everyone affected by the SLA needs to be represented in the creation and negotiation process.

- The creation process is an iterative one. A draft SLA is first created by a work group of representatives. The representatives then take the draft back to their groups for changes, additions, or clarifications. The process continues until all groups are satisfied with the result.

What's in an SLA?

What do you want to include in an SLA? SLAs with customers will be slightly different than SLAs with other levels of support or with vendors, but the structure will be the same. The following are the things you want to include in an SLA with your customers:

- A description of both parties involved in the agreement—you may need to provide different levels of service for different groups and therefore different SLAs.

- The period covered by the agreement—usually one year.

- The services to be provided by the Help Desk.

- The Help Desk's hours of operation and after-hours service options.

- How customers can access Help Desk services.

- The customer's responsibilities.

- A definition of call priorities and required response times.

- The service measures that must be met.

- Escalation procedures.

- The reporting to be generated by the Help Desk.

- The components supported.

- The components considered critical.

- Support fees, if any.

- The pay-for-use services, if any—in this section, include any services that are available to the customers at extra cost, for example, training.

SLAs with other levels of support might include the following items:

- A description of both parties involved in the agreement.
- The period covered by the agreement—usually one year.
- The services to be provided by the support group to the Help Desk.
- The support group's hours of normal operation and after-hours service options.
- How the Help Desk passes calls on.
- The Help Desk's responsibilities.
- A definition of call priorities and required response times.
- The service measures to be met by the support group.
- Escalation procedures.
- A definition of the products or types of problems that the support group accepts.

What Does an SLA Look Like?

The following is an example of an SLA between a Help Desk and its customers in the business's marketing department.

> **Service Level Agreement**
> Between:
> *The Corporate Help Desk and Marketing*
> For:
> *January 1, 1999, through December 31, 1999*
>
> 1. **Services to Be Provided by the Help Desk**
>   Perform first-level support for all standard software applications and all hardware that meets corporate standards.
>   Manage second and third level of support.

Log and track all customer calls.

Carry out quarterly customer satisfaction surveys to rotating client base, 100 at a time. Publish results (see section 8, "Reporting").

Carry out customer callbacks to 50 percent of customers daily. Publish results (see section 8, "Reporting").

2. **Hours of Operation**

Regular Business Hours:

7 A.M. to 7 P.M., Monday through Friday, nonholiday.

After-hours support via pager, 111-222-3333, priority 1 only:

7 P.M. to 7 A.M., Monday through Friday, nonholiday.

24 hours Saturday and Sunday.

24 hours holidays.

3. **Service Access**

Help Desk Service Is Accessible via:

Phone—Call 123-HELP.

E-mail—Send a message to EHELP.

4. **Customer Responsibilities**

Use only the specified phone number or e-mail ID to get support. No other support requests will be processed.

Customers who are new to technology must attend two half-day LAN and PC familiarization seminars before receiving a workstation.

Attend training on all software used. (Percentage of training-type calls will be tracked.)

Read and abide by the *Corporate Security Policy* and *Corporate Standards Policy* documents.

5. **Call Priorities and Response Times**

Priority	*Impact*	*Response*	*Resolution*
1	Critical component down	15 minutes	As required
2	Critical component degraded	45 minutes	4 hours
3	Noncritical component	4 hours	8 hours
4	Other request, question	8 hours	12 hours

6. **Service Measures to Be Met**

By the Help Desk:

First-level call resolution—85 percent or greater.

Average call answer time—90 percent in thirty seconds or less.

Percentage of calls reopened within two weeks—2 percent or less.

By Customers:

Percentage of training-type calls must be less than 10 percent.

7. **Escalation Procedures**

Level	*Initiate when:*	*Call:*	*Phone/Pager*
1	Agreed-upon response time not met.	Help Desk Manager	123-222-222 111-999-999
2	No response two hours after level 1 escalation.	Director, Local Operations	123-222-333 111-999-000
3	No response three hours after level 2 escalation.	V.P., Local Operations	123-333-444 111-999-111

8. **Reporting**

Weekly Reporting:

Distribution—

- Manager and Director, Marketing
- Director and Vice President, Local Operations

Content—

Number of calls.

Call breakdown by percentage for training-type calls, hardware, software, communication, service requests, abandoned calls.

Percentage of first-level call resolutions.

Average call answer time.

Percentage of calls reopened within two weeks.

Percentage of calls meeting agreed-upon response times for each priority.

Percentage of calls meeting agreed-upon resolution times for each priority.

Results of callbacks to customers to check work quality—show number of callbacks as percentage of total calls.
Show percentage of callbacks with positive response.
Quarterly Reporting:
Distribution—

- Manager and Director, Marketing
- Director and Vice President, Local Operations

Content—

- Results of quarterly customer surveys
- Change from previous quarter in number of workstations supported
- Operating costs

Note:
All weekly reporting must show the current week compared to the three previous weeks. All quarterly reporting must show the current quarter compared to the previous quarter.

9. **Systems and Components Supported**
Critical Systems/Components Supported:
Price flow system
Server T1AD
Catalog system
LAN ring 006
All PCs on ring 006
Noncritical Components Supported:
Marketing Search, Competitor System, Marketing Performance.
All standard desktop software as per *Corporate Standards Policy* document.
Hardware Supported:
All hardware that meets corporate standards (as per *Corporate Standards Policy* document) will be supported.

10. **Support Fees**
Cost will be allocated at the rate of $60 per workstation per month.

11. **Pay-for-Use Fees**

Training in standard desktop software packages is available and will be arranged by the Help Desk for the cost of $300 per half day. Course dates and times are available from the Help Desk intranet Web site and are distributed to all customers quarterly.

12. **Signatures Denoting Agreement**

Manager, Help Desk:

_____

Director, Local Operation:

_____

Manager, Marketing Liaison:

_____

Director, Marketing:

_____

Responsibility for revising this agreement on an annual basis lies jointly with the Help Desk manager and the marketing liaison manager.

Measuring Your Performance against an SLA

You have your SLA; now what do you do? Remember, you're looking for ways to improve and eliminate calls. First, you measure how you're performing against each category in your SLA. Just as with objectives, you then recommend improvements based on your performance. You're also measuring how customers met their responsibilities. You may recommend improvements based on their performance as well.

You will use customer surveys, which might be conducted over the phone, to check the customer's perception of your service in accordance with section 1 of the sample SLA. Using the same vehicle you can check if customers were able to get the access they needed in accordance with sections 2 and 3 of the agreement. Call statistics from your Help Desk management system (which we will discuss later in this chapter) will give you response and resolution times for specific priorities, in accordance with section 5. These statistics will also tell you the percentage of calls resolved by the first level and the average call answer time, in accordance with section 6, and the percentage of calls by type, which you can use to measure the percentage of training-type calls, in accordance with section 6.

You and your fellow Help Desk practitioners will be able to provide feedback on customers' fulfillment of their responsibilities (section 4 in the agreement). You can answer such questions as did they go through proper channels or did they try to cajole you away from your other calls to do work for them? Did they abide by corporate standards? Did they take any security risks? Table 9.3 shows a sample of SLA measures.

Looking for Improvements

In the evaluation in Table 9.3, you can see that customers aren't following regular channels when reporting problems. You know this must be stopped to prevent the loss of valuable statistics and disruptions in pri-

Table 9.3 Example of Performance Against Service Level Agreement

Item	*Performance*	*What you learned*
Customer responsibilities: Use only specified phone number or e-mail ID to get support. No other support requests will be processed.	From you: Customers try to get support from practitioners who are en route to fix another problem.	*Need to market to customers the cost of stolen support. Revisit the terms of the SLA with the marketing liaison.*
Service measures to be met: Percentage of training-type calls to be less than 10%.	From Help Desk statistics: Percentage of training-type calls is 30%.	*Revisit the terms of the SLA with the marketing liaison.* *Make sure customers are being kept informed of available training. Are there any types of training we could be providing that would be more convenient for customers?*
Service measures to be met: First-level call resolution to be 85% or greater.	From Help Desk statistics: First-level call resolution is 72%.	*It appears that the standard desktop upgrade was rolled out before Help Desk practitioners were adequately trained. This needs to be addressed for this and all future releases.*

orities and staff workload. An improvement to consider might be a marketing initiative. Table 9.3 also shows that customers are wasting their own time and your time with training-type calls. At 30 percent of calls, this is an area that is just begging to be improved. If you eliminate even just a third of that 30 percent, you will have reduced your call load by 10 percent. An improvement initiative you may want to undertake is to find out why customers aren't taking the required training and if there is any type of training that could be provided (such as just-in-time on-site training) that would be more convenient for them.

Measuring performance can also have some very direct benefits for you. Table 9.3 shows that you and your fellow practitioners are not being trained before software is rolled out. This has affected first-level call resolutions. The measurement against your SLA demonstrates the consequences of a lack of training. To get the training you need you probably won't even have to go through any kind of justification. The evidence is already here.

Customer Evaluation

In the sample SLA presented earlier in the chapter, part of our service responsibility was to do quarterly customer satisfaction surveys. Customer surveys, or various other forms of customer feedback, give us the customers' perspective on performance, which may not be reflected in quantitative measures. Feedback from customers can tell us what they think of the speed and accuracy of our service. Customers' perceptions may be different from the quantitative measures supplied by a call management system.

Feedback will tell us if our customers got emergency service when they needed it. This would give us an indication of whether the definition of an emergency in the four levels of Help Desk call priority specified in section 5 of the SLA was adequate. We will then learn what customers think of the quality of our services, such as purchasing PCs. Was the equipment delivered appropriate for the job being performed? Was it delivered when promised? Was it set up properly?

Getting feedback from customers will tell us what customers think of our technical, problem-solving, communication, and customer service skills. Are customers kept informed of the progress made on their calls?

Are they informed of system outages or planned downtimes and their duration? Are they informed of the training and services available and how to use the services?

How Do We Get Feedback?

Getting customers' evaluations of the Help Desk's performance involves meeting with them, sending out short surveys, or calling them to ask about your service. Specific areas, such as training and purchasing PCs, can be targeted for individual feedback. Perhaps all attendees of your training sessions could be surveyed a few months after they've had some time to begin applying it so their feedback on it will have some relevance. Each person who received a PC might also be asked to fill out a quick survey form to provide feedback on the whole process.

If you are involved in putting together a customer survey, here are a few guidelines to follow to make your survey more effective:

- Target a specific incident or a specific aspect of service. Don't try to cover too much in one survey. Be very focused.

- Be prepared to make changes based on the survey's results. If you are not, don't survey.

- Explain the purpose of your survey to customers.

- Include no more than five questions per survey.

- Always give the customer room for comments.

- Survey customers on an ongoing rotating or random basis rather than everyone once a year. This will give you a much better idea of how things are changing throughout the year and will allow you to react faster to problem areas or suggestions.

- Always, always, report on the survey's results. If customers hear nothing and see no changes, they'll stop responding.

Sample Survey

The following is an example of a survey you may use to check on customers' perceptions of Help Desk service. Remember, you're looking for ways you can improve.

Help Desk Survey

Dear recent Help Desk customer,

Please help us improve the quality of our work by taking a few minutes to respond to the following survey. You may return it via e-mail or print it out and send it via internal mail to the Help Desk. Thank you!

For each question, please choose the appropriate response and enter any comments you may have.

1. Did you feel the Help Desk practitioner who served you was knowledgeable?

   __Y __N

   Comments:

2. Was your problem resolved in a timely manner?

   __Y __N

   Comments:

3. If someone had to visit your workstation, did they arrive when promised?

   __Y __N

   Comments:

4. Was the problem resolved to your satisfaction?

   __Y __N

   Comments:

5. Please rate your Help Desk experience on a scale of 1 to 4, 1 being highest and 4 lowest.

   __1 __2 __3 __4

   Comments:

Measuring Your Performance against a Survey

You've put out your survey and collected the results; now what do you do? You do the same thing you did with objectives and SLAs: You measure your performance against the survey, and you look for areas for

Table 9.4 Survey Results and Observations

Question	Results by Percentage	Notes
Did you feel the Help Desk practitioner who served you was knowledgeable?	Y: 95% N: 5%	
Was your problem resolved in a timely manner?	Y: 71% N: 29%	*This may be the result of those late workstation visits. We need to check your problem resolution statistics and the requirements of the SLA.*
If someone had to visit your workstation, did that person arrive when promised?	Y: 10% N: 22% N/A: 68%	*We need to improve our procedures for scheduling workstation visits.*
Was the problem resolved to your satisfaction?	Y: 97% N: 3%	*Check problem resolution statistics and SLA requirements.* *One comment mentioned that "the problem was solved eventually."*
Please rate your Help Desk experience on a scale of 1 to 4; 1 being highest and 4 being lowest.	1: 32% 2: 43% 3: 15% 4: 10%	

improvement and ways to eliminate calls. Table 9.4 shows the results of the sample survey presented in the last section.

The survey results in Table 9.4 point out a few areas for improvement. You need to assess these and make plans for implementing the improvements. First, the Help Desk is not delivering on the workstation visit times it promises. The workstation visit scheduling procedure must be revised. Suppose you analyze the current process and find that the procedure seems to be "Make a best estimate." You investigate this and propose a solution that involves adopting a new process. Your suggestion is approved. The new process will involve an online scheduling and dispatch system that will schedule the appropriate on-site practitioner and then page that person to inform him or her that a new on-site visit has been scheduled. You send customers an e-mail explaining what you are doing and thanking them for their survey input.

Second, problems are not being resolved in a timely manner in almost one-third of all Help Desk calls. This indicates either that your Help Desk is simply too slow, that is, not meeting your SLA's requirements, or that the SLA agreement is not adequate. You examine the Help Desk resolution times and see that the Help Desk is indeed meeting agreed-upon service levels. You call some of the survey respondents and find that customer expectations were higher than the service levels that were agreed upon. You decide that some kind of marketing initiative is in order. For the next three months you and your colleagues will tell customers what resolution time they can expect whenever you cannot resolve their calls at point of call. You will then do a telephone survey to see if your initiative was successful.

Your Own Evaluation

As a Help Desk practitioner, you also have a perspective on performance, one that you cannot ignore. You need to look at your Help Desk's performance from your point of view and identify areas for improvement and call elimination. The factors you need to look at include the following:

Customer attitude. You are close to the customers. You talk to them all day, and they will notice if and when attitudes on the Help Desk change. The listening skills you worked on improving in Chapter 5 will help you determine whether your customers are satisfied with the service they are getting. If you have a callback program to check on the timeliness and quality of the tasks the Help Desk performs, you will hear very clearly whether your customers are satisfied.

Legitimacy of customer calls. If the Help Desk is being misused, its business value decreases, so the legitimacy of customer calls is not a trivial measure. If you notice that the number of calls that customers could have resolved easily themselves is increasing, this could signal misuse. If customers aren't bothering to look things up or to take training, they are wasting time that you could be spending doing things of greater value, such as making improvements. In addition, those customers probably don't understand the software, so they could be misusing it and making expensive mistakes.

Adequacy of training received (for practitioners). If you aren't getting the training you need to handle the calls that come in then you have identified an area in which improvement is required. You need training.

Availability and performance of tools. If you don't have the tools you need to do your job properly, your performance will suffer. For example, if you don't have a knowledge base and thus no way to check if similar calls have occurred previously you will be solving the same problems again and again.

Workload. If you and your fellow Help Desk practitioners don't have enough time to handle all the work assigned to you, you are going to be tired and stressed and not nearly as effective as you could be. Call statistics might not show this. Reports might indicate the volume of calls, but if you are doing something else besides taking calls the reports won't show this. This is an EWS that you cannot ignore.

Availability and functionality of second-level support. If you aren't getting the support you need from other support groups, your job becomes more difficult, and problems will take longer to resolve. The profitability of the business you support is negatively impacted.

Vendor performance. You and your colleagues may have a lot of contact with vendors. If you do you will be able to report on qualitative measures such as responsiveness, quality of service, willingness to help out when problems occur, the way warranties are honored, and so on.

Value of tasks performed. If you find yourself doing simple tasks over and over or if you are constantly interrupted by time-wasting administrative tasks, you aren't going to attach much value to your job. If this is the case, you need to look for improvements by automating or outsourcing specific processes.

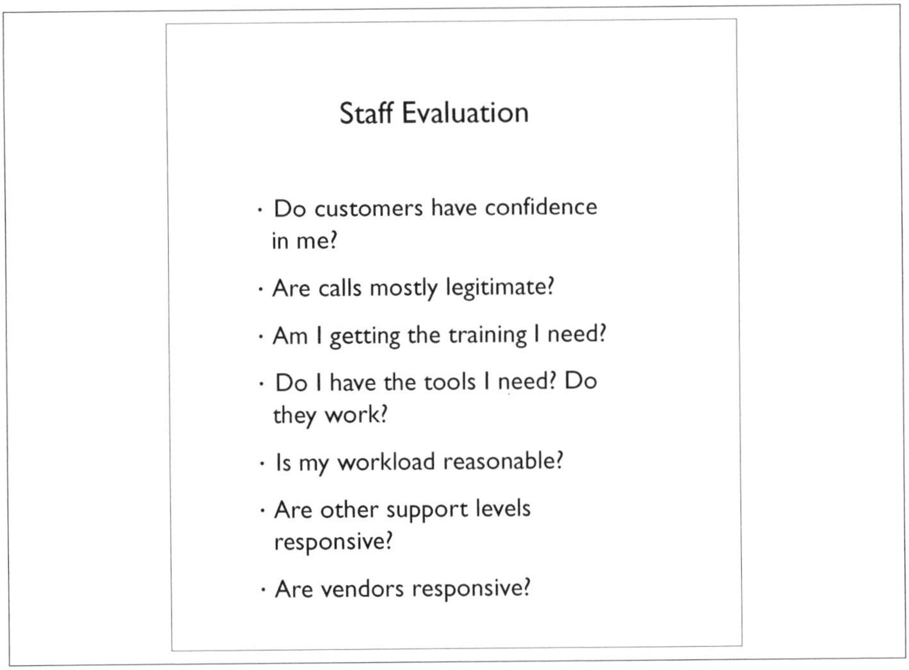

Staff Evaluation

- Do customers have confidence in me?

- Are calls mostly legitimate?

- Am I getting the training I need?

- Do I have the tools I need? Do they work?

- Is my workload reasonable?

- Are other support levels responsive?

- Are vendors responsive?

Figure 9.4   How you, the Help Desk practitioner, evaluate performance.

Your responses to these factors (see Figure 9.4) can give you an early warning of problems developing in your Help Desk and uncover areas where you can make improvements. Review them as part of your ongoing cycle of evaluation and improvement.

Help Desk Management Statistics

Your Help Desk management system provides you with endless statistics about the performance of your Help Desk. They are input into your EWS and are excellent indicators of needed change. You need to keep a sharp eye on these statistics, for if you get too busy and ignore them they're apt to change by leaps and bounds before you notice. Remember, performance is a moving picture, and you need to be looking for significant changes. As a proactive Help Desk practitioner you are looking for trends that negatively impact the profitability of the business, such as an increase in calls, an increase in resolution times, or an increase in the amount of time customers have to wait to get service. Some of the most critical changes to watch for are discussed in the following sections.

Change in Environment and in Call Load

Statistics to watch in the areas of the Help Desk environment and call load include the number of workstations supported, the overall number of calls, the daily call distribution, the number of calls by type, and the number of calls per workstation. Your asset management system should give you information about changes in the kinds of software you are supporting, changes in the type and complexity of hardware you are supporting, and so on.

- The number of workstations supported will tell you whether you are supporting more or fewer customers.
- The overall number of calls will tell you only what is happening to the number of calls. It won't tell you if the increase or decrease is caused by more customers or increases in specific call types.
- Daily call distribution will tell you if your peak and off-peak hours are changing and may explain degradations in service during new peaks that you are not staffed up for.
- Call breakdown by type will tell you whether any specific type of call is increasing.
- The number of calls per workstation will tell you whether any call increase or decrease is due to an increase or decrease in workstations or whether your customers are actually calling you more or less often.

Change in Resolution Times

You need to look at the percentage of calls resolved at point of call to make sure your front line is working at maximum effectiveness. If this percentage has gone down, you need to look at other statistics, such as number of calls by type, to find out why. Some Help Desks report on average time to resolve problems, but this can be a very deceiving measure if there is a wide variance in your resolution times. Better than reporting an average would be to select intervals that make sense for your envi-

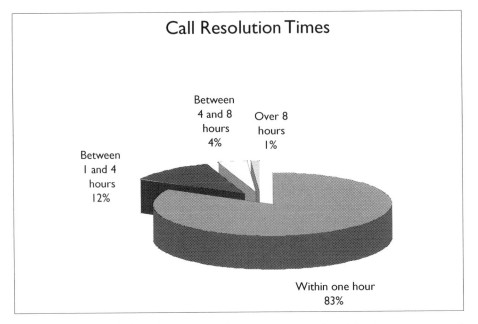

Figure 9.5 Resolution times are often more meaningful when expressed as a percentage of an interval.

ronment and report on these. In Figure 9.5 the percentage of calls resolved is broken down into selected intervals of one hour or less, between one and four hours, between four and eight hours, and more than eight hours. You will have to pick the intervals that make sense in your environment. Experiment to see where the bulk of your calls lie and which intervals are the most meaningful for you.

Another important statistic is resolution times by percentage per interval for calls passed on to other areas of support. This would tell you how well second and third levels of support are doing in terms of response times. This statistic is especially important if your resolution times are increasing and you want to know why and where.

Change in Response Times

Customer wait times and abandonment rates will tell you whether your customers are being forced to wait longer to get service and whether they are actually waiting or are just hanging up.

Interpreting Help Desk Management Statistics

Figures 9.6 through 9.12 show examples of Help Desk management statistics. We will analyze each of these in terms of Help Desk performance.

Figures 9.6, 9.7, and 9.8 show that there has been a 15 percent overall increase in total calls from one quarter to the next, an 8 percent increase in the number of workstations from the beginning of one quarter to the end of the next, and an increase in the number of calls per workstation from 1.5 at the beginning of one quarter to 1.7 at the end of the next. Looking at the calls and workstations separately doesn't tell you much. But looking at the calls per workstation tells you that your calls are not just increasing because you are supporting more workstations; you are actually getting more calls per workstation. You can go to other statistics to find out why. Figure 9.9, which shows call breakdown by type, might hold the answer. Your training-type calls have increased from 15 percent of calls to 30 percent from one quarter to the next. You will have to address this if you want your calls per workstation to come down. The good news is that your abandonment rate is down from 5 percent to 2 percent.

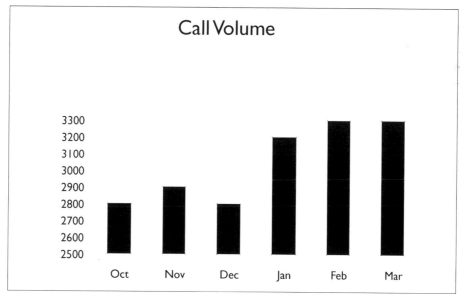

Figure 9.6   Changes in call volume.

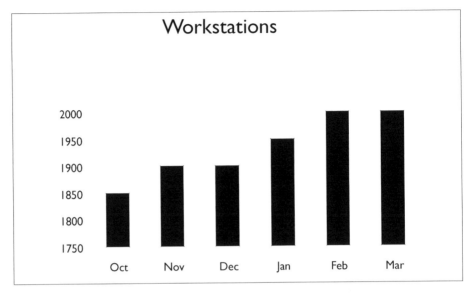

Figure 9.7   Changes in workstations supported.

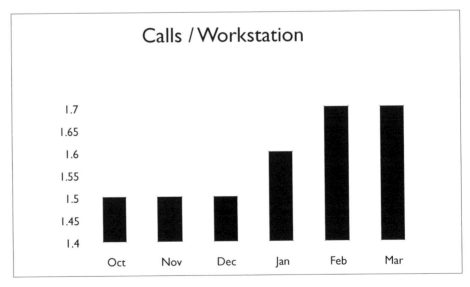

Figure 9.8   Changes in calls per workstation.

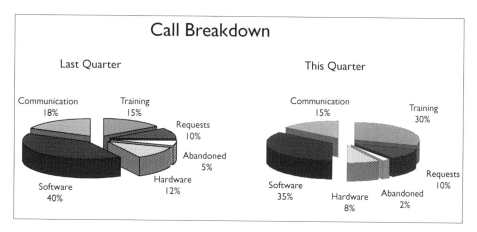

Figure 9.9 Call breakdown.

Figure 9.10 shows changes in average daily call distribution from one quarter to the next. Your call peaks have shifted. Fortunately, you have been watching this on a weekly basis, and you and your colleagues have adjusted your hours accordingly, so your call management has not

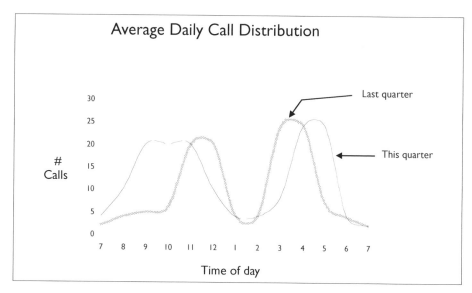

Figure 9.10 Call distribution.

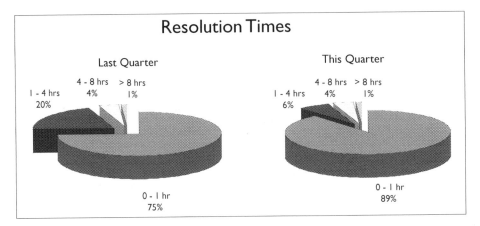

Figure 9.11   Call resolution.

been negatively affected. Figure 9.11 shows that you have increased the calls you resolve within one hour from 75 percent to 89 percent. This is probably due to the increase in the percentage of calls that you are resolving at point of call, which is shown in Figure 9.12.

Figure 9.12 shows you the percentage of these point-of-call resolutions over the past six months (two quarters). You don't have a lot to worry about there. From the beginning of the first quarter to the end of the next, you have increased the percentage of calls you resolve at point

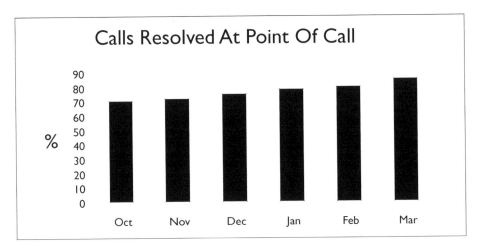

Figure 9.12   Calls resolved at point of call.

of call from 70 percent to 85 percent. If the sample service level agreement presented previously in this chapter was yours, you would be meeting the required calls resolved at point of call dead on.

In summary, the statistics illustrated in Figures 9.6 through 9.12 show the following:

1. **Your calls per workstation are increasing**. This is probably due to the fact that the percentage of training-type calls you are getting has doubled. This is a dangerous trend. You want to eliminate anything that is causing the calls-per-workstation figure to increase. Improvement initiatives you may want to consider are as follows:

- Make basic PC and LAN training mandatory for all customers, to be taken before they get their PCs. You have the data you need to go to the management of your customers' department with this proposal. You may want to do some calculations to show how much money and time this increase is costing the customer and the Help Desk (see Chapter 10 for information on cost justifications).

- Offer various training options to customers. You need to do some investigating to find out why customers aren't taking training. Perhaps it just isn't convenient enough. You might suggest having a trainer come into the customers' areas on a regular basis to work with them as they go about their daily tasks. This just-in-time training might be just the thing to reduce calls to the Help Desk. Customers may be very willing to pay for this kind of help.

2. **Your call distribution has changed.** Your morning peak starts earlier and lasts longer, and your afternoon peak starts earlier. You need to keep an eye on this to make sure you're staffed to handle it. You also need to talk to your customers to see if their requirements are changing. You may have to add hours to your Help Desk's hours of operation to start earlier.

In the preceding examples we looked at statistics from one quarter to the next. In reality, however, you would probably want to look at these figures from month to month, or even more frequently. The sooner you know about a potential problem, the easier it will be to avoid or minimize it.

How Proactive Are You?

To measure how proactive you and your Help Desk are, you need to check to see if your Help Desk is standing still or moving ahead with the business—working to eliminate calls, making improvements, and getting ready for future technology or customer requirements. To do this, you look at your objectives and your improvement initiatives. If you don't have objectives, I would question your level of proaction. It is difficult to achieve when you have no goals.

Are you in an evaluation and improvement cycle (as described in Chapter 7)? If you answer yes, you are proactive. All of the measurements we have talked about in this chapter can be input into your evaluation and improvement cycle. If you answered no, you have some work to do. You might also ask yourself, "Are we doing anything to decrease resolution times or increase calls resolved at point of call?" Positive answers to these questions also indicate proaction. An initiative to undertake to achieve these ends might be to use remote control software to allow practitioners to see and control the customer's screen so more calls can be resolved at point of call and thus eliminating the need to go on site to the customer's PC. Another initiative might be to implement knowledge bases or expert systems to increase the knowledge that a practitioner has access to while resolving a call.

In Chapter 7 we talked about the need to understand where your business is going and what your customers need to be proactive. "What is the organization I am supporting doing? Am I preparing to meet it?" are questions you need to ask yourself when measuring proaction. To answer the second question you need to consider the following factors:

- Are your networks and your assets ready for any improvements that are coming?

- Do you provide the software the business needs? Are your updates timely?

- Are there services you should or should not be offering?
- Are your support hours adequate?
- Are you and your fellow Help Desk practitioners adequately trained? Do you need to pick up different skills?

Proaction isn't really optional. If you want to be able to measure up to your competition—if you want to be able to support your organization effectively—you absolutely must be proactive.

A Summary

This chapter has given you a lot to think about. It has given you performance measures that will help you identify ways to eliminate calls and improve service. Let's do a quick summary here so we can put everything we've discussed into perspective.

Performance has three parts: ROI, effectiveness of call load management, and level of proaction. Measuring ROI involves comparing the operating cost of the Help Desk to the market value of the services the Help Desk provides. This is a number that senior management is typically interested in. Measuring the effectiveness of call load improvement involves looking at several measures to see how well the Help Desk is managing its load of calls from one period to the next and what trends are occurring. The measures used include objectives, service level agreements (SLAs), customer evaluations (e.g., surveys), Help Desk practitioner evaluations, and statistics from your Help Desk management system. You will want to look at your performance against these measures and identify where you can improve and how you can eliminate calls. Your level of proaction is defined by the initiatives you have in place to eliminate calls, to make improvements, and to prepare for the future. If you are proactive then you are in a constant cycle of evaluation and improvement, which was described in Chapter 7.

Traditionally, Help Desk practitioners have not looked at statistics or monitored their performance, but this is changing. One manager cannot do everything, and you are typically much closer to your customers than your manager is. The more you as a Help Desk practitioner can do to use all of these measures to improve your Help Desk, the more effective your Help Desk will be.

Checklist

In this chapter we looked at performance, how to measure it, and how we can use the measurement results we get to improve. To make sure you understand these concepts, ask yourself the following questions and then review the material in this chapter if you need to.

✓ What are the components of performance?

✓ Why do we need to look at performance over time?

✓ What are the different perspectives on performance?

✓ What is ROI?

✓ What is the difference between qualitative and quantitative measures? Why do we have to look at each?

✓ How do we determine the effectiveness of call load management?

✓ How do we measure ourselves against objectives?

✓ What goes into a service level agreement (SLA)?

✓ How do we measure performance against a service level agreement?

✓ How do we measure what our customers think of our performance?

✓ What input do we as Help Desk practitioners have into our performance?

✓ What Help Desk statistics are most useful to us? What do they tell us?

✓ How do we measure our level of proaction?

Cost Justification Made Easy

Knowing how to create a good cost justification is one of the most useful skills you can have on a Help Desk. You can use that skill to justify the cost of anything, from training to knowledge bases and other problem resolution tools. When you have a good cost justification you have evidence that what you're asking for is worthwhile—good for the business. It will be hard for your manager, or whoever has final say, to refuse.

In This Chapter

The topics we will cover in this chapter include the following:

- Come back here!
- Why do you need a cost justification?
- The three secrets
- The formula

- A word about the examples
- Example A: Justifying training
- Example B: Justifying help for peak load
- Example C: Justifying help for a Help Desk in trouble

Come Back Here!

I am always interested in the reaction my students in my seminars have to learning about cost justification: sheer terror. As soon as I start talking about cost justification people lower their eyes, start mumbling about needing a break, and head for the washroom. Not many things empty a room faster than "Well folks, guess what's next? Cost justification!" I have learned to lock the door before making this announcement, with the result that no one gets very far.

"We can't get out!" students say, looking at me in some panic. I look at the door and shake my head, making little "tsk, tsk" sounds.

"I guess it's stuck," I say sadly. "I'll call the maintenance person. Oops, there's no phone in the room. Oh well, someone will be by in about an hour with coffee. They can let us out. We'll do cost justification until then." The lesson continues, and the class practices creating one or two justifications. We start by focusing on the method. Once you know the method you can apply it to anything. If anyone has something they're actually trying to justify at work we use that as one of the exercises.

My reward comes when we've finished the unit and students have had a chance to practice actually creating one or two justifications. Someone always says, "Wow, I'm really going to be able to use that. I can think of several things I'd like to be able to justify to my manager," or "I'm going to use the justification I created in class to justify . . ." and then names whatever it is they're trying to justify at work. The analogy you've heard about teaching people to fish so they will never starve is very true. Once you learn the method of putting a cost justification together you need never go without. You will be able to cost justify anything.

Why Do You Need a Cost Justification?

Something I hear very often from students in my classes is, "Why do we have to justify this? Isn't the need obvious?" The answer to this is that it may be obvious to you but not to anyone else. To illustrate this, I'm going to promote you. You're now the manager of your Help Desk. (Just to keep things fair, if you already were a manager, you're now a senior manager.) There are two methods that people like to use to try to get what they need; each has a very high failure rate. You probably have some familiarity with each of them. They are whining and psychic prediction.

Whining

"We're so overworked," you whine to your boss, Melanie, vice president of technology support. "Can't you see how busy we are? Can't you see we need more staff?" Your boss pretends to be deaf. "We can't handle any more calls!" you persist. "I can't ask people to work any more overtime!" Melanie's hearing still appears to be impaired. Whining is obviously not having any affect on her. Either she really does have a hearing problem or this approach just isn't working. You try another approach . . .

Psychic Prediction

"Melanie" you say, "I just *know* that adding two more staff to the Help Desk will really improve our performance! I *feel* that this really is the way to go." Melanie appears to have fallen asleep. "I *know* that extra staff will allow us to handle our workload more effectively. We *are sure* to have fewer abandoned calls!" You shout so she can hear you. But Melanie's snoring drowns out your words.

Why They Don't Work

"Hmm," you say to yourself, "neither of these proven techniques is working. Melanie is a terrible boss." On the way home that night you stop by the repair shop to pick up a stereo you had dropped off to have fixed. You give the clerk your receipt and tell him that you brought the stereo in two weeks ago. "It must be fixed by now," you say confidently. The clerk looks at you doubtfully then disappears into the back for several minutes. You begin to think he's gone home when suddenly he appears, carrying your stereo.

"It's not fixed yet," he pronounces as he puts it on the counter. "Not fixed!" you shout (you seem to be doing a lot of shouting lately). "But I brought it in two weeks ago! What's the matter with this place; is everyone incompetent?" The clerk draws himself up and faces you angrily. Uh-oh. You've hurt his feelings, and he's a lot bigger than you are. "We are not incompetent!" he shouts back. "We're just severely overworked! There are only two of us trying to deal with about 20 repairs each day. It just can't be done . . . and our boss won't hire any help!"

Eureka!

At that moment revelation strikes you. You tell the clerk to take as long as he wants, apologize for being rude, and leave the store. You are excited. You've discovered why your boss has not been hearing your requests for extra staff. Like you as you listened to clerk's explanations, she simply cannot see what is obvious to you and everyone working on the Help Desk. You see how hard everyone is working, how many calls you're getting, but your boss and everyone outside the Help Desk sees only incompetence. Customers will soon be treating you and the rest of the Help Desk the way you treated that clerk.

When you get home you sit down to find a way to prove that your Help Desk is understaffed because you now realize that the need you thought was so obvious is not obvious to anyone except the Help Desk itself.

The Answer: A Cost Justification

What you come up with, after several iterations and several nights, is a good cost justification for extra staff for your Help Desk. Using estimates of lost customer time and your Help Desk call statistics you put together a justification that proves that you need extra staff. You show that your current understaffed situation is costing the business money because its employees—your customers—are wasting time trying to get support that's too busy to help them.

Melanie suddenly regains her hearing when you show her what you've worked out. She reads over your justification several times, scratches her head and says, "Why didn't you tell me how bad things were earlier? We could have addressed this long ago! Let's see if we can get some contract staff in for next week."

The Truth

If a business wants to stay profitable it needs to scrutinize expenditures closely in terms of their necessity and what they will return to the business. If you want to get funding for your Help Desk improvement you need to put together a good cost justification that shows the return to the business.

The Three Secrets

There are three secrets to a good cost justification: the effective use of estimating, measures that reflect business value, and good organization. We will discuss each of these briefly in this section.

Effective Use of Estimating

Learn how to estimate. The more you practice the easier it will get. You need actual data from your Help Desk management system in your justification, but it becomes much more powerful when it is coupled with estimates such as lost customer time and the future magnitude of the problem. Estimates are typically used for data that can't be specifically tracked.

Measures That Reflect Business Value

Your cost justification should show what the current situation is costing the business and how your solution can help the business. On a Help Desk, one of the most effective measures for showing business impact is the time that customers have to wait trying to get help. As we saw in

Chapter 1, this time has a direct, negative impact on the profitability of the business. The business is getting zero return for its investment in those employees, which in specific terms is their salaries.

Good Organization

The five-part formula outlined in the following section will help you organize your data, estimated and tracked, into a format that presents your case effectively.

The Formula

A cost justification is divided into five parts:

1. A description of the situation
2. The problem or requirement in terms of what it is costing the business
3. Your proposed solution and the benefits it offers the business
4. Solution options and costs
5. Your recommendation

If your cost justification is long, spanning several pages, you may want to preface it with a short management summary.

The Situation

In this part of your cost justification you provide some background for the request you're about to make. You are building the basis for your justification by creating an understanding of the environment or situation in which the problem or need exists. You should state facts without getting into what the problem or requirement is and you use real numbers, not estimates. Using the point or bullet list form will help keep your description brief and help you stick to the facts.

The Problem and Its Cost to the Business

In this second part of your cost justification you describe the problem or requirement and what it is costing the business. Here's where you use estimates. You need to show what it is costing the business not to do what you're asking.

Measures That Reflect Business Value

The cost to the business needs to be defined in terms of something that is valuable to the business. Some examples of these are as follows:

Customer time. If a customer is waiting for a problem to be resolved or running around trying to get it resolved then that customer is not working for the business, or at least not working at full capacity. The business is not moving ahead as quickly as it could be. It is paying for dead time. The more dead time there is in a company the bigger the negative impact on the profitability of the business. Most other measures will relate back to customer time.

Peer support. The customer who could not get support from your Help Desk goes to a peer for help. Now the peer is no longer working for the business. The result is even more dead time for the business.

Certain situations could lead to errors in data. For example, customers failing to take required training could cause errors in the data they work on. The cost of these errors could include the time required to fix them and the resulting loss in business revenue.

Things not done. If the business has problems with technology for one reason or another, not only is time lost but the benefits it could have enjoyed from the things that could have been accomplished in that time have also been lost. Those benefits could be revenue. For example, consider the cost of technology problems that cause a toy manufacturer to enter the market two months late, thereby missing most of the Christmas rush. The loss in revenue would be significant.

Real Data versus Estimates

You won't always be able to get real data to show the cost of the problem to your business. Sometimes you will have to estimate figures such as lost customer time. An estimate is your best guess based on your experience and the facts that you do have. The more experience you have with estimates the more accurate your estimates will become. Estimated numbers are very powerful and are taken very seriously if they are credible. To make estimates credible, make them conservative (as we do in the examples in this chapter). Run them by a few managers, colleagues, or customers to get their input and feedback. It is much better that you should hear "This estimate is ridiculous" from the people you ask to review your estimates than from the decision makers. If you base your estimates on experience; get feedback from customers, managers, or colleagues; and make your estimates conservative, they will be credible.

Some examples of the ways in which you might want to use estimates include the following:

- You might estimate the time a customer loses while waiting for support for each call to the Help Desk that is eventually abandoned (goes unanswered). This, together with real data from your Help Desk, will allow you to calculate the cost of abandoned calls.

- You might estimate the amount of time a customer spends redoing work because of errors generated by a lack of proper training. Use this estimate to calculate the cost of these errors.

- If you want to calculate what peer support is costing your organization you will need to estimate the number of times customers don't even bother calling the Help Desk because they go to their peers for help and then the amount of time they spend with their peers.

Although estimates are important, a cost justification cannot be based solely on estimates. You need real data for your justification, most likely that gathered from your Help Desk management system. If you aren't tracking your calls and don't have real data don't try to do a cost justification. Gather some data first.

Money Talks

The measures you use to express the cost of a problem to the business in your cost justification are most effective when they are expressed in dollar terms. Fortunately, you can translate almost any business cost into dollars. Customer time, for example, can be translated into dollars by using an average hourly salary, including benefits, which is available from your human resources or finance department. If the rate were $60 per hour, five hours of wasted customer time would translate into a very real cost of $300 in employee time. The business therefore received zero return for the $300 it invested in that employee. Similarly, errors can be translated into dollars by estimating the time lost because of the error and then applying the average hourly salary. This figure can then be added to any revenue lost directly as a result of the error to get the total cost of the error.

Proposed Solution and Benefits

After you have described the problem or requirement you need to suggest one or more possible solutions. Sometimes the need is very simple or the solution is obvious, and you don't need to or cannot suggest anything more. Other times there may be several ways of solving the problem or meeting the requirement. For example, if you are facing an upward trend in the number of calls coming into the Help Desk and you want to find a way to decrease the number of calls the solutions you might suggest include automation, such as interactive voice response (IVR); outsourced extra help; or a project to identify and eliminate recurring problems.

One solution that you should always include in your justification is doing nothing. Calculating the cost of doing nothing is a very powerful way of showing what happens if you don't get what you are asking for.

Solution Options and Costs

You often have several alternatives when implementing a solution. The "Solution Options and Costs" section of your cost justification is where you compare the costs of these alternatives.

Options

Considering more than one alternative will give you more confidence that the option you eventually select is the best one. It will also make the best option stand out as the most obvious choice and make decision makers feel they do in fact have a choice and are not being given a "take-it-or-leave-it" ultimatum. Examples of alternatives might include outsourcing versus hiring; various combinations of outsourcing and hiring, for example, outsource help combined with hiring and training new staff; and leasing versus buying.

Costs of Solutions

When calculating the costs of solutions remember to take onetime costs such as technology purchases or hiring costs into account. Show these as being separate from ongoing costs. Also, take into account the fact that the problem will continue until the moment you put your solution into place. You therefore need to calculate the future continuing cost of the problem and include it in the cost of the solution.

Comparing Alternatives and Costs

To make it easier to compare solution alternatives you may want to use a table to compare costs over specific time periods. For example, you might show the cost for the first quarter (including onetime costs), the cost for the first year, and ongoing quarterly costs for each solution option. Doing nothing should always be one of the options you show costs for.

Recommendation

This is the easy part. If you've done your homework well the choice should be obvious. Make your recommendation and explain why you are making it. A table that compares the cost of the options being considered would be a good way to reinforce your explanation and will make your choice even clearer.

A Word about the Examples

Before you plough into the three examples presented later in this chapter, I want to give you a few guidelines to follow so you do not get caught up in the actual numbers or situations but stay focused on the method I am trying to get across to you. The guidelines are as follows:

Focus on the method illustrated in the example, not on the dollar figures or call statistics. For example, if I hear you thinking, "What? Sixty dollars an hour? I don't get $60 an hour," I will know you are not focusing on the method (and keep in mind that that hourly wage includes all employee benefits and overhead and is very realistic in some businesses).

Focus on the method, not on the individual situations. Don't let yourself get distracted by such thoughts as "Surfboard salesperson in Hawaii? That practitioner will never make it as a surfboard salesperson . . . there are already too many surfboard salespeople in Hawaii," or "Thirty-one calls per day? I take 60 calls per day and still have time to eat lunch and take breaks." Remember, the examples are just that, examples. They do not portray everyone's environment.

Focus on the method. I think you get my point now. Enjoy the examples.

Example A: Justifying Training

I'm now going to walk you through the process of putting together a fairly simple cost justification for training. Comments that would not appear in the actual cost justification (my comments) are italicized.

Example A involves a Help Desk that is moving from mainframe support to PC support. The practitioners on the Help Desk who are mainframe experts do not have the knowledge to handle the PC calls and so must pass them on to second-level support or to the other Help Desk practitioners for resolution. We are going to try to justify extensive PC training for the mainframe experts that will enable them to resolve more PC calls. A worksheet of the calculations used in this example is given at the end of this section.

Situation

In this section we want to give the decision makers the background they need to understand the problem. We use real data—the statistics our Help Desk management system gives us. By the way, if you ever wondered, "Why do we have to log every call no matter how simple?" this is the reason. If you didn't have that data you couldn't do this justification. If you only logged some of your calls you might not be able to make a case.

Staff

Currently there are six people on the Help Desk taking calls. Two of these have only mainframe knowledge, three have only PC knowledge, and one has both mainframe and PC knowledge.

Number of Calls and Environment Being Supported

In one week there are, on average, 1,500 calls. Of these, 800 are mainframe and 700 are PC. Last quarter saw the same number of total calls, but the breakdown was 1,000 mainframe and 500 PC. From last quarter to this quarter PC calls therefore increased by 40 percent, while mainframe calls decreased by 20 percent. Two thousand PCs are currently being supported. This is up from 1,500 last quarter.

Table 10.1 summarizes the situation. *We want to put the information about number of calls and the environment being supported into a table to make it easier to absorb.*

The Problem and Its Cost to the Business

We now need to describe the problem in terms of what it is costing the business.

The Problem

The two mainframe experts on the Help Desk cannot resolve the PC issues that are sometimes involved in mainframe calls, and they cannot re-

Table 10.1 Summary of the Situation

	This Quarter	*Last Quarter*	*% Change*
Total number of calls per week	1,500	1,500	0%
Mainframe calls per week	800	1,000	-20%
PC calls per week	700	500	+40%
PCs being supported	2,000	1,500	+33%

solve PC calls that come in when the four other Help Desk practitioners are busy.

Cost of the Problem

Each time one of the two mainframe people passes a PC call on, the customer's problem is not resolved at point of call. The customer must wait for support. Each mainframe person passes on an average of 5 PC calls per day, for a total of 50 calls per week for the two mainframe people combined.

We're now going to use one of the most powerful estimates—customer wait time. Customer wait time is the time the customer has to wait before someone gets back to the customer with a resolution. The customer is not able to work during this time. The profitability of the business is negatively impacted. Even with an estimated wait time of only 20 minutes per call, a loss of 17 customer hours of productivity occurs every week. If we use an estimated average salary of $60 per hour, this works out to $1,020 per week or $13,260 per quarter. *One quarter is 13 weeks.*

This situation is only the tip of the iceberg. The shift toward PCs is a continuing trend that will exacerbate the problem significantly. We need to point this out. The PC environment and related support requirements are growing. Assuming that the growth trend of 40 percent in PC-type calls continues for at least one more quarter and is accompanied by a 40 percent increase in calls that need to be passed on, in the next quarter each of the two mainframe staff will have to turn away seven calls per day. Using the same assumption of an estimated wait time of 20 minutes per call, this would mean a loss of 23 hours every week. At $60 per hour, this works out to $1,380 per week. Over one quarter this would be $17,940.

If we do not consider any further growth of the problem, the first year cost would be $67,080. These losses are summarized in Table 10.2. *Again, we want to use a table here to simplify things. If you're getting lost in the calculations, see the worksheet for Example A later in this chapter.*

Other Costs

Include any qualitative measures that you have in your justification. They can lend a cost justification weight and can sometimes serve to push a fence-sitter

Table 10.2 Cost of the Problem

	Estimated Growth in PC Calls	Estimated Wait Time per Call	No. of Calls Passed on per Week	Total Time Lost per Week	Cost per Week, at $60 per Hour	Cost per Quarter	Cost for One Year
Current quarter	N/A	20 minutes	50	17 hours	$1,020	$13,260	$13,260 first quarter
Next quarter estimate	40% (based on growth to date)	20 minutes	70	23 hours	$1,380	$17,940	$53,820 next three quarters
Total							$67,080

into making a decision. Again, if necessary, estimate what qualitative measures such as low job satisfaction, stress, or employee turnover are costing in terms of lost productivity and lost time.

Other costs that could affect the situation if it is not addressed are as follows:

- Turnover costs caused by people leaving an unpleasant situation
- Costs incurred by stress or illness caused by the unpleasant situation

Proposed Solution and Benefits

This is a simple problem so we choose to suggest only two solutions—training and doing nothing. People in my classes often suggest alternatives such as replacing the mainframe experts with PC experts. (Help Desk practitioners, when unleashed, can be a ruthless bunch.)

The proposed solution is to have the two mainframe experts attend comprehensive training. Get them up to speed in PC knowledge. The benefits of this approach are fourfold:

- More calls could be handled at point of call. As a result, $1,020 per week in customer time currently being lost could be regained. The $67,080 loss over one year could be avoided.

- The weight of calls is shifting from mainframe-type calls to PC-type calls. This quarter saw an increase of 40 percent in PC calls and a decrease of 20 percent in mainframe calls. Getting staff trained to handle PC calls will ensure that the Help Desk is ready to handle this trend.

- Turnover costs caused by people leaving an unpleasant situation would be reduced since the situation would be much improved.

- Costs incurred as a result of stress or illness caused by the unpleasant situation would be reduced.

The alternative solution is to do nothing, leave the environment as it is. The benefit of this solution is that there is no immediate out-of-pocket cost.

Solution Options and Costs

Here is where we compare different implementations of the solution. We give decision makers a choice.

Option 1

Have the mainframe practitioners take a series of three courses from ABC Training over a period of three months. The courses are offered close by so there would be no travel involved. The practitioners would attend class one week each month. The costs of this option are shown in Table 10.3. *Again, using a table keeps things very clear and simple.*

If this were a more complicated justification we could factor in a learning curve. The numbers in Table 10.3 assume that the practitioners will be able to handle all PC calls as soon as they finish the courses, that is, that the losses will stop suddenly. This probably isn't realistic. We could estimate that a steadily decreasing percentage of the losses would continue for a time, three months say, until the practitioners were up to speed.

Table 10.3 Cost of Option 1

Description	Total Cost
Three courses for two people at $1,500 per course	$9,000
Cost of backup support for the 15 days of training	$3,000
Loss of $1,020 per week will continue before and during the training process. Estimate that there will be 10 weeks of losses as the staff start training and gain PC knowledge.	$10,200
Total	$22,200

Option 2

Have staff take an intensive PC crash course from ABC Training. The courses are offered only at the vendor's site so staff would have to travel and would need hotel accommodations. The course would take two weeks to complete. The costs for Option 2 are shown in Table 10.4.

Option 3

Do nothing. Make no changes. Live with the situation. The costs to the business for this option are shown in Table 10.5. *For the option of doing nothing we use cumulative costs to emphasize the loss to the business.*

Besides the costs shown in Table 10.5, we must consider the following costs:

- Any costs incurred through employee absenteeism from stress-induced illness

Table 10.4 Cost of Option 2

Description	Total Cost
Two crash courses for two people at $6,000 per course	$12,000
Cost of travel and accommodations for two people	$4,000
Cost of backup support for the 10 days of training	$2,000
Loss of $1,020 per week will continue until the training ends. Estimate that training will start two weeks from now; so there would be two weeks of losses.	$2,040
Total	$20,040

Table 10.5 Cost of Option 3

Description	Total Cost
Loss of $1,020 per week continuing for this quarter (13 weeks)	$13,260
Loss of $1,380 per week continuing over the next quarter	$17,940
Total cost for six months	$31,200
Total cost for one year, assuming growth does not continue	$67,080

- Any costs incurred by decreased productivity caused by stress
- Any turnover costs caused by people leaving an unpleasant situation

Recommendation

When we recommend a course of action, we show a comparison of the costs of our options over the same time period. This will make the reason for our choice more obvious.

Cost Comparison

Table 10.6 shows a comparison of the three solution options.

Recommendation

We recommend Option 2: Have the practitioners take the intensive crash course. Option 2 is the most cost-effective. The return on investment (ROI) of training happens in less than six months. Six months of doing nothing is more expensive than getting the training.

That's it! We've done such a good job that the decision makers have given us what we wanted. We can train our two mainframe practitioners and get on with the job of supporting the business.

Table 10.6 Cost Comparison of the Three Options

Option	Cost over First Six Months	Cost over One Year
Option 1	$22,200	$22,200
Option 2	$20,040	$20,040
Option 3	$31,200	$67,080+

Table 10.7 Number of Calls and Number of PCs Being Supported

	This Quarter	*Last Quarter*	*% Change*
Total number of calls per week	1,500	1,500	0%
Mainframe calls per week	800	1,000	-20%
PC calls per week	700	500	+40%
PCs being supported	2,000	1,500	+33%

Example A Worksheet

Here are the detailed calculations and the reasoning behind Example A.

Situation

There are six people on the Help Desk: two mainframe experts, three PC experts, and one person who knows both PCs and mainframes. The number of calls and the number of PCs being supported from this quarter to next are shown in Table 10.7.

Cost to the Business

The cost to the business is based on the five calls per day that each of the mainframe experts is unable to resolve at point of call.

The number of calls passed on is as follows:

- Two mainframe experts passing five calls per day each over five days per week = 2 people × 5 calls × 5 days = 50 calls passed on per workweek.

The cost of calls passed on is as follows:

- Assume each customer loses on average 20 minutes for every call that is passed on.

- The cost of calls that are passed on is 20 minutes for each of 50 calls. This is 20 minutes × 50 calls = 1,000 minutes per week. We translate this into hours and get 1,000 minutes ÷ 60 minutes = 16.66, or 17 hours per week.

- Assume an average hourly customer wage, including benefits, of $60 per hour.

- The cost of passed-on calls becomes 17 hours per week × $60 per hour = $1,020 per week. There are approximately 13 weeks in each quarter. The cost becomes $1,020 × 13 = $13,260 over one quarter.

The cost of calls in the future (next quarter) is calculated as follows:

- Assume that the 40 percent increase in PC calls shown in Table 10.7 brings a 40 percent increase in calls that need to be passed on.

- Five calls × 1.4 (a 40 percent increase) = 7 calls. This means each of the two mainframe practitioners will turn away seven calls per day.

- Over a week, this would be 7 calls × 2 people × 5 days × 20 minutes = 1,400 minutes = 23.3, or 23 hours.

- At $60 per hour the cost of passed-on calls becomes 23 hours × $60 = $1,380 per week. There are approximately 13 weeks in each quarter. The cost becomes $1,380 × 13 = $17,940 over one quarter.

Cost of Doing Nothing

If the company selects the option of doing nothing losses would continue at $1,020 per week for one quarter and then increase to $1,380 in the next quarter. We are conservative and assume that the trend tapers off there, and losses stay at $1,380 for the rest of a year. So we have one quarter in which we lose $1,020 per week and three quarters in which we lose $1,380 per week. Using our calculations from the previous section this translates into a loss of $13,260 for the first quarter and losses of $17,940 for each of the next three quarters. This gives us the following figures:

- For the first quarter we will lose $13,260 + $17,940 = $31,200.
- In one year we will lose $13,260 + (3 × $17,940) = $13,260 + $53,820 = $67,080.

Example B: Justifying Help for Peak Load

Example B involves cost justifying extra resources to handle an as-yet-unexplained daily peak in call volume.

Situation

There are six people taking calls on the Help Desk. In a normal week, there are approximately 1,500 calls. In the past two weeks, since our new office software was installed, our weekly call load has increased to 2,200, with almost all of that increase occurring during peak call load times. We don't completely understand the reason for the increase. Significant peaks in call load occur between 10:00 A.M. and 12:00 P.M. and between 3:00 P.M. and 5:00 P.M. *You may want to include an actual call distribution graph from your Help Desk management system in your cost justification.*

The Problem and Its Cost to the Business

The existing staff cannot handle the peak call load. Approximately 100 calls are abandoned each day during our two peak times. Assuming that each of these calls involves, on average, a customer loss of productivity of 20 minutes, we are looking at the following costs to the business:

- 100 calls abandoned at 20 minutes per call translates into 165 hours per week.
- If we assume an average hourly customer wage of $60 per hour, this becomes a loss of $9,900 per week in terms of employee time. Over one quarter this becomes $128,700. Over one year the loss is $514,800.

Other costs are as follows:

- 40 customer complaints have been logged in the past week on our feedback line. We are losing credibility. We suspect that customers are trying to find alternate methods of support, such as their peers.
- Stress levels are increasing on the Help Desk. People are losing effectiveness.

Proposed Solution and Benefits

The options we examine here are getting extra resourcing for the increased call load and doing nothing. The proposed solution is to get help to handle support during the four peak hours each day, at least while the peaks continue. The benefits of this approach include the following:

- We would eliminate the high abandonment rate. The $9,900 per week in customer time currently being lost can be regained. In one month, this would be $39,600.

- The pressure on existing Help Desk staff would be relieved and stress levels would decrease.

- Customer complaints would drop. The Help Desk's image would improve.

The alternative solution is to do nothing, leave the environment as it is. The benefit of the alternative solution is that there would be no immediate out-of-pocket cost.

Solution Options and Costs

We offer two implementation options for our solution to acquire extra resources. The third option we examine is doing nothing.

Option 1

Take on two part-time staff. Hire two permanent part-time staff members to work from home for four hours each day during peaks. Table 10.8 on page 314 shows the costs of implementing Option 1.

In the interests of simplicity we have not taken into account such factors as capital depreciation or equipment leasing options. If your cost justification is more complex than this you may want to include factors like those.

Option 2

Outsource the equivalent work of two part-time staff to Support Happy Inc. Your support could be set up so overflow calls would be automatically routed to Support Happy during the peak periods. Customers would not realize they were speaking to a third party. If your support re-

Table 10.8 Cost of Option 1

Description	Ongoing Costs per Quarter	Onetime Costs
Salary (including benefits) for two people	$24,000	
Cost of backup support for five days (2.5 days each) of vacation	$ 1,000	
Estimated cost of ongoing training	$ 1,000	
Loss of $9,900 per week during the hiring/training process. Estimate this process will take six weeks.		$59,400
Cost of technology to allow new staff to work from home		$20,000
Total	$26,000	$79,400
Total for first quarter: $105,400		
Total for first year: $183,400		

quirements dictated it, at the end of three months the contract could be renewed. Table 10.9 shows the costs of implementing Option 2.

If our problem were more complex, one factor we would want to take into account is the extra cost arising from the Help Desk manager's need to supervise the outsourced staff. This is something that is often overlooked and can become disastrous. Even in major outsourcing initiatives companies forget to include the cost of a full-time management employee to manage the outsourced function. If the outsourced function isn't managed it will, very simply, fail.

Table 10.9 Cost of Option 2

Description	Ongoing Costs per Quarter	Onetime Costs
Three-month contract for two Support Happy people	$30,000	
Loss of $9,900 per week during contract negotiations. Estimate this process will take two weeks.		$19,800
Total	$30,000	$19,800
Total for first quarter: $49,800		
Total for first year: $139,800		

Table 10.10 Cost of Option 3

Description	Ongoing Costs per Quarter
Ongoing loss of $9,900 per week	$128,700
Total	$128,700

Total for first quarter: $128,700+
Total for first year: $514,800+

Option 3

Do nothing. Make no changes. Live with the situation. The costs for this option are shown in Table 10.10.

In this example, we are dealing with an unexplained increase. It may be that this increase is temporary, in which case our losses would not continue for a year, but we don't know this to be the case. Comparing costs over a year, as in Table 10.11, gives a good illustration of the costs of each option compared to the loss being incurred (the cost of doing nothing) over time. Sometimes the startup costs of a solution are such that it is more expensive than doing nothing for the first few months, but after the first few months the savings the solution offers become very visible. Calculate the costs as far out as necessary to show the return (payback) of your solutions.

Besides the costs shown in Table 10.10, we must consider the following costs:

- Costs incurred by employees going to their peers for help. If we needed to, we could use an estimate of this amount to add ammunition to our justification. Peer support is extremely expensive.

- Any costs incurred by Help Desk employees' absenteeism from illness caused by stress.

- Any costs incurred as a result of the decreased productivity of Help Desk employees due to stress.

Recommendation

We recommend Option 2, outsourcing additional help to Support Happy Inc. The comparative costs of the three solutions are shown in Table 10.11. Although Option 2 has a 15 percent higher quarterly ongo-

Table 10.11 Cost Comparison of the Three Options

Option	Cost over First Quarter	Cost over First Year	Quarterly Ongoing Cost
Option 1	$105,400	$183,400	$ 26,000
Option 2	$ 49,800	$139,800	$ 30,000
Option 3	$128,700+	$514,800+	$128,700+

ing cost than Option 1, the startup costs for Option 1 are such that it would take more than two years for those costs to be absorbed. At that point, maintenance and replacement costs for the at-home technology would push the cost for Option 1 higher again. Also, should calls be reduced and extra help no longer needed, the contract with Support Happy could be discontinued. With Option 1, there will be permanent employees and technology investment to consider.

Example B Worksheet

Here are the detailed calculations and the reasoning behind Example B.

Situation

There are six people on the Help Desk. The dramatic change in the number of calls from two weeks ago to the present is shown in Table 10.12. There are two peaks in call traffic, between 10 A.M. and 12 P.M. and between 3 P.M. and 5 P.M.

Cost to the Business

The cost to the business is based on the 100 calls that are abandoned each day during two peak times in call traffic.

Table 10.12 Number of Calls

	Currently	Two Weeks Ago	% Change
Total number of calls per week	2,200	1,500	47%

The number of calls abandoned is as follows:

- 100 calls per day

The cost of abandoned calls is as follows:

- Assume each customer loses on average 20 minutes for every call that is abandoned.

- The cost of abandoned calls each day is 20 minutes for each of 100 calls. That is 100 calls × 20 minutes = 2,000 minutes. This is 2,000 minutes ÷ 60 minutes = 33.33, or 33 hours per day.

- In one five-day week the loss is 33 hours × 5 days = 165 hours. Assuming an average hourly wage of $60 per hour, this gives us 165 hours × $60 = $9,900 per week.

Solution Options and Costs

The calculations for each of the solution options are as follows:

Option 1: Take on Two Part-time Staff

- The estimated cost per quarter, including salary of $24,000, $1,000 backup support costs for vacation, and $1,000 in training costs, comes to $26,000.

- The onetime costs are those incurred during the setup period of the solution. The first onetime cost is the cost of the technology the people will need: $20,000. The next cost is the $9,900 loss per week that will continue for six weeks while the hiring process takes place. The total startup cost is thus $20,000 + (6 × $9,900) = $20,000 + $59,400 = $79,400.

- The costs for the first three months (the first quarter) are onetime costs plus one quarter of ongoing costs. This is $79,400 + $26,000 = $105,400.

- The costs for the first year are the costs for the first quarter plus the ongoing costs of three more quarters. This is $105,400 + (3 × $26,000) = $183,400.

Option 2: Outsource Two Part-time Staff

- The ongoing cost per quarter is the cost of the support contract for two people: $26,000.

- The onetime costs are those incurred during the setup period of the solution. The onetime cost here is the continuing loss of $9,900 per week while contract negotiations take place, over two weeks. The total startup cost is thus $2 \times \$9,900 = \$19,800$.

- The costs for the first three months (the first quarter) are onetime costs plus one quarter of ongoing costs. This is $\$19,800 + \$30,000 = \$49,800$.

- The costs for the first year are the costs for the first quarter plus the ongoing costs of three more quarters. This is $\$49,800 + (3 \times \$30,000) = 139,800$.

Option 3: Do Nothing

- The ongoing cost is constant at $9,900 per week.

- Over one quarter, the cost is $\$9,900 \times 13 = \$128,700$.

- Over one year, the cost is $\$9,900 \times 52 = \$514,800$.

These are all minimum costs. The cost of doing nothing could rise as a result of factors like peer support, which means customers would go to their colleagues for help. Not only would customers not be productive while their problem continued, now their colleagues would not be productive either. Stress and illness among the Help Desk's staff caused by working in a tense, unpleasant situation are another cost. Illness and stress cause absenteeism and loss of productivity.

Example C: Justifying Help for a Help Desk in Trouble

Example C involves cost justifying extra resources to get you out of what threatens to become an out-of-control problem cycle. Last month you had five Help Desk practitioners working on your Help Desk. At the beginning of this month, one of your practitioners quit to become a surfboard salesperson in Hawaii.

"No replacement," said your management. "We're cutting costs." Not only does the Help Desk have to deal with the extra load caused by the departure of the now apparently prosperous surfboard salesperson, but calls have started to rise. The business you support just bought out a small packaging business, and you are now supporting 800 more customers. By the end of this month you have logged 5,000 calls. Next month you are converting the 800 new customers to your standard software platform, so you expect even more calls. Customers are getting fed up and going to peers for support. The Help Desk staff is stressed, and the Help Desk is losing credibility.

You have no time for improvement initiatives. Your environment is getting more and more complex, and customers are starting to ask for extended hours of support. You know your calls will keep increasing, but you have no time to look for ways to decrease calls. "Enough is enough!" you say. "We need help!" Since you are a proactive practitioner, you put together the following cost justification (although you seriously considered taking a course called "Making Surfboards Sell" and joining your former colleague in Hawaii).

Situation

Last month we had five Help Desk practitioners; this month we're down to four. With five practitioners, we were able to deliver a good level of service and do some work on call elimination initiatives. With five practitioners, we could handle 3,200 calls per month, supporting 2,200 workstations. Each person handled approximately 31 calls per day, plus some project work. With four practitioners, the load became 38 calls per person per day. That increase was enough to seriously hamper progress on your call elimination initiatives.

This month, our call load increased to 5,000 calls, largely because of the additional customers we took on from ABC Packaging. We now support 800 more workstations, bringing the total we support to 3,000. The increased call load means each person must handle 60 calls per day. Our calls tend to be about matters that cannot be resolved in a few minutes. Handling a call load of 60 calls per day is simply not possible, and as a result our abandonment rate has gone from almost nothing to 22 percent, or 1,100 calls per month. Average call wait time has also increased, from negligible to three minutes. Table 10.13 summarizes the situation.

We have had to suspend work on our call elimination initiatives. The environment we support is becoming more and more complex, which

Table 10.13 Summary of the Situation

	This Month	Last Month	% Change
Number of people on the Help Desk	4	5	-20%
Number of calls	5,000	3,200	+56%
Call load per person per day	60	31	+94%
Workstations being supported	3,000	2,200	+36%
Average wait time per call	5 minutes	Negligible	
Abandonment rate	22% (= 1,100 calls)	Negligible	

will increase our call load even more, and our customers are starting to ask for extended hours of support. The Help Desk practitioners are becoming very stressed. We have also learned that several of our customers are going to their peers rather than try to get help from the Help Desk.

The Problem and Its Cost to the Business

Existing staff cannot handle the call load. A total of 1,100 calls are abandoned each month. Assuming each of these calls involves, on average, a customer loss of productivity of 20 minutes, we are looking at the following costs to the business:

- 1,100 calls abandoned each month, at 20 minutes per call, translates into 367 hours per month. If we assume an average hourly customer wage of $60 per hour, this becomes a loss of approximately $22,020 per month in terms of employee time. Over one year this is $264,240.

- An average wait time of five minutes for each of 5,000 calls per month comes to 417 hours per month. At $60 per hour this becomes a loss of $25,020 per month. Over a year this becomes $300,240.

- The cost of abandoned calls and wait time comes to $47,040 per month, or $564,480 per year.

Other costs are as follows:

- Customers are going to their peers to try to get support. If only 10 percent of the abandoned calls involve peer support, that is still 110 times per month that customers are trying to get help from their peers. At 20 minutes per peer, that comes to 37 hours, or $2,220 per month—$26,640 per year. *Keeping these kind of estimates very conservative helps keep them credible.*

- Stress levels are increasing on the Help Desk. People are losing effectiveness.

- The Help Desk has no time for call elimination initiatives. Our environment is becoming more complex, calls will be increasing, and the problem will worsen.

The costs are summarized in Table 10.14.

Proposed Solution and Benefits

The options we examine here are resourcing for the increased call load and doing nothing. The proposed solution is to add resourcing to bring the daily call load back to nearly 31 calls per person so the level of service can be returned to what it was before and the work on call elimination initiatives can be reinstated. The benefits of this solution are as follows:

- We would eliminate the high abandonment rate, wait time, and peer support, regaining the $49,260 per month.

- The pressure would be relieved on existing Help Desk staff, and stress levels would decrease.

- Call elimination initiatives could be reinstated. We could get control over the increasing call load.

Table 10.14 Summary of Costs

Factor	Cost over One Month	Cost over One Year
Abandoned calls	$ 22,020	$264,240
Wait time	$ 25,020	$300,240
Peer support	$ 2,220	$ 26,640
Total	$ 49,260	$591,120

The alternative solution is to do nothing; leave the environment as it is. The benefit of this approach is that there is no immediate out-of-pocket cost.

Solution Options and Costs

We offer two implementation options for our solution of bringing in extra resources. The third option we examine is doing nothing. *Note that we do not include an option for hiring full-time staff. In a cost-cutting environment, it is much easier to get funds for outsourced resources than it is to get additional head count.*

Option 1

Hire contract staff from Support Happy Inc. in staggered contracts. We would start with four contract staff for the first four months. This would free up one of our practitioners (on a rotating basis) to work on call elimination initiatives full time so we can regain control of our problems. This would leave seven people handling 34 calls per day each while the eighth person worked on eliminating calls. After three months, we would reevaluate the situation and hopefully reduce the contract staff to three. If the call load stayed at a similar level and we went back to having everyone on the phones, this three-contract-staff arrangement would keep us at about 34 calls per day. If things change, however, and we find we need that fourth person we can always renegotiate our contract with Support Happy. Table 10.15 shows the costs involved in implementing option 1.

Table 10.15 Cost of Option 1

Description	Cost, First Quarter	Cost, First Year	Continuing Yearly Cost
3-month contract for one Support Happy person	$ 20,000	$ 20,000	
12-month contract for three Support Happy people	$ 45,000	$180,000	$180,000
Loss of $49,260 per month during contract negotiations. Estimate this process will take two weeks.	$ 24,630	$ 24,630	
Total	$ 89,630	$224,630	$180,000

Note: A 3-month contract is more expensive than 3 months of a 12-month contract because it is a shorter-term contract. For the sake of simplicity, I have not included any potential increases in outsourcing costs or orientation time for the contract staff. (We could assume that we negotiate a two-year rate and that Support Happy Inc. pays for orientation.)

Option 2

Hire four contract staff from Support Happy Inc. on a yearly contract. This would free up one of our practitioners (on a rotating basis) to work on call elimination initiatives full time so we could regain control of our problems and make service improvements. This would leave seven people handling 34 calls per day each and one person working on call elimination. Table 10.16 shows the costs involved in implementing Option 2.

Option 3

Do nothing. Make no changes. Live with the situation. The costs of this option are shown in Table 10.17. If we do nothing, our calls will keep increasing, so our continuing yearly cost will be even greater than Table 10.17 shows. Also, the costs incurred from absenteeism, the reduction in Help Desk productivity, and turnover, all caused by stress and stress-related illnesses, will push the continuing cost even higher. *If you need to you can actually estimate the increases in calls and the turnover rate so you can put a number to those costs.*

Table 10.16 Cost of Option 2

Description	Cost, First Quarter	Cost, First Year	Continuing Yearly Cost
12-month contract for four Support Happy people	$ 60,000	$240,000	$240,000
Loss of $49,260 per month during contract negotiations. Estimate this process will take two weeks.	$ 24,630	$ 24,630	
Total	$ 84,630	$264,630	$240,000

Table 10.17 Cost of Option 3

Description	Cost, First Quarter	Cost, First Year	Continuing Yearly Cost
Ongoing loss of $49,260 per month	$147,780	$591,120	$591,120+
Total	$147,780+	$591,120+	$591,120+

Recommendation

We recommend Option 1, a staggered approach to outsourcing extra help. The comparative costs of the three solutions we have presented are shown in Table 10.18. If we find that our environment is such that after three months we still need that fourth Support Happy person, we will be able to renegotiate a contract for a fourth person at a rate that does not significantly increase the cost of Option 1 relative to Option 2.

Example C Worksheet

Here are the detailed calculations and the reasoning behind Example C.

Situation

Table 10.19 summarizes the situation. Average wait time is the average time a customer has to wait on the phone before someone answers. An abandonment rate of 22 percent means 22 percent of 5,000 calls, which is 1,100 calls. Last month, both the abandonment rate and the average wait time were negligible. Another facet of the situation is that customers are starting to go to peers for support.

Table 10.18 Cost Comparison of the Three Options

Description	Cost over First Quarter	Cost over First Year	Ongoing Yearly Cost
Option 1	$ 89,630	$224,630	$180,000
Option 2	$ 84,630	$264,630	$240,000
Option 3	$147,780+	$591,120+	$591,120+

Table 10.19 Summary of the Situation

	This Month	*Last Month*	*% Change*
Number of people on the Help Desk	4	5	-20%
Number of calls	5,000	3,200	+56%
Call load per person per day	60	31	+94%
Workstations being supported	3,000	2,200	+36%
Average wait time per call	5 minutes	Negligible	
Abandonment rate	22% (= 1,100 calls)	Negligible	

Cost to the Business

The cost to the business is based on the 1,100 calls that are abandoned each month, the five-minute wait times, and peer support.

The cost of abandoned calls, wait time, and peer support is as follows:

- Assume that each customer loses on average 20 minutes for every call that is abandoned.

- The cost of abandoned calls each month is 20 minutes for each of 1,100 calls. That is 1,100 calls × 20 minutes = 22,000 minutes. This is 22,000 minutes ÷ 60 minutes = 366.7, or 367 hours per month. Assuming an employee cost of $60 per hour, the cost becomes 367 hours × $60 = $22,020 per month.

- The cost of an average five-minute wait time per call over one month is 5 minutes × 5,000 calls = 25,000 minutes. This is 25,000 minutes ÷ 60 minutes = 416.7, or 417 hours. At $60 per hour this becomes 417 hours × $60 = $25,020 per month.

- We estimate that peer support happens in only 10 percent of the calls that are abandoned. Ten percent of 1,100 is 110. Assuming that the peer is bothered for 20 minutes, the loss is 110 calls × 20 minutes = 2,200 minutes. This is 2,200 minutes ÷ 60 minutes = 36.7, or 37 hours. At $60 per hour, this becomes 37 hours × $60 = $2,220 per month.

- The total cost per month is $22,020 + $25,020 + $2,220 = $49,260. Over one quarter, this is 3 × $49,260 = $147,780. Over one year this is $147,780 × 4 =$591,120.

Summing Up

I hope I've left you with a method that will help you justify anything you need on your Help Desk. The best way to ensure you will be able to use this method when you do need it is to practice. Look at a situation on your Help Desk that you would like to change and that you need funding for. It might be something like more training; it might be a Help Desk tool. Then go through the exercise of creating a cost justification for it. Redo your justification a few times until you are satisfied with it. Show it to your peers or manager for their input.

The method I've presented in this chapter will allow you to justify those things that are of value to the business. If you find that you cannot come up with a justification—you just cannot make the dollars go the way you want them to—then chances are what you are trying to justify does not make sense for the business. It may not be a worthwhile expenditure.

Checklist

This chapter has given you a method for justifying improvements for your Help Desk. Practice the method, and pose the questions in the following list to yourself. Revisit this chapter to review anything you don't understand.

- ✓ I don't whine or use psychic prediction when I need something, do I?
- ✓ Do I understand which measures represent business value?
- ✓ Do I understand how powerful estimates are and how to use them?
- ✓ Do I know what factors I can estimate?
- ✓ Do I know how to assign dollar values to my estimates?
- ✓ Do I understand the five steps involved in putting a cost justification together?

- ✓ Do I know how to calculate the cost of problems?
- ✓ Do I understand the concept of calculating the cost of doing nothing? Do I realize how critical it is to my justification?
- ✓ Am I clear about the process of offering different solutions and different implementation options for those solutions?
- ✓ Am I practicing putting together cost justifications?

Can I Interest You in Marketing?

Whether you realize it or not, you are marketing to your customers all the time. Every Help Desk interaction is a marketing opportunity. In this chapter, I want to show you that by making these interactions successful and then by going even further and creating marketing opportunities outside of your regular Help Desk interactions, you can actually reduce calls coming into the Help Desk. You can have a positive impact on the profitability of the business.

I'd like to begin by addressing two fallacies you may have about marketing. First, marketing means telling your customers about your services—period. Marketing does involve letting your customers know what services you offer, but that is only one small part of it. Second, marketing is fluff, not really part of your regular business. Not true. Without marketing, you will be getting more calls than you should, your customers will not be using technology as effectively as they could, and customers and management will not understand the value you are providing. Not a pretty environment.

Let's go to my old friend the vacuum cleaner salesperson for an example. (I actually thought that vacuum cleaner salespeople were extinct, but I got a call from one the other day.) Let's call this salesperson Don.

Don hears that you have twelve-year-old dust balls under your couch, so he decides you might be just about ready to buy a new vacuum cleaner. Don knocks on the door and introduces himself. The first thing Don does is to tell you about his company, ABC Vacuum Cleaners Inc. He wants to convince you that he is a respectable salesperson backed up by a respectable company. He wants you to have confidence in him and in his product. Then he shows you the value that his vacuum cleaner can offer you. To your horror, Don looks under your couch. Before you have a chance to explain that you're having a problem with your cleaning staff, Don looks up, smiles, and says, "There's lots of material there for a good demonstration!" With that, he plugs in the vacuum cleaner and within seconds has eliminated all of your dust balls, along with two dog bones, three watches, three channel changers, and about $6.50 in loose change.

You bend down and look under the couch in wonderment. Don then shows you how to use the vacuum and tells you about its many features. You are delighted and go from one piece of furniture to another, sucking up dust balls and family heirlooms as you go. Don makes sure you understand how the vacuum works, and he watches carefully as you try out all its features. As you're reaching for your credit card, Don tells you about upcoming sales on accessories and gives you a little calendar showing a different vacuum cleaner for every month, when the service center will be closed, and when promotional sales will be taking place. Don gets you a new vacuum from his van, takes it out of its box, and makes sure everything works. He leaves you vacuuming happily, rediscovering treasures that had been lost for years.

As proactive Help Desk practitioners we can learn a lot about marketing from Don. First, Don worried about image. He knew that if you didn't have confidence in him he wouldn't sell you a vacuum cleaner. Second, Don sold you value. He showed you the value the vacuum cleaner offered you. Third, Don educated you. He showed you how to use the vacuum cleaner. You won't have to call him back to ask him how to use it. Fourth, Don communicated information about his company's environment, about upcoming sales and about planned shutdowns. Don used the four components of marketing, which apply whether you're selling vacuum cleaners or working on a Help Desk. They are image, selling value, education, and communication.

In This Chapter

In this chapter, I'm going to talk about what marketing is and why we, as proactive Help Desk practitioners, need to worry about it. I will also talk in detail about each of the components of marketing as well as marketing vehicles and marketing initiatives. The specific topics I will cover include the following:

- Why do I need to worry about marketing?
- Image
- Selling value
- Education
- Communication
- Marketing vehicles
- A Help Desk Web site
- Implementing marketing initiatives

Why Do I Need to Worry about Marketing?

We learned from Don that marketing is about image, selling value, education, and communication. Consider a Help Desk that does no marketing. It would have the following characteristics:

No focus on image. Some customers might base their opinions of the Help Desk solely on an occasional, poorly written communication they may happen to see. This may cause them to avoid using the Help Desk and even to pass their own unfavorable opinions on to their colleagues. They are passing on a negative Help Desk image, even though they may never have actually used the Help Desk themselves. This may cause a customer to go to a peer for help instead of to the Help Desk. The time that customer spends trying to get help from his or her peer has a negative impact on the profitability of the business.

Little or no selling value. Since Help Desk successes go unnoticed and unrecognized, customers and management only remember the problems. If cost cutting or outsourcing comes up, the Help Desk will be on the "endangered department" list.

Little or no education. Customers aren't aware of any of the policies or standards you have in place. As a result, they may introduce non-standard products, which increase the complexity of support, and they may inadvertently breach security, perhaps allowing a virus into the system. Both of these situations would generate extra calls to the Help Desk.

Little or no communication. Customers don't know what is going on in the Help Desk's technological environment. If there are interruptions in service, they are not informed in time, which results in a flood of calls to the Help Desk as well as inconvenience to the customers.

Now let's turn this Help Desk around. The practitioners have all had a chat with Don, the vacuum cleaner salesperson, have taken some training to beef up their customer service and business writing skills, and are now practicing the four components of marketing. The Help Desk has a professional, service-oriented image. All Help Desk communications are professional, and customers have a fair amount of confidence in the Help Desk's ability to actually help them. Management and customers get regular updates on the Help Desk's performance and understand the value the Help Desk offers the business. There is no talk of outsourcing. Customers are aware of policies and standards and have started taking courses suggested by the Help Desk. They are making fewer calls to the Help Desk, which also keeps them informed about all changes and service interruptions in the technological environment. Customers don't need to call the Help Desk about these things.

I think you would have to agree that of the two situations just described, the latter is preferable. If you want to be effective and proactive and to positively impact the profitability of the business, you need to market. A word about marketing vehicles. The Internet has provided us with a perfect marketing vehicle: the Web site. Setting up a Web site for your Help Desk is one of the most proactive things you can do for your marketing efforts. I will be referring to the Help Desk's Web site often, and I will discuss how to put one together later in this chapter.

Image

Image is how you're perceived—all the things your words and actions are saying without you necessarily verbalizing them. You project an image with every customer interaction you have. Consider Scenario 1.

SCENARIO 1

Les is having a hard time getting focused on his Help Desk calls this morning. He's been up most of the night working in his recording studio. He's hoping to become a rock guitarist. Stephen calls the Help Desk, anxious about a problem he's having with his color printer. Les picks up the call and yawns. "Help Desk," he says, with a big sigh and a slow, tired voice. "What can I do for you?" Stephen hesitates. This does not sound like someone who can take care of his problem in a hurry.

Discussion

By his tone and actions, Les has given Stephen the impression that he does not care about Stephen's problem and that he cannot fix it quickly. In Chapters 5 and 6 we talked about the impact of factors such as tone of voice and body language on listeners. What Les said was "Help Desk, what can I do for you?" What Stephen heard was "Hi, Help Desk, I'm feeling really bored and tired, and I am not really interested in your problem."

The image of Les's Help Desk has been tarnished by this interaction. If Les does fix Stephen's problem quickly, Stephen will be relieved, and the tarnish won't be as dark. If for some reason Les cannot fix Stephen's problem quickly, then Stephen's fears will have been justified. He will be convinced that his first impression was correct. Let's look at what Les can do to prevent creating a poor Help Desk image.

SCENARIO 2

We rejoin a tired Les on the Help Desk. He's still not at his best. As in the previous scenario he's been up most of the night working in his recording studio. This is a different Les, however. When the phone rings, he sits up, straightens his shoulders, and tells himself he must act the part of a cheerful, interested Help Desk practitioner—and he does. "Help Desk, Les speaking," he says in a brisk, cheerful voice. "What can I do for you?" The caller, Stephen, is relieved. Here is someone who can help him with his problem.

Discussion

It took no more time and not much more energy for Les to appear cheerful and interested rather than tired and uninterested, yet the difference in the image he projected is dramatic. Even if Les can't help Stephen right away, Stephen will have confidence that Les is doing all he can to help him and to resolve the problem as quickly as possible.

Why Worry about Image?

If the Help Desk has a poor image, customers don't have confidence that its staff can solve their problems, and they don't like to speak to them anyway because they're rude, those customers may try getting support elsewhere or wait longer to call than they otherwise would. "I really don't want to talk to those people," they think. "I'll try solving it myself first." The profitability of the business is negatively impacted.

A poor image also tends to lower your own morale. It is not easy working on a Help Desk when customers don't think very highly of you. Their perception of your service will come through in their comments and general attitude. A poor image means improvements will be more difficult to implement, and complicated problems will take more time to resolve. Customers won't be as eager to cooperate. You won't have their support.

Where Does Image Come From?

Image comes primarily from the quality of your services. If you aren't doing a good job supplying Help Desk services, if you are not fulfilling your promises, or if you are delivering upgrades that don't work the first time, then no amount of marketing will help you. You need to clean up your act. Even if you are doing a good job, however, your image won't automatically become perfect. It will still be affected by you, your tone of voice, your body language, and your words, written and spoken. If your memos or documents are sloppily written, with spelling mistakes and errors, then your customers will think, "They can't even write a decent memo. They're probably incompetent." If your messages are tactless or rude, blaming other people, for example, you will be labeled unprofessional and unwilling to take responsibility for your actions. If you are giving seminars or holding meetings and show up unprepared, customers will think, "This guy doesn't know what he is talking about!"

Image is propagated in a strange way. Let's say that in Scenario 1 Les took a long time solving Stephen's problem and didn't do a very good job of it. Stephen will not tell his friends, "That Les on the Help Desk is pretty useless," he will say, "That Help Desk is pretty useless." If, however, in Scenario 2 Les solves Stephen's problem quickly and accurately, saving Stephen a lot of time, Stephen will tell people, "That Les on the Help Desk is great. When you call there, try to get him!" Poor image spreads like a fungus to the rest of the Help Desk. Good image does not. It's therefore important that everyone on the Help Desk worry about image.

What Can You Do about Image?

If the quality of your Help Desk services is good, there are several things you can do to establish or improve your image with customers. First, make yourself more customer friendly. Be aware of your customers and the image you are projecting at all times. A customer service course will help you here. If you can't take a course, get some good customer service books or reference material, and practice what you read.

Second, learn to act. This can actually be fun. People who do a lot of speaking to groups do this all the time. There are days when even the best motivational speakers are feeling tired, upset, sad, or just not up to par. Their audiences never know it. The speakers tell themselves, "I am going to go out there and be the most bubbly, motivated, interested, energetic speaker these people have ever heard. I'm going to deliver the best talk I've ever given." What happens is that after a while they don't have to act any more. They *become* what they are acting. This will work for you on the Help Desk, as it did for Les in Scenario 2. If you aren't feeling up to par, play the part of an energetic, interested Help Desk practitioner.

Third, make your written communications more customer friendly. Let your communications imply "I care about my customers so I took the time to do this properly." Establish standards and templates for your documents and memos so there's less room for creative writing and you generate a more professional image. Finally, monitor your image constantly. Perform peer reviews so you and your fellow Help Desk practitioners can get feedback from each other on the kind of image you project. Use customer surveys to get a reading on your image and to get suggestions on how you might change it. Make image problems a team issue to be discussed at team meetings.

A good image cannot cover up poor service—customers will soon see through it. But a poor image can tarnish good service. Image is worth looking after.

Selling Value

As we saw in both Chapters 9 and 10, the value your Help Desk offers and the challenges it faces are not necessarily obvious to senior management or to customers. Many of your successes are quiet—for example, preventing disasters rather than delivering a flashy and highly visible result. Your business is always looking for ways to deliver increased value at decreased cost. If senior management does not understand the value your Help Desk brings to the business or if management's perception of that value is false, it might make decisions—for example, outsourcing the Help Desk—that hurt both the business and the Help Desk.

What Does Selling Value Have to Do with You?

Selling value is not a one-person job. It is not only up to your manager. Your manager may take responsibility for putting out formal performance reports, but selling value needs to be more than a four-times-a-year event. A proactive Help Desk practitioner is constantly selling value, constantly communicating performance and successes. The more consistent you are at communicating performance, the more accurately customers and senior management will perceive it.

Selling Performance and Successes

On a Help Desk, we sell value in two ways: formally, via regular performance reports, and less formally, whenever we have something specific to market, such as a decrease in our response times or the prevention of a major customer problem. We market the details of our performance over a period of time, and we also market individual successes.

Formal Reports

Formal performance reports typically cover all aspects of performance over a specific period (e.g. three months) and include the following information:

- Changes in the services you offer or technology you support.
- Changes in call volume and number of workstations supported. You will want to report on changes in calls per workstation, in the percentage of each type of call, and in resolution times.
- Objectives and accomplishments. You include your performance against objectives and service level agreements (SLAs) and your operating cost. You may include a return-on-investment (ROI) calculation if you have one.
- Summary and recommendations. You summarize performance strengths and weaknesses and make recommendations for addressing weaknesses.

You can see a sample performance report in another book of mine, *Running an Effective Help Desk*, second edition (John Wiley & Sons, Inc., 1998). In addition to the traditional paper-based format, performance reports can also be included on a Help Desk's Web site or presented visually at management meetings.

Informal Updates

Performance updates can be published to market such successes as a reduction in resolution times, an increase in the number of customers supported without an increase in resolution times, or work done to prevent problems. How do you tell your customers about these things?

- Include a "What's New" section on your Help Desk Web site. (See the section titled "A Help Desk Web Site" later in this chapter for examples.)

- Include updates in newsletters. Updates might include success stories or information about growth in the Help Desk's environment. For example, "The Help Desk upgraded the network operating software last weekend to accommodate an unforeseen increase in the number of network users. The number of employees on our network has increased from 1,150 to 1,4500 over the past three months! The upgrade prevented a significant network outage that would have brought our sales systems down during our busiest month."

- Use Help Desk report cards to communicate the results of surveys taken previously to gather customer feedback.

- Hold meetings with your customers.

Don't wait for your manager to do these things. You and your proactive colleagues can do them yourselves.

Education

As part of your marketing effort, educating customers involves helping them make more effective use of their technology. No one wants to cause a disaster. No one wants to be inefficient. Ignorance, not intent, is the cause of many disasters and inefficiencies. For example, "Oh . . . was I supposed to check for viruses?" is not something that you want to hear on the Help Desk, but it is probably not what the customer really wants to be saying either. We've all heard stories about customers using CD trays as cup holders, using mice as foot pedals, washing diskettes, and so on. I don't know if any of these stories are true, but if they are, a little education could have prevented them from happening.

The more your customers understand about how to use their technology, the more effective use they can make of it. They will make fewer calls to the Help Desk, make better use of their own time, and cause fewer mistakes and disasters. By helping your customers use technology effectively you will be minimizing a negative impact on the profitability of the business. Let's look at Scenario 3.

SCENARIO 3

Jessica shakes her head. This is the third time this morning someone has asked the same question about the new spreadsheet software. The new version of the spreadsheet does not work quite the same as the original version, and that is causing a lot of grief. Ted, the customer she just spoke to, had created a long and complicated spreadsheet and now has to redo a major portion of it. At break, Jessica mentions the problem to her coworker Mason, and they both chuckle about it.

"Why doesn't anyone ever read the documentation?" Mason asks. Jessica just shrugs.

Discussion

Scenario 3 is a good example of missing out on a great marketing opportunity to eliminate calls. Jessica is inviting more calls to the Help Desk. Not only are Jessica and Mason not proactive, they are ignoring their early warning systems (EWSs), and they are indulging in the creation of some negative filters toward their customers. They are also showing a distinct lack of empathy. Let's look at Scenario 4 to see what Jessica and Mason should have done in the same situation (after they had read this book from cover to cover).

SCENARIO 4

Jessica shakes her head. This is the third time this morning someone has asked the same question about the new spreadsheet software. The new version of the spreadsheet does not work quite the same as the original version, and that is causing a lot of grief. Ted, the customer she just spoke to, had created a long and complicated spreadsheet and now has to redo a major portion of it.

At break, Jessica mentions the problem with some consternation to her coworker Mason.

"I've got to do something about it, but I've been so busy taking calls I've hardly had time to think." "Why don't you add it to the Help Desk FAQ and make it the question of the week? Everyone uses those," Mason suggests. "Oh . . . that's a great idea. I'll do the FAQ update if you do the question of the week update. OK?" "Fine with me. I certainly don't need any more calls."

Discussion

Much better. Jessica and Mason share responsibility for eliminating recurrences of the problem. The small effort required to update the FAQ will mean a reduction in the number of calls to the Help Desk and less time and trouble for customers. The simple solution significantly reduces the negative impact of the problem on the profitability of the business.

What Do You Teach?

You need to educate your customers in two areas: rules and guidelines and effective use of technology. Rules and guidelines include standards, security policies, any Internet usage restrictions or cautions, priorities, procedures such as for reporting a problem or purchasing a PC, and terms of service level agreements (SLAs). Your goal is to make your customers aware of the fact that all these do exist and need to be followed. Your challenges are to keep these in the forefront of people's minds and to communicate updates. Some suggestions for doing this are as follows:

- Keep information online and easily accessible by your customers. Put the documents on your Help Desk Web site so customers always know where to find them. (See the section titled "A Help Desk Web Site" later in this chapter for examples.)

- Avoid paper documents because they become obsolete very quickly and get lost easily (except for severely out-of-date versions. These seem to stay around forever).

- Inform customers of updates. Customers will not keep checking online documents to see if policies or procedures have changed. Use e-mail, notes in newsletters, and your Web site to let people know that something has changed. Try not to inundate people with information. Hit them with the highlights, and tell them where to find the rest. For example, the announcement "Staff found with unlicensed software on their PCs are subject to immediate dismissal—drives will be scanned each night" will catch your customers' attention. If you include the words "See the Help Desk Home Page for this and other new technology-use policies," you can bet people are going to have a look.

The effective use of technology includes anything that helps customers make better use of technology. Some examples are as follows:

- An FAQ option on your Help Desk's intranet Web site. You can take your most frequently asked questions from each week or month and add them to the site. (See the section titled "A Help Desk Web Site" later in this chapter for an example.)

- A regular technology hints-and-tips column in your company newsletter.

- Information sessions to review specific aspects of technology that seem to be causing problems for your customers or to preview new technology. Vendors will be willing to help you with technology previews.

- As your customers become more comfortable with Internet technology, you might want to conduct online forums on specific topics from your Help Desk Web site.

- Hold an open house event to demonstrate standard hardware and software and to show customers how different areas within the company are using technology. You can invite some of your expert customers to give demonstrations. Offer short seminars on topics customers have expressed an interest in.

- If your Help Desk doesn't offer training work with a third-party training provider to provide training options for your customers. Trainers can rotate through customer areas providing just-in-time training as customers work. Trainers can also provide "getting started" training to people who have just received technology.

Let's look at Scenario 5 for a proactive approach to encouraging the effective use of technology.

SCENARIO 5

Neela is a Help Desk practitioner on a busy hospital Help Desk. This morning, her first call is from Grant in the accounting department. "Hi, it's Grant. I need some help with this program." Grant proceeds to tell Neela his problem while Neela looks at Grant's past call records on the Help Desk management system. Grant's current problem, as well as his three most recent calls to the Help Desk, indicate he badly needs training in the software he is using.

As usual, Grant does not really have a specific problem, he simply doesn't know how to use the software. Neela answers Grant's question and then makes a suggestion. "Grant, I see you've called us before a few times about this program. You might want to save yourself some time and aggravation and take the one-day training seminar. It's offered every Thursday in the training room on the third floor."

"Seminar? I'm too busy to take a seminar." "There is another option. The trainer can actually come to your desk for a few hours and help you while you work. I'll pass your name on to her. She'll give you a call and arrange something."

Discussion

Neela was marketing proactively from the minute Grant called. She checked his previous call profile to see if the type of question he was asking was indicative of a need for training and it was. She offered him training options. Neela knew that as long as Grant was not trained he would keep calling. She also understood that the Help Desk did not need any more calls and that the best thing to do was to find a way to eliminate that particular call. If Neela's Help Desk had a Web site and FAQ, then instead of (or in addition to) offering training options, Neela might have recommended that Grant check the FAQ and walked him through it, or she might have sent him an online tutorial for his software. A proactive Help Desk practitioner creates options.

Communication

We've already spent a lot of time and paper talking about communication, and we've run into it again. Communication in marketing involves a two-way information exchange with your customers. To customers, you are communicating news about their technological environment—for example, planned service interruptions, emergencies, bad news (e.g., mainframe down), good news (e.g., "Faster dial-up lines are now available"), and changes in the environment (e.g., software upgrades). From customers, you are also gathering feedback about areas for improvement and about the quality of your service.

All of this information you are exchanging will help you reduce calls to the Help Desk. Every time you give customers an update, it means they don't have to call and ask. If you get input from customers they may give you some suggestions for eliminating calls and making improvements. Improving your communication is one of the easiest ways to eliminate calls to the Help Desk. Let's look at Scenario 6.

SCENARIO 6

It's fairly late in the evening, and Julie is in the process of bringing the network down to put in a fix to the network operating system. Julie's very excited about the fix. Response time should improve considerably. Customers will be a lot happier. Suddenly, the phone rings. Julie answers it cheerfully, thinking that whoever it was will be surprised to get a real person and not voice mail at this hour.

"Hi, this is Kate. I'm working on the sixth floor, and I seem to have a problem on the network. I'm staying late to work on a really critical logistics issue, so I'm glad I caught you. Could you help me?" Oops. Julie hadn't thought to send out a message letting people know about the service interruption. The patch had been an unplanned thing, and everything had been done in a hurry because they had been getting so many complaints about response time. Kate is not going to be nearly as excited about the network upgrade as Julie is—logistics just happens to be the company's top priority.

Discussion

Unfortunately, Julie had to learn a lesson the hard way: that communicating a change is just as important as the change itself. By not sending out any kind of message, Julie not only caused Kate to waste time and stay late for nothing, but the logistics issue could not be addressed, and this could mean a loss in revenue for the company. The profitability of the business was negatively impacted by Julie's actions.

Communicating to Customers

Some suggestions for communicating information about the Help Desk's technological environment are offered in the following sections.

Service Interruptions

Post planned service interruptions to your Help Desk Web site as soon as you know about them, then issue frequent reminders via e-mail and/or logon messages. Customers should also receive reminders the day before and the day of the interruption. Your customers are very busy and can very easily forget about planned service interruptions, even though you may have sent out an e-mail reminder a few days ago.

Emergencies and Bad News

When something goes wrong, how you handle the process of communicating the problem is just as important as how you fix it. First, describe the problem and its impact—don't try to justify it or lay blame. Customers are more interested in getting the problem fixed than in whose fault it is. Second, let people know what you're going to do about the problem. This might be as general as "We do not yet know what the problem is, but we have notified the vendor and are expecting technicians on site any minute." People want to know that you are doing something about a problem.

Third, communicate often. No news is worse than bad news. To a customer, no news means that you are doing nothing. Tell customers how often you will communicate, and then stick to that schedule. For example, you may tell customers, "Call into the Help Desk Emergency Information Line for updates on the problem. Updates will be posted every thirty minutes on the half hour starting at 1 P.M." Make sure that you do change the information message every half hour. Even if nothing new has happened, time-stamp the message and tell as much as you know. Finally, let customers know when there is a resolution. Notify customers as soon as the system is up so they are not sitting there waiting to start work.

Emergencies and bad news situations need to be communicated quickly. Use voice mail messages to let people know there is a problem. Set up a phone group in which you can send a phone message automatically to designated people in each customer area and the designated people can then notify everyone in their departments. Use these same groups to let people know when the problem has been resolved. Set up an option on your Help Desk's phone menu to point people to a system status information line that they can access when there is a major problem. They will then be able to get the most current update on the problem without talking to a Help Desk practitioner.

Other vehicles that might be useful in your company include overhead electronic displays to let people know when a problem occurs, what is being done to fix it, and when it has been resolved; a public address system; and a fax system in which you can fax messages to designated customers to keep them abreast of the status of problems.

Changes and Good News

The kinds of changes that need to be communicated include software upgrades, upcoming technology changes, and new Help Desk services such as expanded hours or interactive voice response (IVR)—in short, anything that will affect the technological environment of the customers. Customers need to know about changes well ahead of time so they can get any necessary training, and they need frequent reminders right up to the moment the changes take place. For example, if word processing software is being upgraded to a new version, let customers know about two months ahead of time. Then remind them on a weekly basis. During the last week, daily reminders might be a good idea. Communicate after the fact as well.

Customers hate surprises. Even if they may have been expecting a specific improvement, don't surprise them with it. Give them time to prepare. A Help Desk Web site is the perfect place to announce changes. You may want to use e-mail if the information is something that needs to be communicated immediately. Other vehicles for communicating news to customers include messages that appear when customers log on and articles in your company newsletter.

Getting Feedback from Customers

Make giving feedback easy for customers. The vehicles you might use to get feedback include the following:

Set up an e-mail ID to receive suggestions and comments from customers. You can set your Web site up so that customers can e-mail comments directly from your Web site.

Provide response lines. Customers can call in, anonymously if they wish, and leave a message.

Do callbacks. Call customers after their problems have been closed to ask if they have any suggestions for improvements and to ensure that the problem was really fixed. If you are already doing callbacks, add a question asking the customer for his or her suggestions for improvement.

Conduct surveys. Chapter 9 will give you some tips for creating effective surveys. You might want to survey customers on a rotating basis so your survey information is always current. For example, you could survey a different department every month or two and then follow the surveys up by attending departmental meetings to communicate the survey results and any planned improvements. Surveys can be sent out via e-mail, on postcards that customers fill in and return, in company newsletters, or at the Help Desk's Web site. You should take into account that the results from some survey ve-

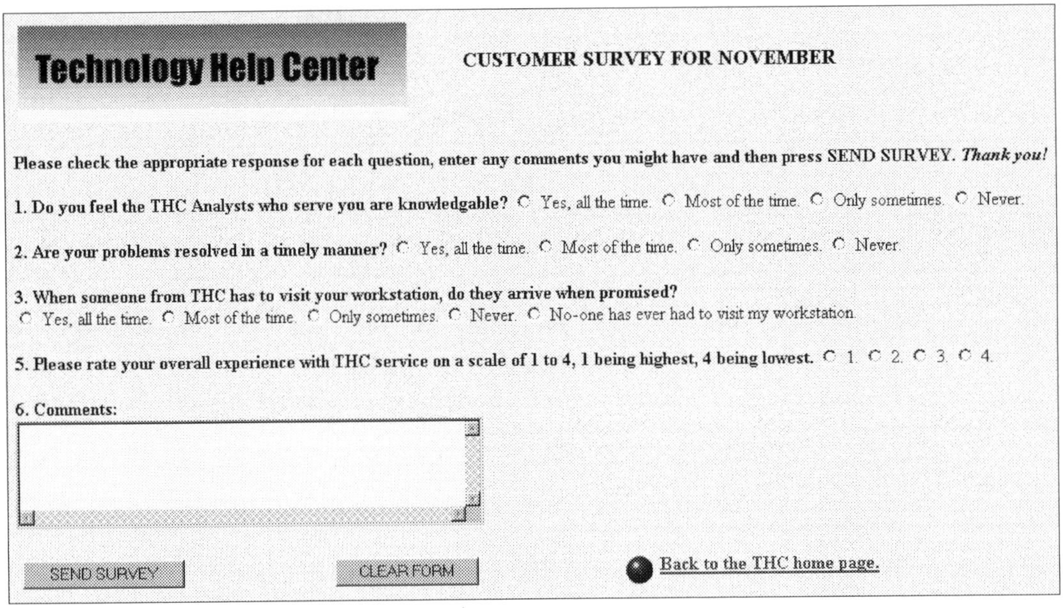

Technology Help Center   CUSTOMER SURVEY FOR NOVEMBER

Please check the appropriate response for each question, enter any comments you might have and then press SEND SURVEY. *Thank you!*

1. Do you feel the THC Analysts who serve you are knowledgable? ○ Yes, all the time. ○ Most of the time. ○ Only sometimes. ○ Never.

2. Are your problems resolved in a timely manner? ○ Yes, all the time. ○ Most of the time. ○ Only sometimes. ○ Never.

3. When someone from THC has to visit your workstation, do they arrive when promised?
○ Yes, all the time. ○ Most of the time. ○ Only sometimes. ○ Never. ○ No-one has ever had to visit my workstation.

5. Please rate your overall experience with THC service on a scale of 1 to 4, 1 being highest, 4 being lowest. ○ 1. ○ 2. ○ 3. ○ 4.

6. Comments:

SEND SURVEY   CLEAR FORM   ● Back to the THC home page.

Figure 11.1   Collecting feedback using a Web site survey.

hicles like postcards or company newsletters will require a fair bit of work to tally, while you may be able to automate the tally process for others. Figure 11.1 illustrates one approach to collecting feedback through a Web site survey.

Attend meetings. Attend customer meetings and ask for feedback. Let people know ahead of time that you'll be there so they can prepare their comments.

Form focus groups. You may already be holding regular focus groups for users of specific software such as spreadsheets. At these groups, you can collect feedback on software performance and the quality of the Help Desk's support.

Host open house events. Gather feedback at any open house events that you host. Have a feedback box prominently displayed and have a designated Help Desk practitioner available so customers can give feedback anonymously or in person. If feedback is given in person, have the practitioner record it so the customer feels that the feedback is being taken seriously and won't be forgotten.

Acknowledging Feedback

Feedback will stop coming in if you don't acknowledge it. You can acknowledge feedback by summarizing it in vehicles such as newsletters, report cards sent to customers, or a feedback option on your Help Desk's Web site. You can also attend customer meetings to talk about the feedback you have received. Besides simply summarizing the feedback, you must tell customers how you plan to act on it. If the feedback comes from an upset customer who includes a name, then you should get back directly to that customer. Similarly, if a customer gives you an idea that you use, thank the customer personally before you publish the feedback results.

Make sure you let customers know how to give feedback and that you welcome it. Mention this at the end of any newsletter articles you submit, on your Help Desk Web site, and in any general communications you send out.

Marketing Vehicles

When selecting marketing vehicles for your customers there are a few points you should keep in mind:

Cater to your audience. Know who your audience is, and design the communication specifically for them. Go back to the customer profile you created when you were getting your Help Desk focused (see Chapter 2). This will tell you whom you need to market to, where they are, how technology-literate and technology-friendly they are, what technology they use, and what they use it for. You need to make sure you send information to your customers in a way that will ensure they receive it. If they have access to and use the Internet, e-mail, and voice mail, then those media are available to you. It's not much use setting up a Web site if your customers aren't on the Internet or an intranet.

Be concise. Your customers are being inundated with information from a variety of sources. They do not have time to read long missives or listen to long, repetitive messages. Make your communications short and to the point. Tighten up meetings and seminars so you use only the time you need to get what you want accomplished.

Think image. The more consistent you are about having each Help Desk communication reflect the image you want to convey, the greater the likelihood your customers will connect that image to your Help Desk.

Be creative. Use graphs, graphics, and humor, and don't be afraid to laugh at yourself. Humor can lighten up even a "Help Desk Report Card" that reflects less-than-desirable performance. If you're afraid your communication vehicle is a little too creative, try it out on a few customers first to get their feedback.

Make use of existing vehicles. Your company already has several communications vehicles in place. Make use of them in your marketing wherever possible:

- **Company newsletters.** Contribute regularly or create your own Help Desk section. Editors who are trying to fill space will welcome your contributions.

- **Company intranet.** Set up your own Help Desk home page.

- **Customer departmental meetings.** Customers often have regular departmental meetings. Make use of these meetings to sell performance, teach, communicate changes, and gather feedback.

- **Performance review meetings.** Your own department most likely has meetings set up to communicate its performance to upper management. Make sure the Help Desk's performance is included, and try to be there to communicate it. If you can't be there, review what is being communicated and make sure it is accurate and communicates the information you want it to.

Some Suggested Vehicles

If you need some suggestions for marketing vehicles, help yourself to the following:

Help Desk Web site. The site could contain all Help Desk-related information such as policies, procedures, hints and tips, priorities, service level agreements, training information, upgrade announcements, performance information, and so on. There could also be a facility at the site to allow customers to give feedback on the Help Desk's service. The process of setting up a Help Desk Web site is described in more detail later in this chapter.

A rolling 6- or 12-month picture of the Help Desk's activities. Present this in graphical format, showing call load, systems supported, call breakdowns, and response times. You can include this in your Web site (update it monthly) or in company newsletters.

Help Desk newsletters. Newsletters are a lot of work. If you can, create a Help Desk Web site instead and just contribute to existing newsletters.

Faxes. You could fax news of coming events, changes, and various updates to predesignated departmental servers. Or, if you have the technology, you could set up a fax-back system that customers could use to request specific documents such as "how-to" information.

Postcards. These can be used for surveys, invitations to seminars or presentations, or upgrade announcements.

Reports (paper or online). Reports are good for formally communicating the Help Desk's performance to management and customers.

E-mail. E-mails are effective for notifying customers of emergencies, sending notes to individual customers, and any kind of information that customers need to receive immediately.

Voice messaging. A phone option could be set up to run off of the main Help Desk phone menu. It could be used as an emergency information line that customers could call for updates when a major service interruption occurs. Options could also be set up to allow customers to leave feedback or to get general Help Desk information.

Scheduled technology demonstrations. Set up demonstrations to showcase new technology or new uses of existing technology.

Seminars. If your Help Desk's call statistics indicate that customers need training in specific software or procedures, a seminar might be just the thing. A seminar could also be used to address recurring questions. If your Help Desk does not provide training, outsource it—bring in a third party to do it for you.

Just-in-time training. If you have customers at remote locations, offer one-day on-site help sessions at regularly scheduled intervals. Use these visits to answer questions, resolve current problems, and update remote customers on the Help Desk's plans and services and on any upcoming technology changes. If you don't have enough staff to provide this on-site service, you may be able to outsource it.

Meetings. Set up information meetings or attend customer meetings to gather feedback and/or communicate changes and Help Desk performance. Attending customer meetings is an excellent way to prepare departments for the arrival of technology.

Focus groups. Focus groups are especially good for introducing new products or upgrades. Customers in the groups will do a lot of free advertising for the Help Desk. If the product is not appropriate and is discarded, it is good to find that out as early as possible. Customers will then feel that you have really listened to their feedback. If the product is appropriate and is purchased, you will have a group of customers already familiar with it and telling others about it. They too will have positive things to say about a Help Desk that listens to their input.

Open houses. Holding an open house increases the visibility of the Help Desk, allows you to meet your customers face to face, and gives you a chance to do a wide range of marketing. Ask some of your expert customers to demonstrate how they use specific software, for example. Give demonstrations of standard desktop software, with lots of time for questions and answers. You can give miniseminars on high-interest topics, offer tours of your computer or server room, show customers what a PC or server looks like inside, and even demonstrate the life cycle of a problem called into the Help Desk. Refreshments and door prizes will add a sense of fun to your open house.

A Help Desk Web Site

Ultimately, the purpose of a Help Desk Web site is to eliminate calls. You want to give your customers as much information and help as you can via your Web site so they don't have to call you. The things you may want to do from your Web site include the following:

- Market Help Desk performance
- Publish documents such as policies and standards
- Provide or suggest training
- Help customers resolve problems
- Communicate changes in the technological environment
- Gather customer feedback
- Accept problems or requests
- Communicate information about your Help Desk

See Figure 11.2 for an example of the home page of a Help Desk Web site.

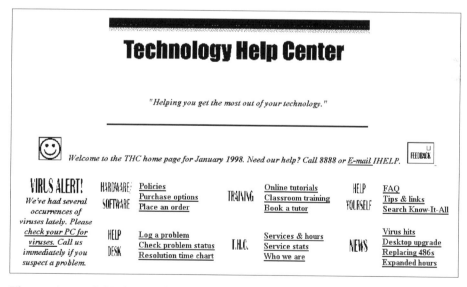

Figure 11.2   A Help Desk Web site home page.

Market Help Desk Performance

A Web site is a great medium for letting customers know what kind of value they're getting. You can showcase information on the following topics:

The environment you support. Using charts and/or graphs, show how your call distribution is changing, and how the number of customers you support is changing.

Resolution times. On your Web site, you can show how your pie chart showing the percentage of calls resolved per interval of time is changing (see Chapter 9). This use is illustrated in Figure 11.3.

Accomplishments. Post the things you have done to prevent service interruptions or reduce the number of calls.

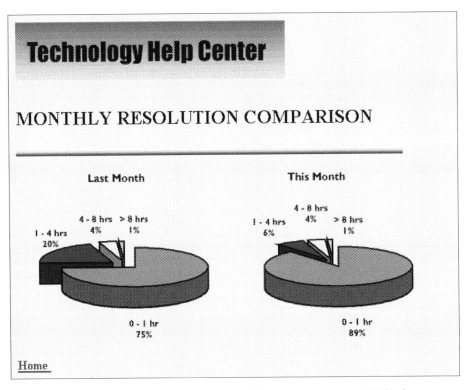

Figure 11.3   Marketing Help Desk performance on your Web site.

See Chapter 8 for more ideas on what information to include on your Web site.

Publish Documents

The kinds of documents you may want to publish on your Web site include the following:

Policies. Security policies that lay out your customers' responsibilities in protecting technology assets and confidential data and Internet use policies that describe the customers' responsibilities and restrictions, for example, regarding distributing data found on the Internet. See Figure 11.4.

Information for new users of the Internet. You may want to put out a package of information for customers who are new users of the Internet to help get them started. See Figure 11.5.

Terms and conditions for product use. A document that describes the responsibilities of a customer in using technology, for example ensuring that hardware is kept in a secured environment, data is kept secure and free from viruses, and no unauthorized or unlicensed software is used.

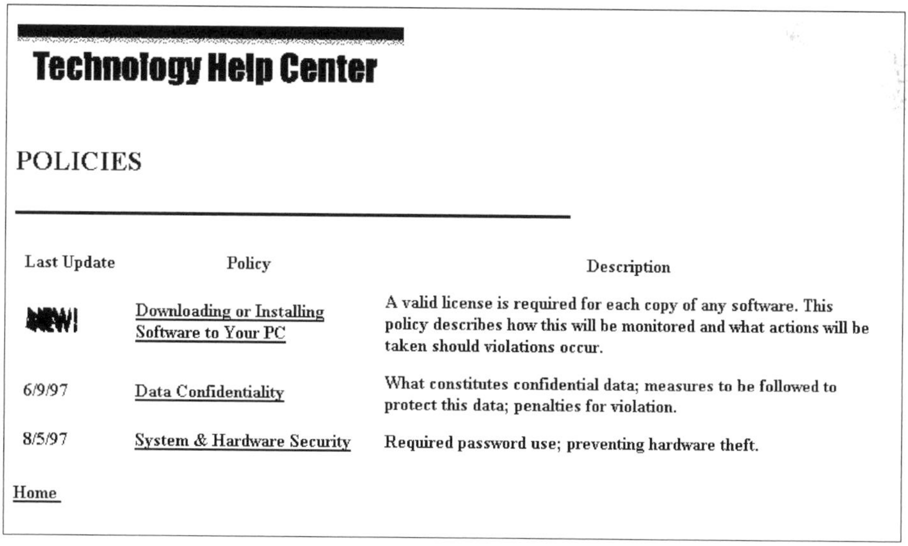

Technology Help Center

POLICIES

Last Update	Policy	Description
NEW!	Downloading or Installing Software to Your PC	A valid license is required for each copy of any software. This policy describes how this will be monitored and what actions will be taken should violations occur.
6/9/97	Data Confidentiality	What constitutes confidential data; measures to be followed to protect this data; penalties for violation.
8/5/97	System & Hardware Security	Required password use; preventing hardware theft.

Home

Figure 11.4   Policies on your Web site.

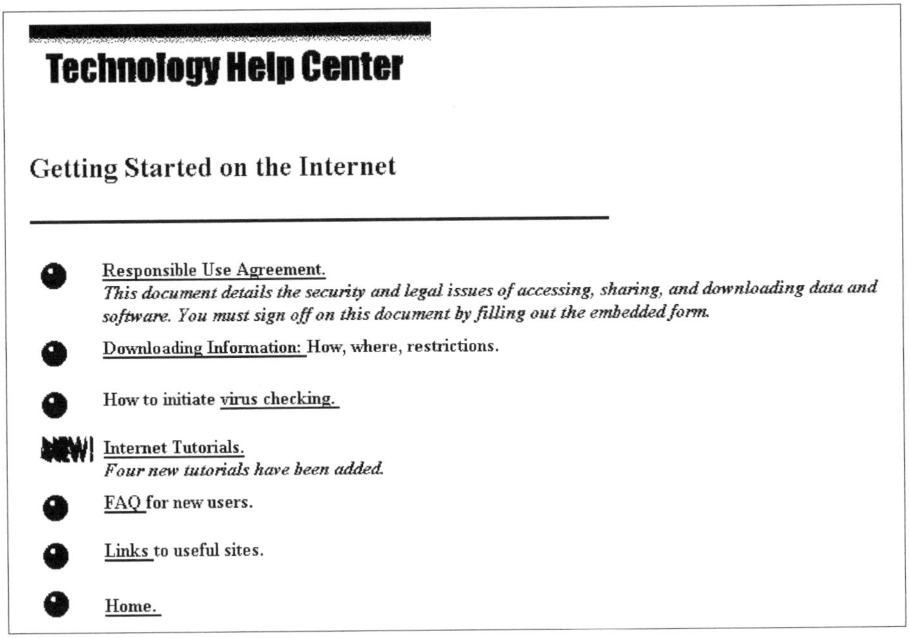

Technology Help Center

Getting Started on the Internet

- **Responsible Use Agreement.**
  This document details the security and legal issues of accessing, sharing, and downloading data and software. You must sign off on this document by filling out the embedded form.

- Downloading Information: How, where, restrictions.

- How to initiate virus checking.

- **NEW** Internet Tutorials.
  Four new tutorials have been added.

- FAQ for new users.

- Links to useful sites.

- Home.

Figure 11.5   Information for the new Internet user.

Standards. The hardware and software standards for your organization.

Procedures. Steps a customer has to go through to perform specific functions, such as ordering a PC.

Service level agreements (SLAs). You may also want to include your performance against service level agreements.

Provide or Suggest Training

There are several ways to make training accessible to customers via your Web site:

Online tutorials. These could be simple documents that you create or buy that deal with specific problems or how-to questions. Customers could select whichever one they wish to see, then simply view it on their browsers. You could also add photos, sound, and even video, depending on your environment. See Figure 11.6.

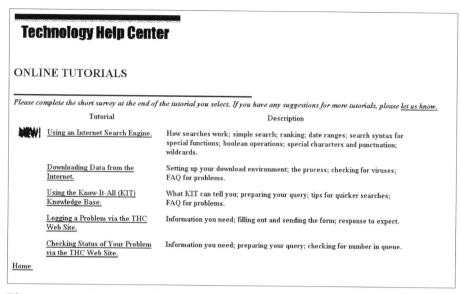

Figure 11.6   You can offer online tutorials on your Web site.

Computer-based interactive training. Vendors offer a variety of prepackaged training modules on many aspects of the most popular software. You could make these accessible from your Web site so customers could select the module they wished to view.

Tutorials. You could include links to other sites that offer tutorials and how-to information.

Schedules. Offer schedules and course descriptions for classroom training that you (or an outsourcer) provide. You could even offer a registration option so customers can sign up from your Web site.

Help Customers Resolve Problems

You can help customers solve their own problems on your Web site in a variety of ways:

FAQ sites. Look at your Help Desk management statistics to find out what the frequently asked questions are. Divide these up by subject area, and list the most frequently asked questions first. This will make it easier for customers to find what they are looking for. See Figure 11.7.

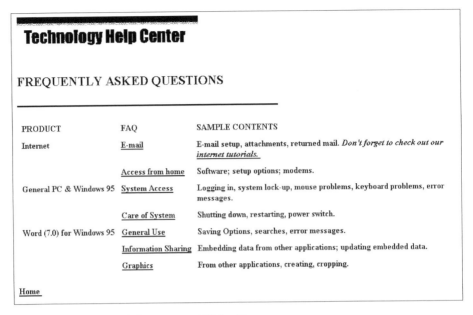

Figure 11.7   An FAQ on your Web site.

Hints and tips sites. Set these up much like your FAQ sites.

Knowledge bases. Your Help Desk Management system may include one or more knowledge bases. If you can, give your customers access to these so they can try to solve their own problems. You may need to set up some tutorials to teach customers how to use your knowledge base(s).

Links to other sites. Don't reinvent the wheel. If you find a Web site that has great problem-solving information for your customers, include it as a link from your site so customers can take advantage of it. (A caution: Many ownership-of-information issues for the Internet are still being thrashed out. If you have a concern about pointing your customers to someone else's site, check with your legal department.)

Communicate Changes

Some of the things you may want to tell people in your Web site include the following:

Product updates. You can post news about upgrades or new software or hardware.

Scheduled service interruptions. You can post a schedule, then issue reminders.

Changes in Help Desk services. You may include new Help Desk hours, new tutorials that are available, or any new functions you offer.

Operational changes. You can post changes in the way customers have to perform a specific function, for example, logging into the network or logging onto the Internet.

Changes in any procedures, policies, or standards. You will want to change the source for these kinds of documents on your Web site, but you will also want to let people know that changes are imminent or have happened.

This information can all be part of a "What's New" or "New this month" option on your Web site (see Figure 11.2). People will get used to going there first to see what has changed.

Gather Customer Feedback

Your Web site provides an excellent medium for you to gather customer feedback since customers are there anyway trying to get help or picking up information. You can collect feedback in several ways:

Have a customer survey as one of your Web site options. You might send e-mails to targeted customers encouraging them to visit your Web site and fill out a survey. See Figure 11.1 for an example of a Web survey.

Set up a "Before you leave this site" button. Have it bring up a short survey form or embed a question or two right into your site so customers don't have to be taken to another page. See Figure 11.8.

Target specific areas for surveys. For example, put survey questions in the areas of your Web site where you want to get feedback. For example, you may want to get feedback on how useful customers think the tutorial is. At the end of the specific tutorial, embed a question about the survey on the tutorial page. Alternatively, you could have

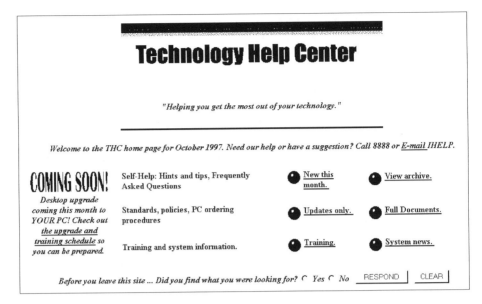

Figure 11.8   An embedded survey.

a button labeled "What did you think of this tutorial? Help us make it better," which initiates a short survey.

Give customers the ability to send you an e-mail with their feedback from your site. For example, in Figure 11.2, clicking on the envelope icon brings up an e-mail screen that will direct the customer's message to the Help Desk. Assign someone the responsibility of answering customers' e-mail.

For each type of information gathering you do, you should know exactly what kind of information you are looking for. Surveys that are too general are a waste of customers' time. You also need to feed the survey results back to customers. Summarize your customers' feedback and let them know what you plan to do based on it. You can do this through your Web site also. See Chapter 9 for more information on collecting customer feedback using surveys.

Accept Problems/Requests

You may want to give your customers the ability to log calls themselves, either through a form on your Web site, through direct access to your

Help Desk management system from your Web site, or via e-mail. Whichever option you choose, you need to make sure of the following:

You do not create more work for yourself. Have a direct interface between your Help Desk management system and the medium the customer uses to input the problem. Don't get into a situation where you have to rekey the data that the customer is sending you.

Customers understand how to log problems and requests. A tutorial might be called for or, more simply, enough instructions so the logging process is very clear.

You acknowledge receipt of the customer's log in some way. Use an autoresponder to let customers know the log was received.

It would be a good idea to also give customers the ability to check on the status of the problem or request from your Web page. To do this, you would need to give them access to your Help Desk management system.

Communicate Information about Your Help Desk

A Web site is a great place to post information about Help Desk services. You could include information on the Help Desk's hours of service, what happens during off-hours, and details about any chargeable services the Help Desk provides (see Figure 11.9). Customers don't often get to meet the people on a Help Desk. The Help Desk's Web site can give them that opportunity. For example, you could have an "About the people on the Help Desk" option that brings up the names and photos of each person on the Help Desk.

You may want to share some (tasteful) humor with your customers in the form of cartoons or quotations. On the Web page illustrated in Figure 11.2, for example, if customers click on the happy face they will get a cartoon. Always make viewing cartoons optional, however. Customers may not appreciate having to wait for a cartoon to load up.

Design Your Site

When you're designing your Help Desk's site you need to work under the premise that your Web site will be visited by busy people who are

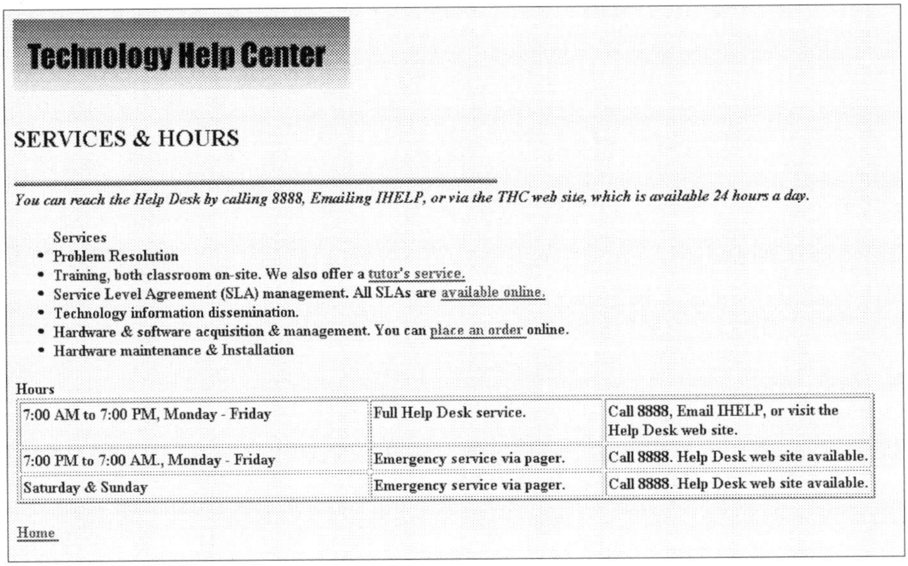

Technology Help Center

SERVICES & HOURS

You can reach the Help Desk by calling 8888, Emailing IHELP, or via the THC web site, which is available 24 hours a day.

Services
- Problem Resolution
- Training, both classroom on-site. We also offer a tutor's service.
- Service Level Agreement (SLA) management. All SLAs are available online.
- Technology information dissemination.
- Hardware & software acquisition & management. You can place an order online.
- Hardware maintenance & Installation

Hours

7:00 AM to 7:00 PM, Monday - Friday	Full Help Desk service.	Call 8888, Email IHELP, or visit the Help Desk web site.
7:00 PM to 7:00 AM., Monday - Friday	Emergency service via pager.	Call 8888. Help Desk web site available.
Saturday & Sunday	Emergency service via pager.	Call 8888. Help Desk web site available.

Home

Figure 11.9 Communicating information about your Help Desk.

looking for help in a hurry. Don't waste their time. Bear in mind the following rules of thumb:

Be concise. Don't just fill pages with data. Give customers the important information they're looking for.

Make your main Web page no more than one screen long. This approach will enable customers to see all of the options at a glance. If the number of options you offer gets too high to fit on one screen, offer a Web site map option.

Make your site easy to navigate. Be careful with frames. Web sites that use frames can be very frustrating if they don't allow you to go where you want to without having to start all over again. Don't nest hypertext to infinite depths. People can get lost.

Keep it simple. Complex graphics and photos take time to load, as does animation. Leave these out of your site. Test your site on a variety of modems so you can see how quickly it loads up. If you want to include graphics such as cartoons, include them as an option so people who have the time can look at them.

Make sure your screens are easy to read. Dark text on light backgrounds is best. Complicated backgrounds interfere with text. Do not use blinking text. It becomes extremely annoying after a few seconds.

Have a "What's New" feature. Such a feature enables visitors to avoid having to wade through information they may have seen before.

Put your logo or identifier on each page. Inserting a logo or identifier on each page and having each page follow a standard template or set of templates ensures that your customers always know they are still within your Web site. Each page will have the same "look."

Test your site. Test the site on a variety of screen sizes, resolutions, and Web browsers. If your customers are all internal, you may have standards for these already. If your customers are external, you will have to assume that "anything goes."

Market Your Site

Your Help Desk Web site won't do anyone much good if people don't know it's there. If your Help Desk serves internal customers, you can send out an e-mail announcing your new site or use company newsletters or any customer gatherings or organizational meetings to spread the word. Include your Web address wherever you include your phone number. If you are a small business, include your Help Desk's Web site address on all promotional material, including business cards and flyers. Include it everywhere you include your phone number. For the first few months of your Web site's life you may want to include a "Visit Our New Web Site!" announcement on all Help Desk communications.

If your Help Desk services external customers, your organization's marketing department will most likely take care of your site's marketing. Your site will probably be an option on the organization's main site. If you are responsible for getting the word out about your Web site to external customers, register with Internet search engines so your Web site will come up when people use specific keywords during a search. Most search engines have options on their home pages that allow you to submit a URL (the address of your Web site), which will be included in the search engine's index of the Web. You may be asked to submit a short description or keywords that the engine can use to index your site. You can also use the META tags in your HTML code to control how your page is indexed. The META tag will allow you to specify both keywords and a short description.

One way of registering your Web site with search engines is through sites such as Submit It! (www.submit-it.com/) and Net Creations (www.netcreations.com/postmaster/). These sites will submit your URL to a number of the most popular search engines for a fee. They also offer other Internet marketing services.

Maintain Your Site

Update your site on a regular basis or people will stop visiting it. Information that is outdated, that people have seen time and time again, has lost its usefulness. If your FAQ only covers Windows 3.1 but your customers have upgraded to Windows 98, your site won't be of much use to them. Tell people when the most recent updates were made. If you perform all your updates monthly, let your home page reflect the month, for example, "ABC's Home Page for December," so visitors will know the site has been updated for that month. Another way to do this is to include a "Last updated" date on your site and/or on the particular option you updated.

If your site has links to other sites, check these on a regular basis to ensure they are still valid. If they aren't, get rid of them. It is very annoying to follow a link that looks interesting, only to find that it doesn't exist. Review FAQs and hints-and-tips options. If the lists are getting too lengthy you need to weed out the defunct information and/or reorganize. Review all information on your Web site regularly for relevance and validity. If your system news includes scheduled service interruptions for January and it's now May, you are wasting space and people's time. Policies and procedures that don't exist should be removed. Those that have changed should be updated. If something such as a policy or standard has changed, mention this in your "What's New" section, but next to the new option itself also include a NEW! icon (or some similar indicator) with a short description of the new item or content.

Implementing Marketing Initiatives

We have talked several times in this book about getting into an ongoing cycle of evaluation and improvement. The same applies to marketing. You need to market constantly to reap the benefits. A marketing plan can help you get organized. A plan will help you make sure your initiatives get carried out, measure their success, and maintain a consistent Help Desk image. A marketing plan will make sure you're prepared for emergencies. If you plan how you will communicate bad news, such as unplanned service interruptions, then chances are you will do a good job communicating to your customers when a service interruption does happen. If you aren't prepared, you may go into panic mode, and the communication will suffer. You will increase the negative impact on the profitability of the business.

A marketing plan will also help prepare customers for future changes in the environment. Customers hate surprises. What may seem like a great surprise to you—"Hooray! The new upgrade is here!"—may be perceived as a disaster by your customer: "What the #$@! is this? What's happened to my old software? How do I do my work?" Putting together a marketing plan will help ensure that customers get adequate notification of any changes and are prepared for them. In your plan, you need to create initiatives for maintaining image, selling value, educating, and communicating. For each initiative in your plan, include the following information:

- Your objectives—what you want to accomplish through marketing
- The information you need to communicate to achieve your objectives
- The marketing vehicles you plan to use
- The audience you are trying to reach
- The frequency of the marketing initiative
- Who is responsible for the initiative

Update your plan at least quarterly. Make it a team effort.

Checklist

The topic of marketing the Help Desk covers a lot of ground—promoting image, selling value, educating, and communicating. As we saw in this chapter, marketing offers the proactive Help Desk practitioner good opportunities for reducing or eliminating calls. Check your understanding of the concepts presented in the chapter by answering the following questions. Revisit this chapter often as you perform marketing on your Help Desk.

✓ Do I understand what marketing is and what the four components of marketing are?

✓ Do I understand why we have to market the Help Desk?

✓ Am I aware of where image comes from?

✓ Am I customer friendly? Are my communications customer friendly?

✓ Do I monitor the Help Desk's image?

✓ Do I understand why I need to sell value?

✓ Do I regularly publish informal performance updates?

✓ Do I ensure that my customers have access to and understand policies and procedures?

✓ Am I doing anything to help my customers make more effective use of technology?

✓ Do I communicate service interruptions, emergencies, bad news, and changes to my customers effectively?

✓ Do I solicit feedback from my customers?

✓ Do I know what marketing vehicles are available to me?

✓ Do I understand how a Web site can help market my Help Desk? Do I know what I can put onto the Web site?

✓ Does my Help Desk have a plan for our marketing initiatives?

SECTION FIVE

Thriving in a Help Desk Environment

It's All in Your Attitude

I'd like to conclude this book by talking about how to thrive in a Help Desk environment. I suspect that many of you are just surviving. A Help Desk environment can be a fairly tough place to work. You try to resolve your customers' problems all day. On a good day you get most of the problems resolved, and your customers are fairly satisfied. On a bad day nothing seems to go right, the problems are difficult to resolve, customers are annoyed that you take so long, and the calls just keep coming and coming. When you're just surviving, it is very difficult to be proactive and play all of your Help Desk roles. When you're thriving, however, being proactive and playing all of your Help Desk roles effectively follow almost naturally.

I assure you that you can thrive on your Help Desk, if you want to. It's a matter of attitude, of refusing to let stress build up, and of taking control.

In This Chapter

In this chapter, I'm going to talk about how stress can force us into a survival-type existence and what we need to do to get past stress and take control of and excel at what we do. The topics I will cover are as follows:

- Attila's secret
- Picking up packets
- Getting a Help Desk attitude
- Lowering your susceptibility to stress
- Changing your outlook
- One step at a time

Attila's Secret

At the dawn of human civilization stress was a good thing. It kept the human race alive. Let's look at Attila, a cave dweller, to see how.

Attila leaves his family in the early morning to hunt something up for dinner. He hunts throughout the day and manages to snare a few rabbits. As he's heading home in the early afternoon he notices a vicious woolly mammoth approaching (it would be hard *not* to notice a vicious woolly mammoth approaching). He starts to walk a little faster. The woolly mammoth starts to walk a little faster too. There's no doubt about it, this woolly mammoth is after Attila. Distinctly worried, Attila decides that this might be the time to pick up a little speed so, with a surge of adrenaline, he takes off. The woolly mammoth follows in hot pursuit, covering ground with surprising quickness despite its bulk. Attila, very anxious now, runs faster, his heart pumping, his body sweating, his brain aware of the fact that he may be crushed by a massive foot or speared by a mammoth tusk at any moment. After what seems like hours Attila arrives home to safety and collapses on the floor, breathing heavily. In a very short time, however, his stress dissipates, and his heart and breathing return to normal. Soon Attila sits resting, reading the evening paper (or the cave dweller's equivalent) by the fire. All of his stress is gone.

Stress saved Attila's life. It gave him the zap of energy he needed to run at a fast enough speed to get away from his predator. Once Attila was back home he didn't need the stress any more so he let it go. That is Attila's secret. He lets the stress go.

Picking up Packets

Unfortunately, we no longer have any woolly mammoths. The stressors we do have don't incite the same level of physical reaction that woolly mammoths do, so they don't encourage the same kind of release. Very simply, unlike Attila we don't let go of our stress. We let it accumulate. If we let it accumulate long enough it makes us ill and eventually kills us. Stress comes in packages that we pick up as we proceed throughout our day. Figure 12.1 illustrates what happens during a typical day on the Help Desk to a typical Help Desk practitioner. I call my stick-figure Help Desk practitioner Sophie.

On her way in to work today Sophie is cut off by another driver. Sophie gets very angry and makes rude gestures at the other driver (which fortunately the other driver does not see), but the physical and mental exertions involved in making the gestures are not enough to dissipate the stress. So Sophie comes into the Help Desk this morning with a packet of stress perched neatly on her head. As she moves through the day Sophie picks up more packets of stress. Two of her customers are very emotional. One of them accuses Sophie of not wanting to help. That really upsets Sophie. It adds a pretty big packet of stress to the ones already on her head. Just before lunch Sophie has a run-in with Emily, the person responsible for the quality of the knowledge base. They disagree about how the knowledge base should be updated, and Emily criticizes the solutions Sophie had been entering. Sophie thought she had done a great job. Sophie picks up another packet of stress. Things get worse as the day goes on. Sophie gets a call from her son's teacher. It seems that her son has been skipping classes. Another packet. To top things off, Sophie's manager calls her into the office and says, "Sophie, you're going

Figure 12.1   Picking up packets of stress.

to have to work much harder at getting along with Emily. I'm disappointed in your behavior." Another huge packet. As Figure 12.1 shows, by the end of the day Sophie is crushed by the packets of stress she is carrying. In the state she is now in, Sophie is not capable of carrying out the roles of the Help Desk practitioner, and she is certainly not capable of being proactive.

Sophie has to learn to go through her day without picking up so many packets of stress.

Getting a Help Desk Attitude

The strategy that Sophie—and you—need to regain control of your day has a prerequisite. You must first decide that you want to change how you deal with the pressures that come at you on and off the Help Desk. This may sound simple but it is not. People are used to dealing with pressure or stress in a certain way. Some internalize it, letting it eat away at their insides. Other people vocalize it, becoming snappish and rude. The way you deal with pressure or stress is a habit, and habits are not easily unlearned. Also, some people simply like the fact that they are stressed and pressured. They don't like the symptoms that the stress brings out in them, but they feel that being stressed is a sign of some kind of strength, a reflection of accomplishment.

Deciding that you no longer want to let your job or your life control you is a big step. When you are controlled it's easy to lay blame when things go wrong. It's also easy to say, "This happened because I was so stressed." But being controlled by your life and your job is a cop-out. If you are really interested in thriving, in becoming the most effective practitioner you can be, you need to decide that you are going to change things and take control. You need to get a Help Desk attitude. How do you get a Help Desk attitude?

First, you need to lower your susceptibility to stress. Refuse to accept more than a minimal amount of stress. Learn from Sophie and don't pick up those packets. Second, change your outlook. Accept that you, and only you, are responsible for what happens in your life or how you handle what happens. Only a very small percentage of the things that happen to us in our lives are things we have no control over: diseases, accidents, hurricanes, and floods are among them. Most things we do have control over, however. People will say to me, "But what about the stock market? I lost a lot of money there." My answer is, "You did it to yourself. No one did it to you. You can't blame anyone. You went out and gambled some money on stocks. There are no guarantees in life, and life is not necessarily fair. The stocks went down. Take your loss, learn from it, and don't repeat whatever mistake you made."

Other people will say, "Oh, but I have suffered so much bad luck." Most of what we suffer is not luck; it's what we do to ourselves. Say you lose your job through a company closedown. Fine. You were hit with a job loss. It's how you handle that job loss, however, that determines how much control you really have over your life. Will you moan and wail about life being unfair and wonder what to do? Or will you say, "That stinks, but I'd better do something about it . . . maybe I'll go after something even better" and start looking for a new job and building a new life. Everyone gets hit with negative things. If you think you are getting more than your fair share I'm sure I can find someone who is getting it even worse than you. Take responsibility. Handle what hits you, and make life go the way you want it to.

In the next sections we're going to look at strategies for developing a Help Desk attitude, lowering your susceptibility to stress, and helping you change your outlook.

Lowering Your Susceptibility to Stress

The following sections present ten ways you can lower your susceptibility to stress and refuse those packets of stress you are offered.

Don't Sweat the Small Stuff

When you sweat the small stuff you are fooled into accepting large packets of stress for insignificant events. For example, recall Sophie's argument with Emily over a knowledge-base update. What Sophie should have done before accepting that packet of stress was ask herself, "How important is this going to seem a year from now? Am I even going to remember it?" We assign stressors far too much importance relative to their true value. We need to learn to place a stressor's value in relation to everything else. Will it be important in a year or so? If not, then it just isn't worth getting stressed about.

In fact, there are very few things that will seem important to us a year down the road. For example, the death of someone close to you will still be there years from now. But an argument with a colleague? No. Don't sweat the small stuff, and most of it really is small stuff. Leave those packets of stress on the ground. They're not worth picking up.

Empathize

The more we try to understand an event or a person's behavior, the easier it is for us to accept it and ignore the packet of stress it offers. For example, if you are driving to work and someone cuts in front of you suddenly and then weaves in and out of traffic, you might get angry and pick up a packet of stress. If you try to empathize, however, you can say to yourself, "What that fellow did was nothing personal. He must really be stressed out about being late. I feel sorry for him. I'm glad I'm not like that."

If someone at work is rude to you or angry with you, empathy can help you accept it. A customer might say to you, "What is the matter with you? Why is this taking you so long? Can't they get someone who knows this stuff?" If you take the words at face value they can be pretty upsetting. They'll have you picking up huge cartons of stress. If, instead, you say to yourself, "This person is not angry at me personally. She's probably having a terrible day. She must really be facing a lot of pressures or problems. Let me see what I can do to help her," you take the focus off yourself and put it on to the other person. You have no reason to get upset; she seems to have a reason. There is therefore no need for you to pick up any packets of stress.

Let Go of Negative Experiences

Human beings can be such strange creatures. Whenever we have a negative experience, we hold on to it. We put it into a pocket where it will be safe, and then if we start feeling really good about ourselves we bring that negative experience out and bring ourselves right down. We examine it and realize that, no, we really are not that good after all.

Negative experiences are very useful. We learn from them. So, take your negative experiences, extract all the learning you can out of them, and then throw what's left away. You do not need the part that's left. It is not the slightest use to you. For example, say you deliver a presentation in front of a large group and you fail miserably. No one laughs at your jokes, people can't hear you because you are talking too quietly, and your presentation comes out all disjointed. You feel totally humiliated and think you will never be able to face anyone who was in that audience again. There are a pile of stress packets there just waiting for you to pick up.

You have a choice here. You can choose to be miserable and wallow in self-pity about the incident, or you can give yourself a mental shake and say, "OK, I screwed up. What did I do wrong? What can I do to make sure it will never happen again?" You think about it, and you decide you did not spend enough time planning the structure of your presentation, you were too nervous to make the jokes successful, and your voice was just too soft. You decide to change a few things so this doesn't happen again. First, you get a book out of the library on giving effective presentations and read it. Then you read it again. You do eventually face the people who were at your presentation, and if the topic of your presentation comes up you say, "Boy, I really messed that up. I certainly learned a lot from that experience." You volunteer for another presentation. This time, you spend a lot of time planning the presentation, structuring it, and thinking about timing and all the things mentioned in the book you read on presentations. You practice it until everyone in your family, including the dog, starts to run away when they see you coming. You even add a little humor, something you're comfortable with, and you practice it some more.

This presentation goes quite differently. It is very successful, and you feel very good about it. Several people give you positive feedback. As you head back to your office you think, "I sure am glad I had that bad experience. I never would have put so much effort into this presentation otherwise. This presentation wouldn't have been nearly as good as it was." Take the excellent learning that comes from a bad experience and use it, but leave the rest of the experience, and all the stress packets that come with it, behind.

Learn to Count to Ten

If you have had teenagers for a few years you probably already know how to control your temper by counting to ten (otherwise you'd be insane by now). When I say count to ten, I don't necessarily mean "count to ten," I mean take a time-out to get yourself back together. Don't pick those stress packets up right away. Start counting, and by the time you're finished you won't need to pick them up. Counting to ten can take various forms. You can actually count slowly to ten, you can mute your phone and scream for ten seconds, you can go out and weed a garden, or you can do 50 laps around your cubicle. What you do doesn't matter as long as it is replenishing your patience and it isn't hurting anyone.

In addition to teenagers, customers can also try your patience beyond normal human limits. Counting to ten can bring your patience back, can make you respond as if they were not driving you crazy: "Yes sir, I know you've called me 11 times about this problem, but we still cannot fix it before we resolve our network issue, and that won't be done for another half hour." Remember, you don't need to pick any stress packets up.

Learn to Recognize Low Moods as Temporary States

We all go through periods where we are feeling low. I'm not talking about depression—that's something quite different and more serious. I'm talking about a temporary feeling of despondency. These moods can be part of our body rhythms, or they may be isolated incidents triggered by anything from the weather to something we've seen or read that is making us feel dispirited. These are times when it is difficult for us to function at full capacity. We start thinking, "Why bother? or "I can't do this . . . I don't know how I ever thought I could do this." We may start to get anxious and begin picking up stress packets.

If we can't see the light at the end of the tunnel and can't see an end to our despondency, it is very difficult for us to get past this anxiety. What we must learn to do is to recognize these temporary low periods when they start to happen. If they recur, we can track them so when they do arrive we can say, "Ah, I know what this is. I know that I will feel better tomorrow or the day after." If they are isolated incidents we can examine them and try to find the cause. Even if we don't understand the cause, if we have paid attention to all of our low moods we will be able to recognize that the mood will be temporary. "I don't understand where this mood came from, but it's probably temporary. I know I'll feel differently in a day or two."

Understanding that low moods are temporary makes a huge difference in how we feel about them. We can face the low mood knowing "you are only temporary, so I am not afraid of you. I am not really despondent; you are just making me feel this way temporarily." We don't have to pick a stress packet up because we don't get anxious. We just get on with things the best we can, and the low mood will pass.

Don't Go Looking for More Work

At the beginning of this book, I mentioned that the trait that makes us really good Help Desk practitioners can also be our downfall. That trait is that we like to help people. We want to help people. We do not like to say no to people. In fact, we say yes even when we are so busy we can hardly do our own work. We pick up someone else's work and several stress packets with it. We pick that work up even as we're thinking, "How am I ever going to get all of this done?"

If you think of each extra bit of work as a stress packet, however, it might be easier to say no to it. For example, Kathy, a Help Desk colleague, says to you, "Can I give these customer callbacks to you to do? I'm running a bit late, and I won't have time for them." Your workload is pretty full. Along with those callbacks will come several packets of stress. You will be anxious and spend the rest of the day rushing around to get everything done. When you're rushing you can't listen effectively, and thus you are less likely to be proactive. You simply cannot play all of your Help Desk roles as effectively when you're stressed and hurried. So, you say, "No, I'm sorry but I can't. My day is packed, I just can't take any more work."

Your manager comes to you and says, "I have a project for you. I need it ASAP, tomorrow noon at the latest." You know that if you take that project on, your calls will suffer, you will have to stay late, and your stress level will increase dramatically—too much work in too little time. You say, "I can't do this and still do all of my other work. I can do the project, but then you'll have to get someone to take over my calls." You might be afraid to say this because after all this person is your manager, but think about it this way. If you do what your manager asks you will be implying to him or her, "Pile as much work on me as you like. I can do it." If you keep implying this, you are giving your manager permission to keep giving it to you. If you don't want your manager to do this, stop accepting work you can't do. You will find this very difficult the first time, but it will get easier.

When you refuse work that will stress you and make you less effective, you are actually doing your manager a favor. You are feeding his or her EWS and forcing him or her to rethink the Help Desk's workload and its focus. Overloading people makes them less effective, which in turn has a negative impact on the profitability of the business. Your manager may have to decide which tasks are the most important and drop the others or get help to handle the extra work.

Learn to Manage Your Time

We pick up packets of stress when we don't manage our time effectively. We don't manage our time effectively if we allow time thieves to waste it and if we work on less important tasks while more important ones sit waiting. We end up with little time to do the most important tasks. Once again, we have too much work to do in too little time, major stress, and a falloff in our effectiveness.

There are two secrets to managing your time effectively. First, understand which tasks are the most important to the business and work on them before all others. For example, your most important task might be to answer calls. Right behind answering calls you might have project work. You might also have various administrative tasks. If you don't know the relative importance of these tasks, ask. Know which tasks you can drop if you run into a time crunch. The Help Desk needs to focus on those tasks that are the most important to the business. For example, a customer requests that you change the color scheme on his or her PC. You have call elimination work to do. Do you work on call elimination or do you help the customer? Your Help Desk may have clear priorities that say that call elimination work comes right after problems that are keeping a customer from working and that customer requests such as the color scheme change are to be done on an as-time-permits basis. If you're playing your role of partner, you will explain these priorities to your customer and get on with your work. If you don't really enjoy the call elimination work you're currently doing or if you don't understand your priorities, you might go and help the customer. Working with color schemes is fun. If you do this enough times, however, you will fall behind in your call elimination work and will be scrambling to catch up, anxious and stressed.

Next, identify and eliminate your time thieves. The easiest way to do this is to run through your workday in your mind, thinking about every activity, no matter how trivial, that you do. You may want to keep a log for a day or two. When I am teaching time management and am working with an entire Help Desk team, an interesting thing happens. I go around the group and ask each person to identify everything he or she does throughout a day. Suppose Wen is giving me that list. Wen will tell me what he does, and I'll write it down on a flip chart. But within a few seconds I'll hear, "Wen, you forgot about . . . ," and someone else will remind Wen of another task he does. Wen's list grows substantially from the one he originally gave me. Pass your list by a few of your colleagues, or do this exercise as a team to make sure you don't miss any of the things you do.

Once you have your list, go through it and identify the most important tasks. Are you working on those before all others? Next, identify your time thieves. This means identify those things that shorten the time you have to work on your most important tasks: for example, people who stop by to chat and go on and on, meetings you don't need to be at, or processes that are taking much longer than they should. An example of the last category is when Help Desk practitioners fail to return software CD-ROMs to the main CD-ROM library. As a result, when someone needs a CD-ROM to update a customer's PC, that person must spend a lot of time trying to find out who has it. The processes surrounding the borrowing of CD-ROMs need to be reviewed so time theft ceases. Perhaps the software could be put onto the server so no CD-ROMs are required. Another example of time theft is going out and looking for someone instead of just paging them (yes, this does happen).

Once you have identified your time thieves you need to eliminate them. They are leaving you less time to work on those initiatives that are most important to the business. They are making your deadlines tighter, they are forcing you to pick up stress packets, and they are making you less effective. If you are working on those things that are the most important to the business before all others and if you are constantly weeding out and eliminating time thieves, then you are probably doing a pretty good job of managing your time. You won't be picking up stress packets unnecessarily. If you don't know how you're managing your time or if you feel you need help managing it, take a time management course. There are many around, and they are typically not expensive.

Do One Thing at a Time

We all always have several things we need to do: projects, problems, documentation, and so on. But at any point in time we should only be working on one of these. We start to pick up stress packets when we try to do too many things at once—for example, answering calls while reviewing knowledge base updates for accuracy. We start to get anxious that we can't get one thing done properly because we're doing the other thing at the same time. Not only do we get anxious and pick up stress packets, but we also start to make mistakes. In Chapter 5 I talked about not being able to listen to two people at once. "Do one thing at a time" was one of the tips for effective listening. Trying to work on two tasks at the same time is no different. If a task requires any amount of thought, it needs to be your sole focus.

Take a Break

Sometimes Help Desk practitioners have strange ideas about what constitutes a break. They go out at lunch, talk about a difficult customer or a difficult problem, and come back more stressed and upset than when they left. That kind of lunch is not what I mean by a break. When I say take a break I mean that you need to get your mind off of what you are doing all day long. If you go home and worry about work, the next morning you won't be coming in refreshed. However, if you watch a movie in the evening, one that completely engrosses you, you will have given your mind a rest. You will be much more refreshed the next morning.

After work, or throughout your day if possible, you need to let your mind switch tracks for a while. If you've been working unsuccessfully on a problem for too long, your mind starts to go in circles. You start cycling through the same thought processes, and you become much less effective. Then you become anxious about the problem and you pick up stress packets, which just makes things worse. Rather than going nowhere, take a break and do something that gets your mind off of that problem. You will get to the solution more quickly if you take a break when you find yourself slowing down mentally or getting anxious emotionally. Taking a break might mean playing racquet ball, running, an aerobics class, playing cards, or just going for a walk. But if your mind is still wrestling with your problem or issue while you are doing any of these activities, you are not getting a break. You need to choose another activity.

If you find yourself picking up too many stress packets it may be time for a few days off. Don't be afraid to ask for time off when the stress you are feeling starts climbing toward your tolerance limit and you don't think you can get it back down. Catch this situation before it becomes serious. It is in the best interests of the Help Desk and the business for you to take a break. You will come back more effective and more able to play all of your Help Desk roles, which will positively impact the profitability of the business.

Get a Sense of Humor

It's impossible to pick stress packets up when you're laughing. The saying "Laughter is the best medicine" is very true. Learn to laugh at yourself, and do what you can to introduce humor into your workplace. For the most part, Help Desk practitioners are pretty good at doing this. When you find yourself getting anxious, when you're starting to pick up packets of stress, try to alleviate things with some humor. You don't need my help in thinking up ideas.

Changing Your Outlook

We've looked at ten ways for lowering your susceptibility to stress. We're now going to look at ten ways that will help you change your outlook, get a Help Desk attitude, and begin thriving on a Help Desk.

Take Responsibility

Taking responsibility goes far beyond being proactive. It involves taking responsibility for making life happen the way you want it to, accepting the fact that life is not fair, and not blaming others for what happens to you. This gives you almost total control over your life and what happens to you. When things beyond your control happen, you can do what is needed to regain as much control as possible.

Let's bring this down to the Help Desk. Your manager has told the team that you are all working toward an objective of 85 percent of calls resolved at point of call. You know this is not possible yet, not until you get the remote control software. You have a choice. One choice is to whine and complain to your colleagues and family about the unrealistic objective, create unnecessary anxiety for yourself, and go on to fail to meet the objective. If you do this you are letting things happen to you and you are not in control, which is a very stressful position to be in.

A second choice is to think about why the objective is not reasonable, write those reasons down, and then go to see your manager. You will present him or her with your well-thought-out list of reasons as well as the impact you think the unreasonable objective will have on the Help Desk. You could even present all of this information as part of a cost justification for remote control software. Chapter 10 can help you learn to cost justify.

If your manager responds positively and agrees that the objective is unreasonable, great. You've removed the problem. If your manager stubbornly refuses to change the objective, saying, "If everyone works really hard we can make it," you have more choices. One choice is to try again. You might get the rest of your team involved this time. You might get another manager involved. Another choice is to accept the situation and acknowledge that you will not meet the objective but work as best you can and not let the situation stress you. If your manager asks why you are not meeting the objective, you simply pull out the evidence that you prepared previously. You are still in control. A third choice is to decide that you cannot work in this environment any longer and start looking for another Help Desk job or ask for a transfer to another department. No matter which one of these choices you make, it is your choice—you are in control of what happens to you.

Be Positive

A Help Desk can, at times, be a very negative environment. It is very busy, people get stressed, customers can be rude and emotional, and so on. If, on top of all of this negativity, you yourself are a negative person, you will become stressed out and ineffective very quickly.

Being positive and optimistic takes no more effort than being negative, yet the results are dramatically different. You are much less stressed, and you can play all of your Help Desk roles more effectively. Let's look at an example. A month ago you asked to go into a rotational position in second-level support. Your manager responded with, "That's a great idea, as soon as the next position comes up I'll slot you in." Today, you came in to work to find that Pat, another practitioner on your Help Desk, was going into second-level support on a rotational basis. You have been bypassed. You have a choice in how to react. You can assume that your manager is out to get you, does not really like you, and is showing favoritism to Pat. You can go about your work angry and tense and bad-mouthing your manager and Pat at every opportunity. That would be a very negative reaction. You are assuming the worst.

Another choice would be to assume that your manager probably had a reason for making the choice and go to her to find out what that reason is. You visit your manager, and she says, "I know, I said you could go into second-level support, but I really don't want you to leave right now. We have a really important call elimination project coming up, and I really need for it to succeed. I want you to head it up. I'm sorry I didn't mention it. It just came up in the last couple of weeks, and I have been so busy. Once the project is over we can look at the second-level support role again." Thus, instead of being negative, you decided to see what the situation was like for yourself. You didn't stress yourself out by making up a negative scenario. Even if you do not agree with your manager's explanation, you now know the truth and can decide what you are going to do about it.

You cannot take control of your life unless you are positive. When you are negative you simply waste too much time on dark speculations and whining.

Accept the Things You Cannot Change

There are certain things in your job that you do not have control over. For example, you may not like your manager or some of your peers. However, you can't get rid of them. Or you may not agree with a reorganization that's going on or with your Help Desk's choice of Help Desk management software. You can't change any of these things either, but, once again, you do have a choice in how you react to them. Choice number one is to let these things upset you, to whine, get stressed out, and talk incessantly about them. That's a very negative choice, and we discussed that in the previous section. Choice number two is to leave the environment. You can get another job. Choice number three is to simply accept the fact that you cannot change these things. Learn to live with the limitations they present. If you find you cannot live with them then go back to choice number two: Get another job.

Living with things you cannot change means you don't complain about them but learn to work with them, accepting them as part of the environment you must work within. You may not like your manager or a peer, but you accept them because you have made the choice that you want to stay there. You interact with them professionally. You don't have to be best friends. You live with the reorganization you don't agree with. You don't bad-mouth it. You accept the fact that you cannot change it and must work within it. You use the Help Desk software without complaining, accepting its limitations and creating whatever procedures you can to improve its usability. (If the software is truly unsuitable you may do a cost justification for changing software, although if your Help Desk just purchased it that may not be an option.)

Worrying about and getting stressed over things you cannot change wastes a lot of energy. If you're doing that I question how well you can be fulfilling all of your Help Desk roles. If there are things you cannot change, accept them or leave.

Live in the Present

You need to plan for the future to make sure your Help Desk is prepared for it, but you don't need to live in the future. If you are constantly worrying about what might happen, about losing your job through consolidation, or about the profitability of the company, you are wasting time and stressing yourself for no reason. You cannot control these things, so worrying about them is a total waste of time. Focus on the present, on becoming as effective a Help Desk practitioner as possible, and on doing the best you can for your business. You can't do more than that.

You also don't want to live in the past. If you keep reliving negative experiences, try to learn something from them and let go of them, as we discussed in the section titled "Let Go of Negative Experiences" earlier in this chapter. If you keep reliving positive experiences, talking about how well you did this or that, and how you wish things could be like they used to be, you are wasting your time. Even if yesterday you were brilliant and your environment was perfect that doesn't really matter now. Things never stay the same for very long. If they did, we'd still be in caves. Focus on your current situation and your current environment. If you are not performing as well as you were, do something about it. If your environment is not as good as it was before, do something about it. You always have choices. Here, your choices may be to improve things, to accept things, or to leave. You are at your most effective when you are living in the present.

Accept the Fact That Relaxed People Can Be Achievers

Our society often equates success with high-energy, Type A personalities who are driven and live in a constant state of stress. The myth that you have to be like that in order to achieve and be successful is just that, a myth. You can be relaxed, quiet, and unstressed and still get things accomplished and be successful. Being driven and doing things in a frenzied way uses up a lot of energy. Being anxious inhibits creativity and thinking. Look around you, at the business you work in, your friends, your relatives, and people you read about. You will find many extremely successful people who are relaxed, gentle individuals. You don't need to be stressed to achieve success.

Redefine Success

You may have a set idea in your mind about what success looks like. For example, you may think you will be successful when you have a corner office with oak furniture and a title of "Vice President of Something-or-Other." You may define success by the amount of money you earn. When you break $100,000 a year, then you will be successful. If these criteria define what success is, you are probably going to be waiting for success for a while. If you define a successful day as one in which you solve every problem and help even the most irate customer, then you will still not have as many successful days as you'd like.

Being successful is good for you, it makes you want to be more successful, it helps you be positive, and it helps you be proactive. Why not redefine what success means to you? Define success in smaller chunks.

For example, you might define a successful day as a day in which you were able to eliminate a particular type of call, resolve a difficult problem, help a very challenging customer, or simply help any customer get working again. In these terms, just about every day will be successful. Why not enjoy these smaller successes instead of waiting for "that really big success," which is probably some way down the road, and in the process becoming anxious, driven, or even discouraged. The more you can redefine success into small, achievable units, the more success you will have and the more effective you will be. You will also be working steadily toward your larger definition of success.

Accept Imperfection Where It Doesn't Matter

I like to think of accepting imperfection as learning to live in a messy house. If you are a parent you have probably already learned that if you try to be a perfectionist about your home and want everything to be sparkling clean and very neat, you are going to end up as one very stressed-out person. Your whole environment will be stressful because you'll be constantly yelling at everyone and constantly getting upset. If you learn to live in a messy house, you will be much happier and much calmer, as will your family.

At work, accepting imperfection does not mean lowering the quality of your services or the quality of your work. It means recognizing when working to make things perfect has no business value and is therefore a waste of time. For example, someone asks you to produce a certain report. You produce the report, look at it, and think, "It would look really great with some graphs, borders, and reformatting." You spend the next few hours frantically making the report perfect, perhaps staying late or working through lunch, and falling behind in your other work. The final report looks terrific, you are very proud of it, and everyone else admires it. The person who requested it says, "Wow, I was just expecting a regular working report. This looks really good." In reality, it was a waste of time. In doing the extra work on the report you may have made other customers wait, got yourself stressed, and then were not as effective with customers as you might have been. If so, then your extra work on the report had a negative impact on the profitability of the business. Another thing to consider is that having done this extra work you have now created an expectation. People have now seen the very fancy report and will expect it. You have created more work for yourself. This was not a proactive thing to do.

Learn to Live with Your In-Basket

In-baskets (made up of your current outstanding work and problems) were meant to have things in them. Problems, requests, and projects do not follow the cycle "Everything starts up slowly at 8 A.M., then starts winding down at about 3 P.M., then completely stops at 5 P.M." They follow their own cycle, which varies from day to day. Those people who told you that your in-basket should be empty before you go home at night were not being very reasonable. If you try to empty your in-basket before going home you will be pressured and stressed at the end of the day. You won't be listening to your customers as well as you should be in the last hours of the day because you'll be worrying about finishing everything that's on your plate. Learn to live with the often unpredictable cycle of problems and requests. Learn to live with an in-basket that always has things in it.

First, Listen to Understand

We spent all of Chapter 5 talking about listening. Listening is a critical success factor in creating and maintaining a Help Desk attitude and taking responsibility. Before we judge and get upset, we must listen to understand. We must make sure we know what the person is saying and what the situation is before we react.

Say one of your colleagues, Anne, comes up to you and says, "I wish you'd update the knowledge base properly! Some of your solutions stink!" Your first reaction is to respond in the same manner, defending your solutions and being rude. But you remember that you're in control and that you've decided to take responsibility. You want to control your reaction and make sure you understand what Anne is really saying. Anne is not the most diplomatic of people at the best of times, but even she does not usually act like this. Instead of reacting in anger, you therefore ask simply, "What happened?" Anne pours out her story. It seems that she was involved in a complex problem with a very challenging customer, and all three steps of the solution you had entered into the knowledge base for that particular problem had been wrong. She knew it was your solution because the system automatically placed the author's name at the end of each entry. Anne told you how embarrassed she had been and how angry the customer became as they tried each step of the solution. Anne finally had to pass the problem to second level. By that time, the customer was livid.

Poor Anne. Now you can understand why she is upset. You can focus on getting the issue resolved, and you can apologize to Anne for causing her so much trouble with her customer. If we listen first, and make sure we understand, we can often circumvent feelings of stress, anger, or anxiety that come from jumping to conclusions and misunderstanding what the person is saying. We stay in control. We can do what is best for the business.

Be Flexible

You're going to see a movie. You've been looking forward to it for days. You get there only to find out the movie is sold out. Your spouse suggests making another selection. You are upset. You wanted to see that movie. How do you react? You have a few choices. You can say, "No way, if I can't see my first choice I don't want to see anything" and go home upset. You can say, "Well, you will obviously be happy with another selection so let's do that," give in with poor grace, and complain all the way home about the movie your spouse chose. You can also decide that, yes, you did want to see that movie, but since it's not there you'll be happy with another movie. You go into the runner-up movie with a very positive attitude and you enjoy it.

Flexible people bend rather than break. Being flexible means that you won't be upset or stressed when things don't go your way. This is especially important on a Help Desk because many times things don't go your way—they go their own way or whatever way the business is going. As the business you support changes, some projects will get put on hold while others will take on new importance. You may have put a lot of work into a project only to find it is being shelved for the time being. You can choose to be stressed, become bitter, and lose effectiveness. Or you can accept that this happened and that you have no control over it, try to make the best of it, and approach the next project positively.

As a Help Desk practitioner you live in a world of change. You need to be flexible so you can move with the change and help make it happen.

One Step at a Time

All of the suggestions for developing a Help Desk attitude discussed in this chapter are fairly substantial. They are "easier said than done." If you decide you want a Help Desk attitude, I therefore suggest you develop it a step at a time. As you implement these suggestions you will sometimes backslide. There will be people who just tick you off so much that you snap back without listening to understand them. There will be projects that you spend far too much time on because you get caught up with some fascinating technical detail. Don't worry about occasionally backsliding. Learn from your mistakes and move forward.

Each suggestion you implement will make you a more effective Help Desk practitioner: in control of your own life, not willing to accept more than a minimal amount of stress, and able to play each Help Desk role in a way that has a positive impact on the profitability of the business. I have one final suggestion. Buy a book titled *Don't Sweat the Small Stuff . . . and It's All Small Stuff,* by Richard Carlson, Ph.D. (Hyperion Press, 1997). The book contains 100 suggestions for avoiding sweating over the "small stuff." It inspired some of the ideas I talked about in this chapter. It's a small book, and each suggestion is short and easy to read. The wisdoms contained within it are perfect for Help Desk practitioners trying to stay in control.

Checklist

In this chapter we discussed how to thrive on a Help Desk by getting a Help Desk attitude. Use the checklist below to make sure you are continuously taking steps toward achieving this attitude.

✓ How often do I pick up packets of stress? Do I drop them or do I hang on to them?

✓ Do I sweat the small stuff or can I ignore it?

✓ Am I able to feel empathy for people instead of getting upset?

✓ Do I take whatever learning I can out of negative experiences and then let them go?

✓ Do I count to ten when I need to?

✓ Can I recognize my low moods as temporary states?

✓ Am I able to say no to work that would cause me stress?

✓ Do I manage my time effectively? Am I working on the things that are most important to the business before all others?

✓ Have I eliminated all time thieves?

✓ Do I work on one thing at a time?

✓ Do I take breaks that refresh my mind?

✓ Do I have a sense of humor? Can I laugh at myself? Do I use humor to alleviate stress?

✓ Do I accept responsibility for my life, my work?

✓ Am I a positive person?

✓ Do I accept with good grace the things I cannot change?

✓ Do I live in the present?

✓ Do I believe that gentle, unstressed people can be successful?

✓ How do I define success? Can I achieve success often?

✓ Have I learned to live with imperfection?

✓ Am I comfortable with an in-basket that has things in it, even when I'm on my way home?

✓ Do I first listen to understand?

✓ Am I flexible?

✓ Do I have a Help Desk attitude?

Index

A

ACD, *see* Automatic call distributor

Active listening, 107, 136, 149, 154–155

Asset management, 223, 225–226, 240, 266–267, 283

Attitude, required on a Help Desk, 29, 107, 149, 158–159, 367–368, 371–372, 380–388

Automated attendant, 224, 229–230

Automatic call distributor (ACD), 229–230

Automation,
in problem prevention, 205, 301
in procedures, 120–121
in senior management expectations, 42

Avoiding mistakes, *see* Support mistakes

B

Budget,
in services, 34
in training, 222

Business value,
in improvement initiatives, 72
in performance, 260, 266, 280
in problem control, 96, 110
see also Performance
see also Profitability
see also Cost Justification

C

Call distribution
in cost justification, 312
in Help Desk management systems, 224
in marketing, 252
in measuring performance, 283, 287, 289
see also Automatic call distributor

Call handling,
in consolidation, 87
measuring effectiveness of, 256, 263–290
procedures for, 122
see also Call load

Do you have these Wiley books on your shelf?

Running an Effective Help Desk, Second Edition
Barbara Czegel

ISBN: 0-471-24816-9, 1998

They're the people who feel the wrath of every system crash. And like the rest of the organization, the Help Desk is being transformed by the potential of intranets, extranets, and the Web. This updated edition to the definitive Help Desk manager's guidebook now offers timely and practical suggestions for upgrading the service of a Help Desk using the latest technologies.

Delivering World-Class Technical Support
Navtej (Kay) Khandpur and Lori Laub

ISBN: 0-471-15534-9

Learn how to develop a top-flight technical support department, offering guidelines on organization and development. Khandpur and Laub discuss such topics as: work distribution, scheduling, and organization; measuring and tracking department performance, outsourcing the tech support function, and taking advantage of the Internet as a departmental tool.

Sales Force Automation Using Web Technologies
Navtej Khandpur, Patricia Bruce, and Jasmine Wevers

ISBN: 0-471-19114-0

This book shows IT managers, LAN administrators, and Webmasters how to implement automation into an organization, providing strategies for implementation using the Web, Lotus Notes, and intranets. It gives readers the core information necessary to implement sales force automation across an organization, and it shows how to create templates for forecasting, lead generation, sales kits, order processing, and links to other departments.

Available at bookstores everywhere

Wiley Computer Publishing
Timely. Practical. Reliable.

Made in the USA
San Bernardino, CA
01 November 2012